COLLINS COBUILD

COLLINS Birmingham University International Language Database

ENGLISH GUIDES

5

REPORTING

Geoff Thompson

THE UNIVERSITY
OF BIRMINGHAM

COLLINS
COBUILD

S0-BRZ-107

HarperCollins*Publishers*

HarperCollins Publishers
77-85 Fulham Palace Road
London w6 8jb

COBUILD is a trademark of William Collins Sons & Co Ltd

ISBN 0 00 370566 8

Computer typeset by Tradespools Ltd, Frome, Somerset

Printed in Great Britain by HarperCollins Manufacturing, Glasgow

For Susan

Corpus Acknowledgements

We would like to thank those authors and publishers who kindly gave
permission for copyright material to be used in the Bank of English. We
would also like to thank Times Newspapers Ltd, the BBC World Service,
and National Public Radio of Washington for providing valuable data.

Acknowledgements

The author and publishers are grateful to the following for permission to
reproduce material on the pages indicated:
The Guardian, 152-153; Daily Mail/Solo, 157-159; Doris Lessing for the
extract from *The Good Terrorist*, published by Jonathan Cape, 171-172;
New Community for the extracts from *Black children in local authority
care: admission patterns*, by Ravinder Barn, published in New Community
Vol 16 no 2, 180-181; Daily Mail/Solo, 201-202; 206.

The Author would also like to thank the following people: at COBUILD,
Gill Francis for her perceptive comments on the text; in the English
Language Unit at the University of Liverpool, all colleagues for helping to
reduce his teaching load when deadlines were uncomfortably close, and
Mike Scott for advice on dealing with computers as well; at home, Rose
and Frank for all their help; and above all, Susan Thompson for her ideas,
stimulation, and support.

COBUILD

Editor in chief   John Sinclair
Editorial Director Gwyneth Fox
Senior Editor   Jane Bradbury
Editorial Advice   Susan Hunston
Index   Hazel Harrison
Computer Staff   Tim Lane & Andrea Lewis

HarperCollins *Publishers*
Annette Capel
Gillian McNair

Contents

Foreword

The *Guide to Reporting* is one of a series of COBUILD ENGLISH GUIDES to particular areas of difficulty for learners of English.

One of the special features of a human language is that it can talk about itself. No other communication system has this power. Musical themes can recall each other, parrots can mimic other noises, but they cannot refer to each other. A dog cannot build into its barking and whining some reference to the noise a neighbour's dog has been making. But the dog's owner, using language, can say 'The neighbours have been having an awful row' and go on to report what they shouted at each other.

The ability of language to report – to build into the talk a reference to other talk – extends the power and flexibility of language enormously. Not only can distant actions be talked about (with the use of verb tenses) but distant talk as well.

This thorough description of reporting in English shows the range of expression and the variety of techniques that are available. The author gives priority to the talk within which the report occurs, which is helpful for the learner as well as being closer to reality. A lot of learning time has been wasted in exercises to convert Direct Speech (the presumed original talk) into Indirect Speech (the report itself). The author shows clearly that the decisions about verb tenses and other timing words and phrases depend on the situation of the reporting, and not the often hypothetical situation of the 'original' talk. The conversion rules are best abandoned in favour of the explanations given in this book.

The exact reproduction of previous talk is hardly ever attempted, except in telling jokes that depend on accents or voice quality. Mimicry in humans is usually considered offensive. In reporting there is always some change made – by adapting the talk to the present situation, by shortening it, by adding descriptive or evaluative phrases, and so on. No rules are given in this process, no more than there are rules that relate physical objects to the descriptions that are made of them in language. Instead, the author offers a rich variety of ways of making reporting effective.

This book, like all COBUILD books, is derived from the evidence obtained from studying corpora – in this case the Bank of English, containing over 200 million words. The examples are taken directly from the corpus and the frequency of patterns affects the prominence given to them here. It shows that reporting is not a great and complicated mystery with many rules to be learned, but a common and natural means of expression, simple to master and powerful to use.

I hope that you find this book helpful and easy to use. Please write to me with any comments or suggestions about how to improve COBUILD publications.

John Sinclair
Editor in Chief: COBUILD ENGLISH GUIDES
Professor of Modern English Language
University of Birmingham

Introduction

You use language to talk about events and objects in the world around you. Some of the events that you talk about are language events – what other people say or have said, what you yourself think or have thought, and so on. You can also treat these events as things – you listen to *a speech* or make *a suggestion*. Any language has particular ways of talking about events and things which happen to consist of language. This book looks at how English deals with referring to other bits of language.

There are three basic ways of referring to other bits of language:

- to repeat the bit of language more or less as it originally occurred:

  'I'd forgotten he was a gourmet cook,' Walter joked.

- to report the bit of language in your own words:

  He admitted that much work still needed to be done.

- to report the occurrence of a bit of language without actually saying what was said or written:

  In Sweden, Descartes was forced to rise at 5:00 a.m. in cold weather in order to converse with the queen.

In traditional terms, the first of these options is called **quotation** or **direct speech**; the second is called **reported speech** or **indirect speech**; and there is no special term for the third option. For the purposes of this book, they will all be considered as kinds of **language reports**.

When you report what someone else has said you have a choice: you choose the way of reporting which seems most appropriate for the meaning that you want to convey and which is most likely to have the effect on your listener that you want. In order to understand the reasons why you choose to use a quote, for example, you need to consider all the main options that you might have chosen. The effect of any choice is partly the result of what was not chosen. For example, the words below (spoken by a government minister) could be reported in many different ways.

But our policy has not changed and it will not change.

Someone might report this as a quote; or they might use reported speech: 'The Minister pointed out that the government had consistent policies'; or they might reduce the information about what was said even further: 'The Minister repeated his position'. Each of these choices would give a different picture of the event.

The three ways of reporting language are described separately in this book, but many of the examples of language reports that you come across will show a mixture of features from two (or occasionally all three) of the options.

The following examples all have a mixture of features. How far is it possible to decide what was actually said in each case (and by whom)?

Disraeli, for instance, predicted that its author would take an eminent position in our future literature.

The King congratulated him again on his patriotism and loyalty.

The Prime Minister made no secret of the difficulty of getting an agreement.

The adage that time heals seems true.

Edward was adamant: he wanted to join the company then and there.

It's a case of reform or die, according to Jasper Becker.

This book describes in general the range of structures and vocabulary that we use for the purpose of reporting language, and then investigates in more detail the various kinds of reporting that people do and the way in which these functions are carried out by particular structural features.

In **Chapter 1**, the focus is on the ways that different grammatical structures can be used in reporting language.

Chapter 2 concentrates on the function of the reporting signal and shows what information can be given about the report by the reporting signal. In particular, it shows how speakers can indicate different attitudes towards the report through the reporting signal.

In **Chapter 3**, attention turns to the message, that is, what is reported, and its functions. The chapter shows how different message types can be chosen for different purposes and explains the uses of tense, pronouns, and similar features in reported clauses.

Chapter 4 describes the ways that speakers can use the structures of reporting to express thoughts, ideas, opinions, and feelings. This chapter also focuses on other reasons for using reporting structures, in particular for politeness.

Chapter 5 introduces four longer texts, to demonstrate how different choices in reporting language go together to give a consistent message. The texts – from journalism, from conversation, from a novel, and from academic writing – show reporting being used in different situations and for different purposes.

A Note on Terminology

It can be complicated to talk about reporting because, amongst other things, there are usually at least two different people involved (the person being reported and the person doing the reporting) and two different bits of language (the bit being reported and the bit in which the reporting is being done).

To try to make the explanations as clear as possible, the following terms are used with the particular meanings set out here:

- **speaker, writer**: the person who said or wrote what is being reported

- **hearer, reader**: the person to whom the speaker or writer was talking or writing

- **reporter**: the person who gives the report of the language event
- **language event**: the original act of speaking or writing by the speaker or writer
- **report**: the whole account of the language event (which may or may not include identification of the speaker/writer; and may include a direct quotation or some indirect speech, or both, or neither)
- **message**: the part of the report which represents what was said or written in the language event
- **reporting signal**: the part of the report which tells you that this is a report, for example, a reporting verb such as 'say'. In some cases punctuation marks such as inverted commas may act as reporting signals

The following example, taken from a novel, illustrates these terms:

> <u>Michael said 'Take care' to the businessman</u> and followed Wilfred through the mob.

In this case:

- the **speaker** is *Michael* (a character in the novel)
- the **hearer** is *the businessman* (another character in the novel)
- the **reporter** is the narrator or the author of the novel
- the **language event** is the conversation that is taking place between Michael and the businessman, and in particular this farewell
- the **report** is the part of the sentence that is underlined
- the **message** is *Take care*
- the **reporting signals** are *said* and the inverted commas

The next example, also from a novel, does not include a quote, but the components of the reporting can still be identified:

> *He told his wife that he was going to Florida to look for a car.*

In this case:

- the **speaker** is *He*
- the **hearer** is *his wife*
- the **reporter** is the narrator or the author of the novel
- the **language event** is the conversation between the man and his wife
- the **report** is the whole sentence
- the **message** is *that he was going to Florida to look for a car*
- the **reporting signal** is *told*

It will not always be possible to identify clearly all these features. In the following example, which is part of an account of a job interview, there is no speaker in the report. Also, the reporting verb (*thanked*) acts simultaneously as the reporting signal and as part of the message.

I was thanked for coming and left.

In this case:

- the **speaker** is not mentioned
- the **hearer** is *I* (the person who has just been interviewed for the job)
- the **reporter** is also *I*
- the **language event** is the act of thanking at the end of the interview
- the **report** is *I was thanked for coming*
- the **message** is *thanked for coming* (note that part of the message is conveyed by the reporting verb itself)
- the **reporting signal** is *thanked*

This terminology is used throughout the Guide.

1 Structure

1.1 This chapter describes the range of structures that can be used to report language.

Reports usually consist of two parts: the **reporting signal** and the **message.**
The **reporting signal** is the part of the report which shows that you are reporting someone else's words rather than expressing your own ideas.

When he arrived, <u>the General told reporters</u> the meeting would not be a negotiation.

The **message** is the part which shows what was said or written.

When he arrived, the General told reporters <u>the meeting would not be a negotiation.</u>

In structural terms, there are two main types of reports: **direct quote structures** and **indirect report structures**.

Direct quote structures

1.2 A **direct quote structure** is any structure which shows that you are reporting what someone said or wrote (or sometimes thought) as if you were using their own words.

The basic type of **direct quote structure** consists of two clauses: a **reporting clause** (the reporting signal):

<u>I said,</u> 'I'm going out'.

and a **quote** (the message):

I said, <u>'I'm going out'.</u>

1.3 If you read a direct quote, you do not know whether the quote is exactly the same as the words used in the original language event. In a newspaper report, for example, the quote may only be roughly what the original speaker said: quite often, different newspapers quote the same speaker as saying different words. If someone is telling a story, they may use a direct quote even if they do not remember exactly what was said. In a novel, there is no original speaker and no original language event. The words exist only in the writer's imagination. In an academic paper, on the other hand, there is a convention that the words of the quote will be accurately copied from the original piece of writing. In all these cases, however, the **reporter** – the person making the report – is implying that the quote does represent the original words.

signals of quotes

1.4 The most frequent reporting signal for direct quote structures in writing is the use of **inverted commas** (' ' or " ") around the quote. Inverted commas can signal a quote even if there is no reporting clause.

> *Mark still shook his head in disbelief. 'And what's he doing about it?'*
> *She asked him how old he was. 'Twenty-three.' 'Do you work?' 'I will*
> *when I get back home. I'm a lawyer.'*

Note that inverted commas are sometimes called **quotation marks**. For the use of punctuation in direct quote structures, see 1.19–1.24

reporting clauses in direct quote structures

1.5 In addition to inverted commas, direct quote structures are very often signalled by a **reporting clause** containing a **reporting verb**. In the following examples, the reporting clause is underlined.

> *'I'm all right,' said Jarvis.*
> *He paused and asked, 'How much do you remember?'*
> *Then he said gently, 'How have you been, Hannah?'.*
> *'So how's things with you?' he asked.*

position of reporting clauses in direct quote structures

1.6 The reporting clause usually comes before or after the quote.

> *But Flashman, who at first refused to comment, later said 'As far as I am concerned Barry has not been sacked.'*
> *'Get out of here,' Carlyle said.*

It can also come in the middle of the quote, especially in written narratives such as novels.

> *'It's a captain's job to lead from the front,' he said afterwards, 'and that's what I felt I had to do.'*

1.7 In speech, it is more usual to put the reporting clause first, to avoid ambiguity as to whether the speaker is quoting someone else or not.

> *And then he said, 'Why is his name on the electoral register?'*

In writing, the inverted commas normally indicate clearly that the writer is using a quote, and the reporting clause often follows the quote, particularly in narratives.

> *'In the cupboard?' said the Captain. 'Yes,' said Jonathan. 'How do you know?' asked the Captain. 'I put it there,' said Jonathan.*

However, you often find the reporting clause before the quote in writing as well. This is the normal position in formal, academic writing, but it also occurs in other kinds of writing.

> *Charles Raven once wrote: 'Religion involves adventure and discovery and a joy in living dangerously.'*

I said to Felicity: 'You'd like that, wouldn't you?'
Accounts clerk Catriona Valentine said: 'It was a terrifying experience which I shall never forget.'

There are some reporting verbs which rarely appear before the quote, although they often appear after it. These include 'agree', 'command', 'promise' and 'wonder'.

reporting clauses in mid-position

1.8   When the reporting clause comes in the middle of the quote, you have a great deal of choice as to exactly where you place the reporting clause, although some positions are not possible. Notice in the examples below that mid-position reporting clauses very often come after a complete first element of the quote (for instance, the subject of the quote clause).

The main positions are:

● after 'answer words' such as 'yes', 'no', 'okay' (which imply a question from someone else)

'Oh yes,' I said a trifle impatiently, 'we know the Gows are rich.'
'No,' I said, 'I can't see.'

● after the first noun group in the quote

'Your need,' he said, 'is for a man who really loves you.'
'The problem,' I explained, 'is quite simple.'
'All we have done,' Paula explained patiently, 'is to cut two branches off this cherry tree.'

● after a clause, if the quote contains more than one clause

'You keep it,' she said, 'and let's start.'
'If you don't mind my saying so,' Connie said, 'this is something you'll want to look at immediately.'
'The thing is,' he told Mary Ann, 'surprises are very, very good for people.'
'So tell me,' he asked, 'how did you get into the police department?'

● after an adverb or prepositional phrase

'Unfortunately,' he wrote, 'your portrait of Eula Hall was not very good.'
'In the final analysis,' he once said, 'we must rely on man's ingenuity.'

● after a 'wh'-word in a question

'Why,' he asked, 'don't you let me buy you a meal or something?'
'How long,' he asked, 'shall I be held hostage?'

● after a vocative

'Mom,' she asked, 'where am I going?'
'Ladies and gentlemen,' he rasped, 'there is only one verdict you can possibly reach.'

● after an exclamation

'Oh hell,' Castle said, 'who would ring us at this hour?'

reporting clauses with long quotes

1.9 If you want to use a quote of several sentences, it is common to use a reporting clause with the first sentence only, especially in writing. The reporting clause often comes at the end of the first sentence.

'He's a curious guy,' Paul said to Tom Latimer. 'The things he asked! How old I was. Was I an only child? Maybe he just meant to be pleasant, but really!'

In some cases, the reporting clause comes before the whole quote.

She said: 'But you're not to register them in your name until you finish paying for them. I want to keep some control over you. Is that a deal?'

In speech, it is common to repeat the reporting clause several times in a long quote, to make it clear that the quote is continuing.

I said to him, 'Isn't that odd?' 'No, it's the usual thing now,' he said, 'there's so much industrial espionage goes on,' he said, 'that, you know, firms that have secrets, you know, sort of things they want to protect,' he said, 'it's an insurance to make sure their building is...' now what was it? I can't remember the word he used.

1.10 Particularly in written stories, quotes often appear without reporting clauses, usually when it is clear who is talking to whom. The change of speaker is often shown by starting a new line, as well as by the quotation marks.

'Doyle ain't here,' he said.
'Call him.'
'He's gone.'
'He ain't gone. He's hiding.'
'No, I told you he's gone.'

inversion of subject and reporting verb

1.11 When the reporting clause comes after the quote or in the middle of the quote, the subject is often put after the reporting verb.

'Thank you,' said Brian.
'For how long?' asked my stepmother.
'Shall we sing it as we go?' 'Yes!' shouted the boy.
'We no longer believe in anything,' wrote Zuenir Ventura, one of Brazil's most observant journalists.

This inversion is common in written quotes, but it also happens occasionally in speech.

'Oh,' says Pam, 'I didn't know they did that.'

1.12 The subject and verb are not usually inverted in this way when the subject is a pronoun. Note that none of the examples above has a pronoun as subject.

You also do not invert the subject and verb when the hearer is mentioned. In the following examples, the hearer is underlined.

'Why don't they attack our centre with infantry?' Doggett asked Sharpe.
'Shut up,' Thomas said to her.
'It's the Tunis plane?' Nortier shouted at me.

As you nearly always mention the hearer with 'tell', this means that 'tell' is not one of the verbs which can be inverted with the subject when it follows the quote.

'I'm not responsible to you for anything,' Cross told her.

1.13 Occasionally, newspaper journalists put the subject after the verb even when the reporting clause comes before the quote. The verb in these cases is usually 'say', although other verbs can be used.

Said a delighted Ferguson afterwards: 'Andy is in tremendous form.'
Added Smith: 'If I've got to bring in new players before the transfer deadline I will.'
Admitted Sir Lawrence, who refused to reveal yesterday's voting figure: 'We would have liked an opening bowler.'

In Britain, this structure is associated with 'popular' rather than serious journalism, and is used especially in sports reporting.

quotes in speech

1.14 In speech, of course, there are no punctuation marks, so you have to indicate that you are using a quote in other ways.

As mentioned above, in speech you normally use a reporting clause with a quote. But you also normally signal the quote by using a particular tone of voice. For example, you can raise the pitch of your voice for the quote. You can also pause slightly before and after the quote and use a separate intonation pattern for it.

1.15 The intonation of spoken quotes generally imitates the way that the quote might be said by the original speaker, although the imitation is not necessarily an accurate one (just as the quote itself may not be an exact repetition of the original message).

The quoted question in the following example was spoken with a typical intonation for 'wh'-questions, with a fall on *person*.

We all went, 'Who is that person?' and then I realized it was me.

Note that, in this book, the punctuation that seems most appropriate is added in spoken examples simply to make them easier to read.

1.16 Occasionally, quotes are used without reporting clauses in oral narratives. In this case, the reporter will often show a change of speaker not only by imitating the intonation that the original speaker used but also by using a different tone of voice. In the underlined part of the example below, the reporter used a higher tone of voice and spoke slightly more softly to signal that she was quoting another speaker.

Hariklia says she doesn't mind, you know, I keep saying, you know, 'I feel awful taking your bed.' <u>'I don't mind, Nanny, at all. I'm comfortable on this bed.'</u>

1.17 When you quote someone's thoughts, in telling a story about your experiences for example, you normally mark the quote off like other quotes, with pauses and an appropriate intonation pattern.

I thought <u>'Ooh my God,'</u> you know, <u>'she won't be a bit pleased.'</u>
A lot of the time you see it as: <u>'Oh well, they're doing self-access, phew! That takes the pressure off us teachers.'</u>

1.18 Particularly in formal speech situations, such as reading an academic paper aloud, the reporter may say 'quote' to signal the beginning of the quote and 'unquote' at the end.

Halliday defines this as, <u>quote, 'the starting-point for the message', unquote.</u>

You can also do this in conversation, especially if you want to emphasize that you are quoting something in an ironic way.

What about the, <u>quote, inequality of our circumstances, unquote?</u>

If the quote is very short, the speaker may say 'quote, unquote' before the word.

They call this sort of person, <u>quote unquote, 'perseverative'.</u>

Punctuation for quotes

1.19 As you may have noticed in the examples above, the punctuation for written quotes varies slightly from writer to writer, but there are some general conventions. These are explained below.

inverted commas

1.20 You can use single inverted commas (' ') or double inverted commas (" "). In Britain single inverted commas are used in most published material except newspapers, while in the United States double inverted commas are more widely used.
Double inverted commas are more usual in handwriting in both countries. Those used at the beginning of a quote are called **opening inverted commas** and those at the end are called **closing inverted commas**.
In dictating punctuation, you normally say 'open inverted commas' or 'open quotes' and 'close inverted commas' or 'close quotes'.

other punctuation marks in quotes

1.21 Note the position of the inverted commas in relation to other punctuation marks. When the direct quote structure consists only of a quote, all other punctuation marks are placed inside the inverted commas.

> *'But who would have taken the ice?'*
> *'I haven't the slightest idea.'*

When the direct quote structure includes a reporting clause following the quote, there is a comma before the closing inverted commas, unless the quote finishes with a question mark or exclamation mark (which is also placed before the closing inverted commas).

> *'That's right,' the guard said.*
> *'Who else?' Maria asked.*
> *'That's not her, I told you!' he shouted, pointing at the drawing.*

When the reporting clause comes before the quote, it is followed by a colon or a comma before the opening inverted commas. The quote begins with a capital letter.

> *I joked a bit and Steve said: 'This is serious.'*
> *She answered, 'Don't ask, just go.'*

When a quoted sentence is separated into two parts by the reporting clause, there is a comma at the end of the first part of the quote before the closing inverted commas, and another at the end of the reporting clause before the opening inverted commas. The second part of the quote does not begin with a capital letter.

> *'But I can assure you, Ginny,' he added, 'that you couldn't do better than Vogel.'*

Compare the punctuation in the example above with the next example, where there are two complete sentences in the quote. In this case, there is a full stop after the reporting clause; and the following quote begins with a capital letter.

> *'I just need to talk to him about something,' Ben said. 'Have you seen him lately?'*

When the end of the quote is also the end of the direct quote structure, any final punctuation mark (full stop, question mark, or exclamation mark) is placed inside the closing inverted commas.

> *She didn't return his affection, but said: 'I have had to make an important decision.'*
> *He said only, 'May I walk home with you?'*
> *Then Ros shouted: 'He killed him!'*

quoting thoughts

1.22 Quote structures are normally used to report something that someone has said or written – where the original message existed in the form of words. However, thoughts are also sometimes reported using a direct quote structure: this happens particularly with characters in a novel or when people tell stories about themselves. In this case, the quote is sometimes signalled in writing by inverted commas just like an ordinary quote.

'No,' he said to himself. 'It's not going to be like that.'

Usually, however, inverted commas are not used.

He thought, I ought to be alone.
Why did I marry so quickly, so foolishly, she thought to herself.
What would he say, she wondered, if he could see that now?

long quotes

1.23 If the quote is longer than one paragraph, you put opening inverted commas at the start of each paragraph, but you put closing inverted commas at the end of the last paragraph only.

She said: 'The pictures are fun and they brighten the morning.
'There's enough misery in the world, so if it spreads happiness, why try and ban it?'

In academic writing (see Chapter 5) long quotes – that is quotes that are more than two or three lines long – have a different punctuation and layout from short quotes. For example, they begin on a new line and do not have inverted commas round them. They are also indented (that is, they have wider margins on both sides than the rest of the text).

quotes within quotes

1.24 When you have a quote inside a quote, you use one kind of inverted commas for the outer quote and the other kind for the inner quote. So if you use single inverted commas for the outer quote, you use double inverted commas for the inner quote. If you use double inverted commas for the outer quote, you use single inverted commas for the inner quote.

Here are two examples.

'It's coming,' he said. 'It's coming very soon. You know our expression "the iron rice bowl"?'
He said: "I heard this voice saying: 'Tell my dad he's an old fool.'"

All the other punctuation marks come in their usual places. If you take away the outer (single) inverted commas in the first example, the question mark will come at the end of the complete question (*You know our expression "the iron rice bowl"?*). As usual, the inverted commas ending the whole quote (the single ones) go right at the end after any punctuation marks.

If you take away the outer (double) inverted commas in the second example, the quoted words are a complete sentence which ends with a full stop (*Tell my dad he's an old fool.*). The single inverted commas ending this inner quote therefore come after the full stop; and, of course, the outer inverted commas come last.

Indirect report structures

1.25 An **indirect report structure** is used to show that you are reporting what someone said or wrote in your own words rather than in the words they actually used. You can also use indirect report structures to report what someone thought or felt.

indirect report structures with reporting verbs

1.26 There are several different types of indirect report structures. The first ones discussed here are those which involve a **reporting verb.** This kind of indirect report structure consists of two parts: the **reporting clause,** which carries the reporting signal and contains the reporting verb, and the **reported clause,** which carries the message. The two-clause structure is sometimes called **indirect speech** or **reported speech.** In each of the following examples, the reported clause is underlined; the rest of the sentence is the reporting clause.

The nurse said that I could see him.
The friend asked what had happened to Clara's mother.
I asked him one morning if he had slept well.
Somebody's told you to talk to me.
Last night he admitted experiencing difficulties in his marriage.

1.27 Indirect report structures consisting of a reporting clause and a reported clause with a 'that'-clause are described in 1.28–1.38; with a 'wh'-clause in 1.39–1.44; with a clause beginning with 'whether' or 'if' in 1.45–1.46; with a 'to'-infinitive clause in 1.49–1.54; and with an '-ing' clause in 1.55.

'that'-clauses

1.28 One very common way of reporting someone's words or thoughts in your own words is by using a reported 'that'-clause. The reported clause is underlined in the following examples.

He replied that he couldn't help.
The report also points out helpfully that there are more sheep than people in the north of England.
She explained that it is quite unnecessary to hurt a patient, and that a firm but gentle pressure is quite enough.
Is it true your mother thought that sunshine coming through the windows would destroy the furniture?

'that'-clauses without 'that'

1.29 Often, the 'that'-clause is not introduced by the word 'that'. The term **'that'-clause** is still used to describe these clauses.

Dooley said <u>he stood between the man and the referee as the teams were leaving the pitch.</u>
Finland's Deputy Ambassador to the UN told a news conference in New York last night <u>she was worried about the possibility that medical supplies could be converted into chemical weapons.</u>
Now Osborne claims <u>the mine has shown a low profit for the last five years.</u>
I swore to myself <u>I would not dream of staying in Ramsdale under any circumstances.</u>

'That' could have been used in all these sentences. For example, the journalist who wrote the first sentence above could have written 'Dooley said that he stood between the man and the referee'.

1.30 In formal situations, and particularly in writing, 'that'-clauses without 'that' are relatively rare – the more formal the context, the more likely you are to find 'that' used wherever it can be.

In less formal situations, there is often no 'that' after the reporting verbs 'say', 'tell', or 'think'. 'That'-clauses without 'that' are less often found with reporting verbs that give more information about the original speaker, the way of speaking, or the reasons for speaking. These are verbs such as 'complain', 'maintain', and 'whisper'.

The Bank <u>said</u> it met union representatives yesterday to discuss a review of the branch operation. Privately, bankers <u>complained</u> that the union was trying to stoke up support for ballots for industrial action.
Mr Shemyov <u>said</u> he suspected that the KGB was behind the move.
I think she <u>thought</u> I was trying to cheat her.
And then I <u>had</u> to <u>convince</u> them that I was a student at a different university.

1.31 You are also more likely to keep 'that' when the reported clause does not follow the reporting verb immediately. In the examples below, the 'interpolations' between the reporting verb and the reported clause are underlined.

He said <u>when he got home</u> that it was exactly a year since he had his last drink.
The others said <u>of Squealer</u> that he could turn black into white.
He'd thought <u>a couple of months earlier</u> that Catchpole was coming along nicely.

position of reporting clauses

1.32 With indirect report structures there are no quotation marks in writing to signal that there is a report; and in speech the reported clause does not have the kind of 'quoting intonation' that we find with quotes. Therefore, the reporting clause normally comes before the reported clause, to make it clear that you are reporting rather than speaking or writing for yourself.

A government spokesman told the BBC such a move would be illegal as only a court can make this kind of decision.

My husband says his sister was the only child his father ever paid any attention to.

1.33 However, it is possible to put the reporting clause after the reported clause, though even in writing this position is less frequent than it is with quotes (see 1.7). In this case, 'that' is not used.

My old car could not get out up the steep slippery hill. Nor could any tractor, the foresters told me.

The cash dividend paid on the common stock will also apply to the new shares, the company said.

The employment report's most important information will be the level of manufacturing jobs rather than the total employment numbers, Mr Resler asserted.

She swore back and threw wire baskets at the man, Runcorn magistrates heard.

reporting clauses in mid-position

1.34 It is also possible to put the reporting clause in mid-position in the reported clause, although this is not common.

The situation, I told them, was similar to being in a state of mild hypnosis.

One of them, he admitted, had been befriending and arming the enemy.

None of us wants war, he said, but none of us is prepared to accept a partial solution.

indirect report structures in relative clauses

1.35 Note the usual position of the reporting clause when it appears in a relative clause where the relative pronoun ('who', 'whose', 'which', 'that', 'what', 'whom', 'where', or 'when') belongs to the reported clause.

They came out at the foot of a mountain which she said they must climb.

This example could be paraphrased as 'She said (that) they must climb the mountain'. Grammatically, *which* (standing for *a mountain*) is the object of *climb*.

Here are some other examples of reporting clauses inside relative clauses.

At least twenty people have been killed in clashes which the government said began after the killing by bandits of a senior army officer.

The deposit – which the agency said was capable of producing forty thousand cubic metres of oil a day – was found about 250 kms from the port of Vung Tau.

Reporting clauses of this kind are not normally followed by 'that'.

Occasionally, the relative clause does not begin with a relative pronoun: in the following example, the underlined clause is a relative clause which could have been written 'which he always said he loved'.

It was a home, the first home he had ever had, the house he always said he loved more than any other material thing.

indirect report structures in 'wh'-questions

1.36 When you want to check what someone has said, you can use a reporting clause inside a 'wh'-question.

Who did he say he'd talked to when he went there?
Sorry, who did you say was calling?

In this case it is actually the reporting clause which is interrogative in form (with inversion of subject and auxiliary verb), while the reported clause remains declarative.

As with reporting clauses inside relative clauses (see 1.35 above), there are no commas round the reporting clause, and the reporting clause is not normally followed by 'that'.

punctuation for reported clauses

1.37 When the reporting clause comes before the reported clause, you do not put a comma between the clauses.

Old Evan says it is the worst winter that he can ever remember.
Syd Fielden says that the coaching must be improved and natural talent encouraged.
He asked her if she was a poor woman.

Sometimes you may see a comma before 'that'. This only happens when there is a pair of commas before and after an interpolated word or phrase, and it is not part of the reporting structure itself.

The government have insisted, for example, that Air France continue to use the unpopular Roissy airport.

1.38 When the reporting clause comes after the reported clause, there is a comma between the two clauses. The reporting clause does not start with a capital letter (compare the punctuation for quotes, 1.21).

Once they became engaged, they could no longer keep their relationship a secret, he explained.

When the reporting clause comes in the middle of the reported clause, there is a comma before and after the reporting clause. (But note that there are usually no commas in the special cases illustrated in 1.35–1.36 above.)

The wise use of chemicals, said the Commission, could not be ensured by the restraining effect of high prices.

'wh'-clauses

1.39 Many reported clauses begin not with 'that' but with a **'wh'-word**: 'what', 'why', 'where', 'when', 'who', 'whom', 'whose', 'which' and 'how'.

Finally she asked <u>what I'd brought with me in the way of shelter, clothing and money.</u>
I asked the two men <u>why they were taking the risk.</u>
She rang Tom and asked him <u>who Anne was.</u>
I asked him <u>how this would affect the company policy concerning promotions.</u>
I asked <u>how much two aquamarines would be.</u>

These clauses can be used to report 'wh'-questions (see 3.27). They can also be used to report exclamations (see 3.30), and to give a summary of statements (see 3.53).

1.40 Even when a question is being reported, the reported clause is not usually interrogative in form: there is no inversion of subject and auxiliary verb. In the last example above, although it is a report of a question, the subject **two aquamarines** and the auxiliary **would** are not inverted. Also, the reported clause does not have a question mark.

1.41 You use the same word order, with no inversion of subject and verb, when you report questions in which the subject of the clause is the 'wh'-word itself.

When you report this kind of question, the word order remains the same as in the corresponding direct question. In the first example below, the corresponding direct question is 'Who else has visited the place recently?'

I asked him <u>who else had visited the place recently.</u>
I asked <u>what had happened.</u>

1.42 Very occasionally, if the verb in the reported clause is 'be', you may find examples of subject-verb inversion in reported questions.

I asked him <u>what was the matter.</u>
We asked Dr Tulloch <u>what are the prospects for a vaccine to prevent infection in the first place.</u>

1.43 The 'wh'-word can appear after the reporting verb with no following clause. This happens especially with 'why', but can also happen with other 'wh'-words.

I did not see or hear one bird. Not even a sparrow. I asked the boys <u>why.</u>
Stranger things have happened. Don't ask me <u>what.</u>

1.44 When the 'wh'-word is the object of a preposition, the preposition usually appears towards the end of the clause, not in front of the 'wh'-word.

Someone asked us who we were looking for.
He asked us where we came from.
If you ask me what he died of, I don't know.
Do you mind if I ask what you live on?
Mattie had not asked what Henry had been up to in London.

Occasionally, the preposition appears at the beginning of the 'wh'-clause before the 'wh'-word. This is generally associated with more formal speech or writing.

They will usually ask you in what denominations you want the money.

'whether' and 'if'

1.45 Another type of reported clause begins with 'whether' or 'if'.

I asked him whether it was still raining.
One of the journalists at the Press Conference queried whether sabotage could have been involved.
That's why I asked if I could spend the night here.
She was asked if she would like to join the team.

Although there is no inversion of subject and verb in the reported question, you do use some of the words normally used in questions rather than statements. For example, you usually use 'any' and 'ever' rather than 'some' and 'never'.

I asked her if she had any children.
I resisted the impulse to ask her if she ever took a rest.

'Whether' and 'if' clauses can be used for reporting 'yes/no' questions (see 3.19). They can also be used for reporting when people are uncertain about something (see 4.29).

1.46 You can add 'or not' to a reported question starting with 'whether'. This either comes immediately after 'whether', as in the first example below, or at the end of the reported clause, as in the second example.

I asked him whether or not he actually had done any experiments for the CIA.
For the first time since he was a little boy he asked himself whether he loved his father or not.

1.47 With indirect report structures of the kinds described in 1.39–1.46, the normal position for the reporting clause is before the reported clause. However, the reporting clause sometimes appears in the middle of the reported clause (see 1.34). This happens fairly commonly with reported 'wh'-questions, especially when you are reporting thoughts. The reporting clause normally comes immediately after the 'wh'-word.

When the reporting clause is in this position, the reported question is interrogative in form, with inversion of subject and verb where necessary, as in the second and third examples below.

Who, he asked himself, would want to kill him?
What, <u>I wondered</u>, could things have been like on the day that it actually happened?
How then, <u>I asked him</u>, did men and women meet each other socially?

These reports are a kind of indirect quote structure – see 1.61–1.66.

'wh'-words with 'to'-infinitives

1.48 There is another kind of reported clause beginning with a 'wh'-word, in which the verb is in the 'to'-infinitive form. Any of the 'wh'-words listed in 1.39 can appear in this kind of clause except 'why'. 'Whether' can also appear, but not 'if'.

She stopped someone else and asked them <u>how to get down town</u>.
I wondered <u>how to keep the whole arrangement plausible</u>.
This information left us wondering <u>what to expect for our child's future</u> or even <u>where to focus our efforts</u>.

These clauses are used to report questions asking for advice (see 3.42) and uncertain thoughts (see 4.31).

'to'-infinitive clauses

1.49 A reported clause can also be a 'to'-infinitive clause.

I promised <u>to play bridge with Lady Penrith</u>.
The Secret Army Organisation had sworn <u>to kill De Gaulle and bring down his government</u>.
They claimed <u>not to have read it</u>.

In the last example the reported clause is negative: *not* is placed before *to*.

1.50 In the examples above, the subject of the reporting clause (the original speaker or writer) is also the understood subject of the reported clause. In the first example, for instance, the *I* who *promised* is also the person who will *play bridge*.

In the examples below, on the other hand, the understood subject of the reported clause is not the speaker or writer but someone else. In many cases, it is the hearer or reader – the person to whom the message was originally spoken or written. In the first sentence below, for instance, *I* does the telling but 'she' will *write about Nancy Reagan*. Note that if a pronoun is used to refer to this person the object form is used (e.g. *her* in the first example rather than 'she').

I told <u>her to write about Nancy Reagan</u>.
I asked <u>him to give me a week to think of something</u>.
I got into trouble one mealtime for calling one of the teachers rude names when she ordered <u>me to eat something which looked awful</u>.

A number of foreign embassies are advising <u>dependents and non-essential staff to leave the country.</u>

1.51 With the indirect report structure shown in 1.50, the reporting verb is sometimes passive, with the hearer or reader being the subject.

An MGM director was told to film a series of short newsreels under the title 'The Inquiring Reporter'.
Colonel Wentworth had not been ordered to start the broadcasts.

1.52 There are certain reporting verbs which can only be used with a 'to'-infinitive clause when they are in the passive.

<u>She was alleged</u> to be able to add up pounds and dollars with the speed and accuracy of a computer.

For a list of these verbs and a discussion of their functions, see 2.78.

1.53 With some reporting verbs which can be followed by a 'to'-infinitive clause, you use a prepositional phrase to mention the person who will carry out the action in the reported clause.

The Chair neither rebuked Mr Wigg nor <u>called on him to withdraw.</u>
She <u>appealed to people in the UK to help fund the establishment of hospital facilities.</u>

For more information on these verbs and the prepositions used with them, see 2.94.

1.54 When the meaning of the 'to'-infinitive clause is obvious from the context, it is possible to leave out most of the clause. However, the word 'to' is kept.

She always kept her mouth shut when told <u>to</u>.
Flecker seems to be writing things down, even though he told Patrick not <u>to</u>.

Compare report structures with 'wh'-clauses where only the 'wh'-word is kept, see 1.43.

'-ing' clauses

1.55 There are a fairly small number of reporting verbs which can be followed by a non-finite reported clause with the '-ing' form of the verb.

They had admitted <u>taking the drug</u> allegedly for medical complaints.
The World Health Organisation recommends <u>eating five small portions of fruit and vegetables or about one pound in total every day.</u>
Witnesses have reported <u>seeing refugees forced to work as cooks and manual labourers.</u>

The reporting verbs which can be followed by '-ing' clauses can also all be followed by a noun group as object – see 1.98.

See also 1.93–1.94, on '-ing' clauses as part of prepositional phrases in reports.

partial quote structures

1.56 The two types of reports that have been dealt with so far – **direct quote structures** and **indirect report structures** – have been treated as if they were entirely separate. However, many reports in fact have some features of both types. There are two main 'mixed' types of reports: **partial quote structures** and **indirect quote structures**.

1.57 As mentioned above, an indirect reported clause does not claim to represent the actual words used by the original speaker or writer. However, in a reported clause you can include some words which are marked as representing the actual words used. You mark them by putting inverted commas before and after them. These words need not form a complete clause – in fact, you can mark just one word in this way. The only condition is that the partial quote must fit grammatically into the reported clause in which it appears.

Mr Nott said sovereignty could 'never' be given up. That would be 'absurd'.
He admitted that he adopted the name simply 'because it occurred to me at the moment'.
In February 69% of Britons told opinion polls they were satisfied 'with the way the American government is handling the situation'.

The partial quote need not be a complete part of the clause. In the first example below, the partial quote begins in the middle of the verb group, between the modal and the main verb; while in the second it begins between the article *the* and the rest of the noun group.

They said they were not able to make desert landings using normal hovering as this would 'envelop the helicopter into a ball of swirling sand'.
Javed said he was quitting in the 'greater interest of the game and the country'.

1.58 It is fairly common, particularly in academic and other formal writing, to find a type of partial quote in which 'that' is used after a reporting clause to introduce a grammatically complete quote rather than a reported clause.

Haig admitted that 'the situation developed more favourably for us than I had dared even to hope'.
The Annan Committee supported this policy, and added that 'foreign holdings in television companies should be severely limited'.
She said that 'his resignation would suit all parties'.

1.59 Especially in academic writing, you sometimes find 'that' used to introduce a long quote. The quote begins on a new line, and there is often a colon after 'that'.

> *Dudley-Evans and Johns (1981:33) argue that:*
> *to talk of 'listening to lectures' or 'teaching lecture comprehension' may be misleading; it may be better to talk of 'listening to lecturers' or 'teaching lecturer comprehension' as a reminder of the idiosyncratic nature of lecturer performance.*

1.60 Note that the punctuation of partial quotes is different from that of full quotes (see 1.19–1.24). Except for the inverted commas, the sentence is punctuated as if the partial quote were not there: it is not necessary to have commas or colons before or after the quote; and punctuation marks such as the final full stop come outside the inverted commas.

indirect quote structures

1.61 Particularly in narratives, you often come across reports which are not exactly direct quote structures or indirect report structures, but a mixture of the two. These structures are called **indirect quote structures** (they are also sometimes called 'free indirect speech').

> *How long, Kershaw asked himself, was he going to lie here, knowing that he would have to get up and be sick sooner or later?*

This example looks at first sight like a quote, though without inverted commas. But it is clear that the nearest thing that *Kershaw* could have said to himself was something like 'How long am I going to lie here, knowing that I will have to get up and be sick sooner or later?'

On the other hand, the question remains in the interrogative form, whereas reported questions normally do not (see 1.40 above). If the reporter used an indirect reported clause, he would probably write 'Kershaw asked himself how long he was going to lie here'.

1.62 Normally in reported clauses the **interactive features** are changed or omitted. For example, interrogative clauses (questions) are changed to declarative clauses (statements). The **reference features** (tense and pronouns) are also changed so that they relate to the time of the report rather than that of the original language event (see 3.77–3.98).

What happens in indirect quotes is that the reference features are changed, but some or all of the interactive features of the original language event are kept.

With some indirect quotes there is a reporting clause (*Kershaw asked himself* above); but not all indirect quotes have a reporting clause.

Indirect quotes are most often used to report the words that pass through people's minds (see 4.3), but they can also be used to report what people say.

interactive features in indirect quotes

1.63 Interactive features are those which are associated with face-to-face communication. There is one main grammatical structure which is always interactive: questions (including tag questions). Questions are interactive because they normally imply the presence of another person to answer them. The following examples show indirect quotes of questions; the first three have reporting clauses, while the last does not.

> *And she said <u>could they possibly do the operation in Gosport.</u>*
> *What did she think, he asked, <u>was it adequate?</u>*
> *He had shrugged, saying it depended on the quality, <u>didn't it?</u>*
> *Pointless, he thought, obviously they're going to check. <u>Why should she lie about things that could be so easily verified?</u>*

1.64 Other interactive features include:

● exclamations and interjections

> *The overwhelming beauty of the music filled her brain. <u>How beautiful it all was,</u> Karen thought.*
> *But <u>what the hell,</u> you couldn't do everything in one day, Johnny thought.*

● 'answer words' such as 'yes', 'no', and 'okay' (which imply a question from someone else)

> *I asked the girl who served me whether they were open in the evening. <u>Yes,</u> they were, until ten o'clock.*
> *I said to her, 'Do you get off at Runcorn?' She said <u>no,</u> she goes through to Liverpool.*

● conjunctions at the beginning of a sentence which show that it is an answer to a question (e.g. 'Because') or a continuation of what was said earlier (e.g. 'And')

> *'You've got me, I'm here.' <u>And</u> when had his own presence been a help or a consolation to anyone, ever, he thought.*

● certain conversational markers, particularly 'well' and 'so'

> *I thought <u>well</u> if there was a fire in this house I'd take my teddy bear.*

● prosodic features: this is shown in writing by underlining (as in the first example below) or italics suggesting the speaker's tone of voice; in speaking, the reporter may 'imitate' the original speaker's way of speaking – in the second example, *he* in the second sentence was spoken with an exaggerated rise then fall in pitch both times

> *Alice tried to keep her mind on what next had to be done. The cleaning. The <u>cleaning!</u>*

He was eighteen this year so he was able to vote. He was going to vote Labour, he didn't like Mrs Thatcher.

1.65   Sometimes the indirect quote is signalled in less obvious ways, though there is still the connection with conversational interaction. In the example below, the colloquial phrase *the hell* belongs to the Australian rather than the reporter who is telling the story, and this suggests that the underlined clause is an indirect quote of the character's words.

After about four days an Australian on board asked him <u>who the hell he was</u>.

1.66   Certain interactive words and phrases can be reported in a particular kind of indirect quote structure. The words include particularly 'yes', 'no', 'thank you','sorry', 'hallo', 'goodbye', and 'good night'. The reporting verb in these cases is normally 'say', though other verbs are occasionally used, such as 'bid' with 'goodbye' and 'good night'.

She was also <u>saying no</u> to her husband and children.
'I'm just going in to <u>say goodbye</u>,' he said.
Hey, doesn't anyone <u>say thank you</u> any more?
We really ought to <u>say hello</u> to the minister.
We drove in silence to the doctor's house. We <u>bade one another good night</u>.

Reporting adjuncts

1.67   In the reports that have been described so far, the reporting signal has been carried by a reporting clause. It is also possible to have the reporting signal carried by a **reporting adjunct** instead of by a reporting clause. Reporting adjuncts may be:

● adverbs, e.g. 'apparently'
● prepositional phrases, e.g. 'according to (the speaker/writer)'
● non-finite clauses, e.g. 'to quote (the speaker/writer)'
● subordinate finite clauses, e.g. 'as far as (the speaker/writer) is concerned'

Reporting adjuncts are used in both direct quote structures and indirect report structures. They are usually marked off from the rest of the sentence by commas (except the one-word adverbs, which are often not marked off).

<u>As Haig admitted,</u> French fears were not without foundation.
<u>According to Simon,</u> they spent an interesting evening looking at photos.
<u>To quote McCullough:</u> 'The ocean breezes at Long Branch do not suffice, so off he is taken to Saratoga.'
'The world is not hostile, nor yet is it friendly,' <u>in the words of J.H.Holmes</u>. 'It is simply indifferent.'

French peasants, too, worshipped a Napoleon, who 'sent them rain and sunshine from above', in Marx's classic phrase.

An important feature of reporting adjuncts is that you use some of them to signal that you agree or disagree with the speaker or writer whose words you are reporting – see 2.48.

1.68 When phrases such as 'in John's opinion', 'as far as Gwyneth is concerned', 'for Mellors', and 'for the students' part' are used, it is often not clear whether the 'report' is really a report of the speaker's/writer's words or simply a comment by the reporter. These adjuncts rarely appear with quotes.

The two men had seemed friendly enough tonight, in Alexis's opinion, and of course the wives seemed friendly.
And anyway, as far as Judy was concerned, the discussion was purely theoretical, so she didn't much mind what was said.

'as'-clauses

1.69 A very frequent type of reporting signal that can be regarded as a reporting adjunct is a special use of 'as'-clauses. Like the other adjuncts listed above, the 'as'-clauses are marked off from the rest of the sentence by commas. 'As'-clauses are, however, different from the other reporting adjuncts in that they are finite clauses which include a reporting verb. This reporting verb is usually one which can be followed by a 'that'-clause (but see 1.70 below).

'As'-clause adjuncts are used with quotes and reported clauses with roughly equal frequency. As with other adjuncts, when they introduce quotes a colon is often used instead of a comma before the quote.

As one of the prince's friends said: 'It has all been so one-sided, but there is nothing I am able to do.'
As he said, 'Only a fool would venture out into the desert alone.'
As Patricia Rowan points out, it would give parents greater control over their children's education.
He told the camera crew that he never watched television. Well, almost never: as he then admitted, there is one programme that he can't bear to miss.
As de Costa had promised, Ryle learnt a lot about the Civil War.

1.70 'As'-clauses functioning as reporting adjuncts often include the verb+object phrase 'put it'.

But as one astronomer put it, 'At least now there is something to study instead of just theories about how galaxies are born.'
Then he managed to get into drama school and finally Hollywood, where, as he would put it, 'the rest is history'.
Social breeding, then, creates a governing class equipped, as Burke put it, to be the 'soul' of the body politic.

1.71 Much less frequently, you also find 'have it' used in a similar way as 'put it', except that the subject of the verb is less often a person than a word like 'story' or 'tradition' (see 2.73).

I've always wondered about the extravagances that are told about your life and how, <u>as the story has it,</u> you married both God and the army.
<u>As an advertisement for a series of such tapes has it,</u> they provide 'A gentle stream of music that floats upon one's consciousness with scarcely a ripple'.
In the middle work there began to emerge an artist who, <u>as Morris had it,</u> dwelt less often 'in the world of the imagination'.

1.72 As with all reporting adjuncts, when an 'as'-clause is used in an indirect report structure,'that' is not used to begin the reported clause. You can say, for example, 'As he said, it's late' or 'He said that it's late', but you can not use both 'as' and 'that'.

adverbs as reporting adjuncts

1.73 An adverb which can be included as a reporting adjunct, although it is rather different from the others discussed so far, is 'apparently'. This can be used to indicate that what you are saying is based on what someone else has told you rather than on first-hand information. It therefore signals a kind of report, but without indicating who the original speaker or writer was. Other adjuncts which function in the same way but are less frequently used include 'reputedly','allegedly', 'reportedly', and 'supposedly'.

<u>Apparently</u> he would often sing popular songs when he went to a party.
There was more violence there when one of the women of the house <u>allegedly</u> flung boiling water on the crowd in the street.
He also <u>reportedly</u> jotted down the license plate numbers of cars spouting black smoke from their exhaust pipes and sent the culprits' numbers to the police.
<u>Supposedly</u>, Augustus, an admirer of Virgil, issued an edict that none of his writings be destroyed.

Unlike the other reporting adjuncts, this group of adjuncts is quite often not marked off from the rest of the sentence by commas, as the examples show.

See also 'so-called', 1.82

position of reporting adjuncts

1.74 The most common position for reporting adjuncts, as many of the examples above show, is in front of the quote or reported clause. However, like reporting clauses, the adjunct may also come after the quote or reported clause, or in any of the mid-positions listed in 1.8. 'As'-clauses and 'apparently' are particularly likely to appear in these other positions. Indeed, in writing it is relatively rare for 'apparently' to come at the beginning, although this is more common in speaking.

At least seventy-two people have been killed in a fire off the southern coast of Norway, according to the Swedish rescue service.
Sugar is in increasingly short supply, and meat, according to officials, cannot be rationed because there would still not be enough to go round.
Harvard is perhaps best described, in the words of Charles W. Eliot, as 'the oldest, the richest and the freest' American university.
We understand that students are only 'passing through', as one administrator put it.
By 1957, hundreds of families from East London had been housed, as one wit put it, 'in the middle of nowhere'.
Under deep hypnosis some subjects allegedly can be carried back in memory not only to early childhood but even to before this time.

Reporting nouns

1.75 So far this chapter has looked at report structures with reporting clauses and reporting adjuncts. The reporting signal may also be carried by a **reporting noun**. Reporting nouns appear in direct quote structures, with the message carried by quotes, or in indirect report structures, with the message carried by 'that'-clauses, 'wh'-clauses and 'to'-infinitive clauses.

A summary of these structures is given below. Note that the punctuation after reporting nouns is exactly the same as after reporting clauses. A comma or colon is normally used before a quote; but no comma is used between the noun and any of the reported clauses. Lists of the reporting nouns which are used in each of the structures are given in 2.97; and the function of reporting nouns is discussed in 2.125.

reporting nouns with quotes

1.76 Most of the reporting nouns which this book concentrates on are related to reporting verbs (e.g. 'explain'–'explanation'). These reporting nouns are usually used in indirect report structures.

However, there are some reporting nouns which are not related to reporting verbs. As the examples below show, you most often use quotes following this kind of reporting noun.

The pledge ends, of course, with the words 'liberty and justice for all'.
Perhaps the first lesson I learned was the old dictum 'one hand for the ship and one for yourself'.

If you do use a quote following a reporting noun which is related to a reporting verb, in many cases the complete quote is introduced by 'that' (see 1.58).

Control from the centre incurs the valid <u>criticism that 'they only talk and do not do anything'</u>.

I agree with Mr Herber's <u>assertion that 'reconciliation of man with the natural world is no longer merely desirable, it has become a necessity'</u>.

This gave substance to Helena P. Blavatsky's <u>statement that 'nature ever builds from form and number.'</u>

1.77 When the message is a question, however, you fairly frequently find quotes in this structure. The reporting noun is usually 'question'. Even if inverted commas are not used, it is clear that these questions are quotes rather than reported clauses because they remain interrogative in form, have a question mark at the end, and are normally separated from the reporting noun by a comma or a colon.

We return to the question, <u>what has been tested?</u>

The whole matter can be summed up in the question: <u>what is education for?</u>

But what she needs the most is to find realistic answers to the repeated question: <u>How can I raise my children properly?</u>

We should ask the question <u>Why, if satisfactory traditional designs have been evolved, should we try to change them?</u>

The quoted question may appear in the middle of a sentence. In this case, the form is interrogative but there is usually no question mark. The question is still marked off by commas.

This chapter has posed the question, <u>who takes the decisions</u>, by showing that a whole range of decision-making can be looked at under three broad headings.

Notice that these examples, although they are expressed as quotes, do not necessarily refer to specific language events. For example, the question *What has been tested?* may summarize a general idea rather than quote an actual question.

The question may be signalled as a quote of a specific language event by the use of inverted commas.

If asked the <u>question 'What does a plant need to grow'?</u> he answered 'Earth, water and sun!'

One newspaper report asked the <u>question: 'How can she justify spending this sort of public money?'</u>

reporting nouns with reported clauses

1.78 The indirect report structure consisting of a reporting noun and a reported 'that'-clause is very common.

A new, alarming note was his <u>admission that reports on the scandal had been given to him continuously by his closest advisers</u>.

They may recall Thoreau's <u>advice that we should distrust any enterprise that requires new clothes</u>.

Later press enquiries were met with the <u>explanation that it had been a</u>
<u>motor-cycle with a faulty silencer</u>.
The Consumers' Association has given a <u>warning that dangerous goods</u>
<u>could enter Britain after trade barriers in the European Community are</u>
<u>lifted</u>.

These 'that'-clauses typically include the word 'that'.

1.79 A small number of reporting nouns can be followed directly by
reported clauses with a 'wh'-word or 'whether' (but not 'if').

This is not irrelevant to the <u>question whether we can expect biology to</u>
<u>turn out to be reducible to chemistry and further to physics</u>.

1.80 A number of reporting nouns may be followed by a reported
'to'-infinitive clause.

The Embassy cannot guarantee help to anyone who ignores our <u>advice to</u>
<u>leave immediately</u>.
I can tell you that NBC's <u>claim to have the most musical workers in</u>
<u>Birmingham</u> was no idle boast.
I told him about Koornhof's <u>offer to sponsor the trip</u>.

As with reporting clauses followed by 'to'-infinitive clauses (see 1.53) the
understood subject of the reported clause may appear in a prepositional
phrase.

Lebel related his <u>request to Thomas in London</u> to trace every missing
passport over the previous fifty days.

Reporting adjectives

1.81 There are many adjectives that can be followed by 'that'-clauses.

Polanyi (1958, ch. 6) is particularly <u>insistent</u> that science is guided by
passions every bit as much as by politics.
The prime minister is <u>adamant</u> that he will not resign. To do so, he said,
would be a betrayal of democracy.
Sometimes parents with little money feel <u>sad</u> that they can't buy toys for
their children.
The next moment he was <u>aware</u> that he had made some sort of mistake.

A few of the adjectives with 'that'-clauses can be used to report language
events (see 2.110), but most are used to talk about feelings or about
knowing facts (see 4.38).

Many of these adjectives can also be followed by 'to'-infinitive clauses
and 'wh'-clauses.

He was <u>happy</u> to see his son married.
This was a great occasion which I was <u>sad</u> to miss because I was in
America.
But I was still <u>unsure</u> whether I would be able to study at the level
demanded.

These are also used to talk about feelings and about knowing facts (see 4.40).

See also 1.96 on reporting adjectives followed by prepositional phrases.

1.82   One adjective, 'so-called', is used in a noun group and has a meaning similar to the reporting adjunct 'apparently' (see 1.73). It signals that you are reporting what some other people call something, but without saying who these other people are. It also normally indicates that you think that the term they use is incorrect or inappropriate.

A great deal of concern has been expressed about the presence of <u>so-called</u> 'additives' in foods.
He felt they were trying to pull the wool over his eyes, baffle him with their <u>so-called</u> cleverness.

'So-called' is sometimes used in a way that is similar to a reporting adjunct. The phrase is added immediately after the term that you are reporting. It is marked off by commas and is often not written with a hyphen.

He has a philosophy, <u>so-called,</u> which he kindly explained to me once.
The invasion, <u>so called,</u> was a farce which they had no hesitation in describing as probably the most ludicrous in living memory.

Separating the reporting signal from the message

the reporting signal as subject

1.83   There is a type of report in which the reporting signal appears as the subject of the clause, the verb is 'be', and the message functions as the complement of the clause.

Does it matter? Well, <u>the answer is</u> it doesn't really matter all that much.
To the first question <u>my answer is,</u> up to a point, yes.
But <u>the question is,</u> why does he still need to go there?

Less frequently, the message is the subject and comes before the reporting signal. This only happens when the message is carried by a quote.

'It's not what you know, it's who you know' is <u>a maxim</u> that has special relevance if you're in business today.

1.84   The reporting signal can be of two kinds. The first is a reporting noun.

<u>The argument is</u> that once you are labelled as a secretary you will never become anything else.

Her complaint was that the meeting had been boring and unconcerned with the real issues.

The second kind of reporting signal is a 'what'-clause, also functioning as subject of a clause with 'be'. The verb in the 'what'-clause is a reporting verb.

What I am trying to say is that I felt different about Jennifer.
That isn't exactly what he said. What he said was that teenagers aren't fully civilized yet, and so they're dangerous.
What she would have liked to tell him most was to change his clothes.

Sometimes phrases such as 'all (that)' and 'the thing (that)' are used instead of 'what'.

All that they would tell me was that Uncle Nick was ill.

1.85 The message may be carried by a reported clause, as in most of the examples above; or it may be carried by a quote.

'Do you know what assets your husband has?' I say. Their reply is 'No, but all I have to do is ask him.'
'I understand,' was the bishop's reply.

This happens frequently with questions.

The question is, what happens next?
The central question then was: are they testable?

1.86 The message may also be carried by a reported 'wh'-clause. In this case, the reported clause is not interrogative in form, and there is no question mark. If the question being reported is a 'yes/no' question, the reported clause begins with 'whether' (but not 'if'). The noun is most commonly 'question', although other nouns such as 'issue' are sometimes found.

These nouns may report specific language events, but they more commonly refer to general ideas.

The question that concerns me is how the care of children is arranged.
The question the council would ask itself is whether a significant number of girls would be silly enough to believe it.
The second issue was what on earth to do about the problems on the long southern border of the new EEC.

discontinuous reports

1.87 The types of reports described so far have all been structures which are grammatically linked – a reporting clause and a reported clause making up one sentence, for example. In many cases, however, the reporting signal is carried by a grammatically separate structure, which could stand alone. These structures are not strictly speaking direct quote structures or indirect report structures, but they are clearly related. They are called **discontinuous reports.**

1.88 The message in discontinuous reports may be a quote. The verbs in the reporting signal, which are underlined in the examples below, are often those which are not used in reporting clauses. For example, you do not say 'He spoke that he could swim'.

> *Finally he lifted his chin and spoke. 'I could swim when I was five. Daddy taught me.'*

In some cases, the reporting signal may be separated from the quote by a colon rather than a full stop.

> *A taut look appeared on his face and he spoke sharply: 'God help them if that's whom they follow.'*
> *'It's appalling.' Only the director agreed: 'Yes, we know.'*

1.89 In journalism, a particular type of discontinuous report involving quotes is quite often used in reports of interviews. A question from the journalist is given as an indirect quote in interrogative form – see 1.61. The interviewee's answer is then given as a direct quote, normally with no reporting clause.

> *Did playing a tyrant make him act like a tyrant? 'No, but all of those things I just put off to the side, really.'*

1.90 'That'-clauses may appear in discontinuous reports. If the reporting signal includes a reporting verb, the verb is typically followed by both a noun group and a 'that'-clause. The noun is an 'empty' noun such as 'something': although it is the object of the reporting verb, it does not carry the message – the message follows in the 'that'-clause. The reporting signal is normally separated from the reported clause by a colon.

> *She realized something: that she could not put Mr Turner off.*

Instead of a noun group as the object of the reporting verb, the object may be a 'what'-clause which itself contains a reporting verb (compare reporting signals as subject, 1.84).

> *You have already heard what Etta has said: that I'm spoiling you.*

1.91 Reporting nouns are also used as reporting signals in discontinuous reports with quotes and 'that'-clauses.

> *Over two decades ago he posed a question: 'How does it feel to be on your own?'*
> *A description of the golf course penned in 1892 holds true: 'The Aberdovey course lies partly among the sand-hills and partly on the low ground just inside.'*

Non-clause messages

1.92 All the kinds of reports that have been described so far have the message carried by a clause, even if the reporting signal is not a separate clause. However, there are also reports where the message is carried by a prepositional phrase or a noun group.

prepositional phrases as message

1.93 Many reporting verbs are followed by a prepositional phrase which carries information about the message.

The two politicians were arguing about the election results.
Local residents have long complained about oil storage and gas plants near the airport.

You can also use a structure with an '-ing' clause following the preposition. This means that you can give almost as much information about the message as with a reported 'that'-clause.

Park hadn't talked much, and the first real exchange was when he had insisted on halving the bill when it came.
He confesses to not being so interested in Turner's paintings.

The last example above could be paraphrased as 'He confesses that he is not so interested in Turner's paintings'.

Note that the subject of the verb in the '-ing' clause may not be the same as the subject of the reporting verb.

Waite created regular chaos by insisting on a large part of his library travelling with him.

This example could be paraphrased as 'Waite insisted that a large part of his library should travel with him'.

1.94 A number of reporting verbs can be followed by a noun group and a prepositional phrase. Both the noun group and the phrase carry information about the message.

Finally he thanked her for the tea.

One of these reporting verbs – 'describe' – is particularly frequently used in this structure. In many cases, the prepositional phrase contains a partial quote (see 1.57).

The Foreign Office confirmed that Mrs Parish had been released, describing it as good news.
The Foreign Ministry has now responded to reporter's questions about his health, describing it as 'quite good'.
Mrs Smart hit the headlines when, describing herself as 'Absolutely Disgusted of Tunbridge Wells', she accused the Tories of betrayal after a lifetime of her support.

A similar structure with an 'ing'-clause can also be used.

The report criticizes senior police officers for not being better prepared for trouble.

See 2.28–2.32 for a list of these verbs and a discussion of their function.

1.95 Many reporting nouns can also be followed by a prepositional phrase telling you about the message.

Friends of the Brigadier said last night it was significant that he had made not one, but two, positive denials of the relationship.
He offered his government's congratulations on having defeated the coup.
Their computer rivals made a written apology for indulging in the same practice.

With some reporting nouns, the prepositional phrase may contain a quote. This happens particularly with nouns such as 'shout'.
The preposition in these cases is 'of'.

Some hearty stamping and whistling followed, and a shout of 'Give us another!'
Napoleon ended his speech with his usual cry of 'Long live Animal Farm!'

1.96 There are also a number of adjectives which can signal that a language event is being reported and which give information about the message in a prepositional phrase.

Some British firms are critical of BT's failure to provide enough capacity, particularly for data communications.
Bank of England officials were dismissive of suggestions that measures were needed against speculators.

These adjectives are related to reporting verbs. For example, 'critical' and 'dismissive' are related to 'criticize' and 'dismiss'.

See also 1.81 on adjectives followed by 'that'-clauses.

noun groups as message

1.97 Another way of reporting a language event is by using a structure with a noun group as the object of a clause with a reporting verb when the verb is active. When the verb is passive, the noun group is the subject of the clause.

This structure of reporting verb+noun group can be of two basic types. The first is where the noun refers to language (including thoughts) in some way. Most of these nouns are reporting nouns.
The combination of verb+noun together summarizes what was said or written.

In December Pitt issued orders to his commanders in North America which were similar to those they had already received.
As Lithuania faces the Soviet Union's threat to cut off supplies of gas and oil, the Unites States has issued a warning to Moscow.
In Moscow, President Gorbachov expressed regret and said that an investigation was already under way.

Note that, since many reporting nouns can be followed by reported clauses (see 1.75), prepositional phrases (see 1.95), or preposition and '-ing' clauses, the object can be expanded to give a great deal of information about the message.

> *On 12 February an Express article made the curious assertion that 'The present worries of Europe only make war more unlikely'.*
> *It's considered likely that any annnouncement that full agreement has been reached will be made when the two presidents meet in London next week.*
> *The owner also made a public apology for the team's performance.*
> *She continued to gaze into space as the captain expressed his insincere regrets for inconveniencing her.*

1.98 The second type of reporting verb+noun group combination is where the noun refers to events or facts in the outside world. In this case, the verb clearly refers to a language event, and the noun group tells you what is being talked or written about.

> *Your article quite rightly criticizes 'cut-price' company cars.*
> *Please do not mention the fact of our building a power machine to anybody.*
> *The Black Madonna was frequently carried in procession and many claimed cures as a result of her intercessions.*
> *A woman wished a heart attack on me two days, ago, didn't she? She said, 'I hope you have a heart attack.'*

reports without messages

1.99 There are a number of reporting verbs which you can use to refer to a language event without giving any information about the message.

> *'You can't live without friends, you know,' she called over to the silent girl. Aurora didn't answer.*
> *Those who felt themselves attacked have complained loudly.*
> *He walked down the stairs towards the library, still muttering.*
> *When reports were brought of the damaging remarks he made, I often found that I agreed with him.*

These are not strictly speaking reports of the language event, and are not dealt with in any detail in this book.

Summary of reporting structures

1.100 A typical report structure consists of a reporting signal and a message.

The reporting signal is one of the following:

```
reporting clause
reporting adjunct
reporting noun
reporting adjective
reporting verb
```

The message is carried by one of the following:

```
quote
reported clause:
    main clause
    'that'-clause
    'wh'-clause
    'to'-infinitive clause
    '-ing' clause
prepositional phrase
noun group
```

There are, of course, a few restrictions on which combinations of signal and message are found: for example, reporting nouns cannot be followed by '-ing' clauses or noun groups.

A quote may appear on its own, signalled only by inverted commas.

2 Function: the reporting signal

2.1 This chapter and the next discuss some of the main functions that are carried out by the different structures described in Chapter One. The chapters deal with 'central' types of reporting: those which report what someone has said or written and which therefore clearly refer to another language event. Chapter Two deals with the reporting signal, and Chapter Three looks at the way the message is expressed.

Other ways in which report structures can be used to represent thoughts, opinions, feelings, and perceptions are discussed in Chapter Four.

Many of the reports discussed in Chapters Two and Three can refer either to speaking or writing. To simplify matters, the terms 'speaker' and 'hearer' are normally used in talking about these reports; but, unless it says so, the statements also apply to 'writers' and 'readers'.

2.2 In Chapter One, it was pointed out that many reports include a reporting signal such as a reporting clause. You can show a lot of different kinds of information by the reporting signal that you choose. You can, for example, report how the speaker spoke.

'Come closer,' Debilly <u>whispered</u>.
She heard Helen <u>shout</u>, 'Look at it.'

You can also, for instance, show whether the 'speaker' is human or not.

<u>He says</u> he doesn't understand why he did it.
By a yellow circle on the pavement <u>a notice</u> says: 'Take pictures here'.

One of the main ways in which you can use the reporting signal to give information about the report is by your choice of reporting verb. The following section looks at the different kinds of information that you can give depending on which reporting verb you choose.

Functions of the reporting verb

2.3 You can choose a reporting verb which simply shows that you are reporting what someone else has said or written without adding any extra information. These are **neutral** reporting verbs (see 2.4).

He <u>said</u> several tons of assistance is being sent to the refugees daily.

On the other hand, you can choose reporting verbs which give information about the speaker's purpose or attitude (see 2.10).

His English was poor and he <u>joked</u> that even his Italian was not too good.

You can also report how they spoke (see 2.18).

'That's not her, I told you!' he <u>shouted</u>.

You can choose a reporting verb which in itself gives information about what the speaker actually said, especially about whether the speaker said positive or negative things (see 2.28).

The Agency had been <u>criticised</u> for being slow off the mark.

Function: the reporting signal

Your reporting verb can show how the reported message fits in with the rest of the language event (see 2.34).

'Is he all right?' 'No,' he <u>answered</u>.

You can draw attention to the particular words used by the speaker (see 2.39).

Lapointe <u>described</u> Pollard as 'a habitual practical joker'.

You can also show your own attitude to what you are reporting (see 2.40). In the following example, the reporter indicates that, in his opinion, the story printed in the newspaper is not true by choosing to use the verb *claiming*.

'The Sun' printed a story <u>claiming</u> that I had told their reporter that I didn't care about England any more.

And you can report the effect of what the speaker said, on you or on other people (see 2.54).

I <u>persuaded</u> Gabriel, the strongest of our porters, to stay with us.

Finally, although most reporting verbs can be used to refer to speech or writing, you can show explicitly whether the reported language event involved speaking or writing (see 2.59).

He <u>wrote</u> that the situation was neither new nor surprising.

neutral reporting verbs

2.4 The basic reporting verb is 'say'. You use this as a neutral signal, to show simply that you are reporting what someone said and that you do not want to add any more information about the speaker's purpose or manner. The verb 'say' can be used to report any kind of language event – statements, questions, commands, suggestions, and so on. The language event may be spoken or written.

'I'll talk to them' Leaphorn <u>said</u>.
'Why are you not Orthodox?' people <u>say</u>.
Basic food aid was an urgent necessity, he <u>said</u>.
Other people <u>said</u> they were now afraid to go out at night.
I remember the look on his face when I <u>said</u> look I want this.

The above examples show 'say' used in the reporting signal for direct quotes, indirect reports and indirect quotes. The verb can also be used in a number of other types of reporting structure.

I had a dream that <u>said</u> to read Carlos Castaneda's 'Journey to Ixtlan'.
What she's <u>saying</u> to herself is: 'Be yourself'.
About fifty civilians were <u>said</u> to have been killed.

2.5 If you want to use a neutral reporting verb, and you want to mention the hearer, you can use 'tell'. The verb 'tell' can be used to report statements, instructions, and suggestions, but not questions.

'I am convinced this would be the wrong move,' he <u>told</u> Eleanor.
Anthony <u>told</u> him the proposal was out of the question.

Professionally, I was told, they all thought it a fascinating story.
He told Henry to touch nothing.
They were told at first that they should simply expel the refugees.

2.6 The verb 'ask' can be used as a neutral verb for reporting questions.

'When can I go home?' he asked almost daily.
I asked them where they were taking her.

It can also be used to report requests.

I was the one who asked her to marry me.

2.7 The verb 'write' can be used as a neutral verb to report written language events.

He wrote that 'he is a truthful narrator, but he is not a scientific discoverer'.

2.8 All the above verbs can also be used without a separate reporting clause. 'Write', 'ask', and 'tell' can be used with the message given in a prepositional phrase:

Then Knox told her of the cable he had received from Ginny.
I asked the man for his address.
On one occasion she wrote about the opening of a new, expensive private school.

They can all be followed by a noun group as object.

Did he say anything to you?
We don't know why you have asked the question.
I wrote a letter to the car rental agency.

They can also be used by themselves.

'What about the stars?' 'He didn't say.'
I had no idea why I had been asked.
But he wrote and requested that I join him there.

2.9 If you only want to give a summary of the message in a prepositional phrase, or if you do not want to give any information about the message, you can also use the verbs 'speak' and 'talk' as neutral reporting verbs. If there is a summary of the message, the language event may be spoken or written; if there is no information about the message, it can only be spoken.

As she spoke of her father, her eyes reddened and she turned away.
Those reports also spoke of two young hijackers.
The health care equipment you talk about in this book, is it actually being used somewhere?
They talked on and on. Dinner was announced and served. They talked of unimportant things while the butler was present. Later, in private, they talked again.

Function: the reporting signal

If you want to use a neutral reporting verb, but with the emphasis on the fact that the speaker put their opinions or feelings into words, you can use 'express'. The verb 'express' is always followed by a noun group as object.

As many as fifteen companies have expressed an interest in entering the field.
The friend expressed her concern that JJ might 'do something foolish'.

showing the speaker's purpose

2.10 You can also choose a reporting verb which is not neutral in the way that the above verbs are. There is a large group of reporting verbs which you use when you want to show the speaker's purpose.

'It's cold,' she complained, 'and there's no one here.'
Mrs Carstairs explained that Sybil had a nasty sore throat.
Interestingly, one study reported that adolescents who perceive their parents as 'democratic' are more likely to perceive their parents as happy.
The script stipulates that members of the show's chorus line should dress as angels.

Here is a list of the major verbs which indicate the speaker's purpose and which you can use in an indirect report structure with a reported 'that'-clause. You can also use the verbs marked with an asterisk (*) in a direct quote structure.

acknowledge*	confide*	notify	remark*
admit*	confirm*	object*	remind*
advise*	contend*	observe*	report*
affirm*	counsel*	ordain	request*
allege*	declare*	order*	reveal*
announce*	decree*	plead*	rule*
argue*	demand*	pledge*	specify
assert*	disclose	postulate	state*
assure*	divulge*	pray*	stipulate
avow*	emphasize*	preach	stress*
bet	explain*	predicate	suggest*
boast*	foretell	predict*	swear*
brag*	grumble*	proclaim*	teach
caution*	guarantee	promise*	testify*
certify	inform*	prophesy*	threaten
claim*	insist*	propose*	vow*
comment*	joke*	protest*	warn*
complain*	lament*	reassure*	
concede*	maintain*	recommend	
confess*	moan*	record	

The phrase 'let someone know' and the phrasal verb 'point out' are both used with a 'that'-clause, and 'point out' is also used in a direct quote structure.

With the verbs 'advise', 'assure', 'inform', 'notify', 'reassure', and 'remind' you must mention the hearer (see 2.82).

2.11 There are a few reporting verbs which you use when you want to report that a speaker did not say explicitly what they really meant. You use these verbs to report the real purpose behind the speaker's words.

The Minister of Defence implied that the document was a fake.

Here is a list of the major verbs of this type. Since they do not introduce a report of what the speaker actually said, they are not used to introduce a direct quote.

hint	imply	insinuate	intimate

2.12 There is one reporting phrase, 'let slip', which you can use to show that the speaker did not in fact intend to say what they said.

Gretchen was a little surprised when Lou let slip that the divorce had happened twenty years ago.

2.13 There are also reporting verbs which you can use to show the speaker's purpose but which can be used with a reporting 'to'-infinitive clause. Some of these have already appeared in the list above, but others are not normally used with a 'that'-clause.

He had promised to take his eldest son to a football match that Saturday.
They appealed to the country's leaders to respect free expression and not resort to violence.

Here is a list of the major verbs which are used in this way. You can also use the verbs marked with an asterisk (*) in a direct quote structure.

admonish*	command*	incite	recommend*
advise*	counsel*	instruct*	remind*
appeal*	direct*	invite*	request*
beg*	encourage	offer*	threaten*
beseech*	enjoin	order*	urge*
caution*	entreat*	plead*	vow*
challenge*	exhort*	pledge*	warn*
claim*	forbid	promise*	
coax*	implore*	propose*	

Note that the phrasal verb 'egg on' is used in a similar way.

With most of these verbs, (except 'claim', 'offer', 'pledge', 'promise', 'threaten', and 'vow'), you must mention the hearer when they are used with a 'to'-infinitive clause (see 2.87).

2.14 There is a small number of reporting verbs which you can use to show the speaker's purpose which are followed by a reported 'wh'-clause.

He questioned why no action had been taken.

Here is a list of the major verbs which are used in this way. You can also use the verbs marked with an asterisk (*) in a direct quote structure.

enquire*	inquire*	query*	question

2.15 A small number of reporting verbs showing the speaker's purpose can be followed by a reporting '-ing' clause.

She said the main thing was not to marry too young. She recommended waiting until you were twenty-four like her.

Here is a list of the major verbs which are used in this way.

admit	recommend	suggest
propose	report	

2.16 Some of the reporting verbs which you can use to show the speaker's purpose can also be used with a prepositional phrase giving a summary of the message.

He joked about their hasty marriage and his good fortune.
The ambassador has protested against today's meeting.

Here is a list of the major verbs which are used in this way. The preposition normally used with each of them is given in brackets.

admit (to)	confess (to)	object (to)
advise (against)	enquire (about)	plead (for)
appeal (for)	explain (about)	pray (for)
argue (for/against)	grumble (about)	protest (against)
beg (for)	hint (at)	remark (on)
boast (about/of)	inform (about/of)	remind (about/of)
brag (about/of)	inquire (about)	report (on)
caution (against)	insist (on)	testify (to)
comment (on)	joke (about)	warn (about/against)
complain (about/of)	moan (about)	

Most of these verbs (except 'appeal', 'beg', 'comment', 'inform', 'plead', 'pray') are also sometimes followed by a preposition and an '-ing' clause.

Only 42.7% of men in the former East Germany admitted to being useless around the house.
My father often joked about winning the million dollar prize.

With 'inform' and 'remind' you must mention the hearer (see 2.82).

2.17 Note that with all the verbs and nouns which you can use to show the speaker's purpose, it is actually your interpretation of the purpose that you give. In most cases, your aim will probably be to give an honest and accurate interpretation, but sometimes the speaker might in fact have had a different purpose.

In some cases, the reporter may choose a particular reporting verb to impose his or her own interpretation of the language event. This can be seen by comparing the following reports of exactly the same interview by two different newspapers.

Dr Ali Bacher <u>admitted</u> he had been 'leant on by a third party'.
Dr Bacher <u>said</u> the two groups met after 'an influential third party' had prevailed upon them to try to reach an accord.

The choice of *admitted* in the first report implies that Dr Bacher was unwilling to say what he said and had to be forced to say it, perhaps by persistent questioning from the reporter who already knew the truth. This negative implication is missing from the second report. (Notice also the difference in the wording of the partial quotes and the difference between *leant on* which suggests threats and *prevailed upon* which suggests reasoned persuasion). For further discussion of interpretation in newspaper reports, see Chapter 5.

showing the manner of speaking

2.18   There are many reporting verbs which you can use to show the way in which something was said. These can normally only be used to report spoken language events (see 2.67 for verbs which report the manner of writing). They are most often used in direct quote structures, although many can also be used in indirect report structures with 'that'-clauses. You normally use these verbs when you want to indicate or suggest the speaker's emotions at the time that he or she was speaking. The verbs are used particularly in written stories, although some of the more common verbs, such as 'shout', also occur in spoken stories and newspaper reports.

'Let's see the colour of your money,' the Admiral <u>cried</u>.
'Shut up, Archie!' Anne <u>shouted</u>.
'We still haven't got a penny!' Malcolm <u>sighed</u> irritably.
Three young women tried to break the line, only to be dragged clumsily off towards the trucks, <u>shouting</u> that they were being hurt.

2.19   These verbs can be divided into several groups according to the main aspect of the speaker's manner that they refer to, but it should be remembered that individual verbs may also give other information about the manner. For example, if you use 'storm', you mean that the speaker spoke very loudly, but also very angrily. If you use 'quaver', you mean that the speaker spoke slowly and unsteadily, but also in a nervous or uncertain way. Some of the verbs can also show your opinion of the speaker or of what they said. For example, you can use 'simper' to show that in your opinion the speaker was rather silly. If you use 'chatter', you mean that the speaker spoke quickly, but also that they were not saying anything important. (For more on the reporter's attitude, see 2.40.)

2.20   One group of verbs refers particularly to how **quietly** or **loudly** the speaker spoke. Here are the major verbs of this type.

bawl	declaim	rave	shrill
bellow	exclaim	scream	storm
boom	holler	screech	trumpet
breathe	mumble	shout	whisper
call	murmur	shriek	yell
cry	mutter		

The following phrasal verbs are used in the same way.

bawl out	call out	rap out
boom out	cry out	shout out

Then Harry <u>bellowed</u>, as only he could, 'I'm not having my grandchild brought up in Germany!'
<u>Muttering</u> that he would be back in a moment, he went upstairs.
'My God,' Pantieri <u>murmured</u>, 'I think I've got it.'
She flung the bag down. 'That woman has been spying on me!' she <u>screeched</u>.
'Jeanne?' I <u>whispered</u>. She was asleep.
We'd stand outside in the hall and <u>yell</u>, 'Daddy, don't forget to wash your hair!'

2.21 Another group of verbs refers particularly to the **speed** of talking. Here are the major verbs of this type.

babble	drawl	gibber	stammer
blurt	falter	quaver	stutter
chatter	gabble	snap	

The following phrasal verbs can be used in the same way.

blurt out	burst out	prattle on	stammer out

He <u>blurted</u>: 'Is it true?' His voice was shocked.
'I'm not special and I don't want to be!' she <u>blurted out</u>.
'You wouldn't like that, Mr Bird, would you?' 'No need for that, sir,' Bird <u>gabbled.</u>
'Tim here is quite the expert,' he <u>prattled on</u> pleasurably, 'not only in paintings.'
'What university?' I asked. 'Grimsby,' <u>snapped</u> Mary.

2.22 Another group refers particularly to the speaker's **general behaviour** as they spoke, especially the expression on their face or the other noises they made (for example, laughter). The list below gives the most frequent examples, but you can in principle use any other verb of a similar kind to introduce a quote.

beam	fume	hum	sob
blaze	gasp	laugh	splutter
blush	giggle	moan	sputter
bluster	gloat	sigh	titter
bristle	grin	simper	wail
chortle	groan	smile	whimper
chuckle	guffaw	smirk	
explode	gulp	sniff	
exult	gurgle	snigger	

'I can see spirits wandering in the ruins,' Mirella giggled and raised her full glass of wine.

'I missed you, oh, I missed you,' she simpers to Rick as she recalls their college days.

'Pardon?' asked the receptionist. 'Oh. Nothing,' spluttered Dennis.

2.23 Almost any verb used to describe the noises made by animals can also be used as a reporting verb. As with the group above, you can in principle use any other verb of a similar kind to introduce a quote.

bark	coo	purr	squeal
bleat	croak	roar	trill
bray	growl	snarl	twitter
cackle	grunt	snort	whine
chirp	hiss	squawk	
cluck	howl	squeak	

'Put the chair down,' she brayed. 'Put the chair down. Now.'

'It's beyond luxury,' coos Analisa Maduro, the hotel's glamorous public relations manager.

'Who asked you? Stay out of it!' Conti growled.

'I was just saying, our garden's better than this,' squawked one woman from the home counties.

2.24 A number of other verbs do not fall easily into any of the above groups. They refer to various aspects of the speaker's manner of speaking. For example, if you use 'huff', you are indicating the speaker's mood, whereas if you use 'rasp' you are describing the sound of their voice. Here are some examples of verbs of this kind.

burble	ejaculate	lisp	sing
chant	gush	pipe	witter
chorus	huff	pontificate	
croon	intone	rasp	

A number of phrasal verbs can be used in the same way. Here are some examples.

drone on	jerk out	pipe up	spit out

'Why aren't there more salespeople here?' one well-dressed lady huffed as she elbowed competitors out of the way.

Function: the reporting signal

*'Occasionally,' he <u>pontificated</u>, 'the mind converts some shock or other
into a physical symptom rather than a mental one.'*
'Where've you put it?' he <u>rasped</u>, in a cautiously controlled voice of fury.

2.25 There are a number of verbs which refer to the manner of
speaking but which can be used without a quote or a reported clause.

With these verbs, you can give a summary of the message in a
prepositional phrase, usually with 'about' (where another preposition is
used, it is given in the list below). Here is a list of the major verbs you
can use in this way. Some have already been included in the above lists,
but others can only appear in this kind of report.

babble	fulminate (against)	mumble	scream
blether	gab	mutter	shout
chatter	gabble	prattle	shriek
clamour (for)	gossip	rant	whisper
crow (over)	grizzle	rave	

The following phrasal verbs can be used in the same way.

prattle on	ramble on	rant on	rattle on

*To get on in the world, one had to sell one's soul <u>blethering</u> about how
relevant and meaningful the changes were.*
Mathers <u>fulminated</u> against them for even considering the matter.
*The media, press and local politicians <u>ranted and raved</u> about pointless
violence, gun control and vicious criminals.*

2.26 A number of verbs which refer to the manner of speaking can be
followed, when active, by a summary of the message in a noun phrase
functioning as object. Here is a list of the major verbs that can be used
in this way.

bellow	intone	scream	whisper
breathe	lisp	shout	yell
chant	mumble	shriek	
enunciate	murmur	sing	
gabble	mutter	stammer	

The following phrases and phrasal verbs can be used in the same way.

bawl out	call out	rattle off	spout out
belt out	cry out	read out	stammer out
blast out	gasp out	reel off	
blurt out	let slip	shout out	

The driver dived from his car and <u>screamed</u> a warning to police.
*She <u>rattled off</u> this monologue while pouring the white wine like pints of
beer.*
*She <u>spouted</u> the kind of cliches you usually only hear from the lips of a
publicity-seeking model.*

In the end it had been Aunt Dulcie she told. Finding her alone, she
stammered it out. 'Something awful's happened.'

2.27   Note that you can also show the speaker's manner by using an
adverb or a prepositional phrase with the reporting verb.

'I've got the key!' he announced triumphantly.
Then a child spoke up boastfully: 'Yesterday a soldier came.'
'Senora,' she said imploringly, pulling harder at Amy's sleeve.
'OK, tell me where?' he asked in some surprise.
He answered with studied casualness that it had 'just happened, if you
know what I mean.'
'Well, who has been condemned?' said the woman with a snarl.
'Bastards,' he swore under his breath.

showing what was said through the reporting verb

2.28   There are many reporting verbs which in themselves give some
idea of what was actually said or written. In the example below, you
know that *Balestre* said bad things about the *tribunal he created*
(although the report does not tell you what bad things he said).

It's strange for Balestre to criticise a tribunal he created.

Like the verbs discussed in 2.10–2.15, these verbs also show the speaker's
purpose, but they are not used with a reported clause or quote. The
message in this case is not given in a separate clause but is partly or
mainly contained in the reporting verb itself. The reporting verb
therefore acts as reporting signal and message at the same time.

With all of these verbs, you must say who the **target** is. The target is the
person or thing being spoken or written about. The target may be the
hearer but it is often someone (or something) else. In the example above,
the target is *a tribunal he created.*

You can also say good things about the target rather than bad things. In
the example below, the target is *her performance.*

Unconscious or not, her performance was still highly praised by her
teammates.

You can often add more information about the message in a prepositional
phrase, or an '-ing' clause introduced by a preposition–note that, as the
second example below shows, the prepositional phrase or clause may
include a partial quote (see 1.56–1.60). The most common prepositions are
'for' and 'as'.

The Agency had been criticised for being slow off the mark.
The judge criticised the trial as a 'costly disaster'.

2.29   The following are the major verbs which mean roughly 'say
something bad about the target'. Where you can add more information
in a prepositional phrase or in an '-ing' clause, the preposition that
you normally use is given in brackets.

Function: the reporting signal

abuse (for)	charge (with)	dismiss (as)	reprove (for)
accuse (of)	condemn (as/for)	disparage (as)	revile (for/as)
attack (for)	criticize (as/for)	insult	ridicule (as/for)
belittle	curse (for)	lampoon (as/for)	satirize
bemoan	decry (as)	libel	slam (for)
besmirch	defame	malign	slander
bewail	denigrate (as)	mock (for)	slate (for)
blame (for)	denounce (as/for)	pillory (for)	upbraid (for)
castigate (for)	deplore (as)	rebuke (for)	vilify (as/for)
censure (for)	deprecate	reproach (for/with)	

The following phrases and phrasal verbs can be used in the same way.

call names	run down
pour scorn on	slag off

Social scientists have tended to <u>belittle</u> earlier child protection work.
Those lower down the scale are now going to be <u>slated and abused</u> for what they did, when they did it with the best intentions usually.
She feared being <u>lampooned</u> by the press as a vindictive and overbearing bossy-boots.
In Hobson's earlier review he had <u>rebuked</u> Le Bon for overstating the degree of permanence of a race.

Note that 'bemoan', 'bewail', and 'deplore' are used only when the target is a fact or a way of behaving, not when it is a person.

2.30 The following verbs mean roughly 'say something good about the target'.

acclaim (as/for)	commend (for)	endorse	flatter
applaud (as/for)	compliment (on)	eulogize (as)	laud (as/for)
bless (for)	congratulate (on)	extol	praise (for)

I <u>blessed</u> her silently for being so willing to accept my curiosity without question.
Many of the rescuers who were <u>lauded</u> as heroes four years ago are today being denied proper treatment.
'Casablanca' was shot entirely in the studio, although it has been <u>praised</u> many times for having the authentic feel of the Paris streets just before the war.

Note that 'endorse' is used only when the target is a fact or a way of behaving, not when it is a person.

2.31 There are other reporting verbs which are similar to those listed above, in that they give an idea of what was actually said or written and show the speaker's purpose. However, in these cases, what is said is addressed directly to the hearer, who must normally be mentioned in the report. With some of these verbs, you can also give more information about the message in a prepositional phrase, again usually with 'for'. Here is a list of the major verbs you can use in this way.

admonish (for)	greet	nag (about)	soft-soap
berate (for)	hail	reprimand (for)	taunt (with)
cheek	heckle	scold (for)	tease (about)
chide (for)	jeer	shush	toast

The following phrasal verbs can be used in the same way.

answer back	tell off
bawl out	tick off

The phrase 'give someone a piece of your mind' can also be used in this way.

> *He admonished the officials for allowing too many observers to invade the fairways.*
> *Dietle turned on the guards, berating them for leaving the gates unlocked.*
> *'What I mean...' Jonathan started, and Lee shushed him.*

2.32 A few other reporting verbs can be used to give some idea of what was actually said and to show the speaker's purpose, but the hearer is often mentioned in a prepositional phrase. Again, you can give a summary of the message in another prepositional phrase. In the following list of the major verbs of this kind, the first preposition is the one used to mention the hearer, and the second is the one used to give the summary.

apologize (to – for)	jeer (at – for)
argue (with – over/about)	quarrel (with – over/about)
carp (at – about)	remonstrate (with – over/about)
commiserate (with – over/about/on)	scoff (at – for)
expostulate (with – against)	

> *When we finally got home Gemma apologized to Mother over and over for her irresponsiblity and the anxiety she had caused.*
> *She's constantly carping at him about all the things he's 'not doing'.*
> *When people commiserated with me about Sam's death, I said, 'It's a great tragedy.'*

2.33 There are a number of verbs which are sometimes used with separate information about the message or the target but which can also be used by themselves. The verbs themselves give an idea of what was actually said and show the speaker's purpose. Here are the major verbs of this type.

apologize	confess	jeer	quibble
argue	equivocate	joke	squabble
bellyache	flannel	nag	swear
bicker	gripe	object	waffle
bitch	grouch	pray	wheedle
blaspheme	grouse	preach	whine
boast	grumble	protest	whinge
brag	haggle	quarrel	yammer
complain	heckle		

The following phrasal verbs can also be used in this way.

answer back   talk back

> *When it is being worked, the operators are apt to <u>bicker</u> and <u>squabble</u>.*
> *Remember how you <u>griped</u> all the way back from that concert in town?*
> *Said you couldn't make head or tail of it.*

indicating how the message fits in

2.34 Some reporting verbs can be used to show how what is being reported fits in with the rest of the language event.

In the example below, 'reply' shows that there has been a question before.

> *'He is just old, sir,' <u>replied</u> the soldier.*

In the next example, 'repeat' shows that what the speaker is saying has been said before.

> *Her husband moved aside and she came into the hall. Webb <u>repeated</u> his introduction.*

In the third example, 'add' shows that the speaker has already said something else; it also suggests that *the team were doing badly* is not the speaker's or writer's main point but something extra following after the main point.

> *He <u>added</u> that the team were doing badly.*

You can use the verbs in this category in many different ways: some, like 'add', can be used with direct quotes, indirect reported clauses or noun groups giving information about the message; others, like 'digress' normally give no information about the message (except that it was not related to what was said before).

2.35 One group of verbs indicate that what is said is a response of some kind to something that has already been said, usually by someone else. Here are the major verbs that are used in this way. Those marked with an asterisk (*) can be used in a direct quote structure.

agree*	counter*	rejoin*	respond*
answer*	deny	reply*	retort*
concur*	disagree		

> *When a young man asked Carlyle how he should go about reforming the world, Carlyle <u>answered</u>, 'Reform yourself. That way there will be one less rascal in the world.'*
> *'Did you two kids have a fight last night?' he asked. 'About what?' she <u>countered</u>.*
> *He said he understood that I had met Senator Robert Kennedy, and I <u>replied</u> that I had.*

A small number of verbs are similar to this group in meaning but are normally used with a noun group only, not with a quote or reported clause.

contradict	rebut	refute

'You still haven't <u>contradicted</u> my explanation for your desertion,' Jimmy said.

2.36 Some reporting verbs can be used to indicate that what is said has already been said, either by the speaker or by someone else. The major ones are given below. You can show that the speaker is using more or less the same words (e.g. 'echo') or simply reporting the general meaning (e.g. 'paraphrase').

The verbs in the list below can be used in a direct quote structure or can be followed, when the verb is active, by a noun group acting as object. Except for 'echo' they are also sometimes used in an indirect report structure with a 'that'-clause.

echo	reiterate	repeat

To whatever question is asked, he <u>repeats</u>, 'But I brought home my pay cheque every Friday!'
He correctly <u>repeats</u> that the European authors know nothing of the religious doctrines of the Assassins.
He spoke in English first, then <u>repeated</u> the warning in German and French.
Most of the next day's headlines <u>echoed</u> the minister's line and hailed the agreement as a triumph.
He <u>reiterated</u> that he had made no private deals.

The verbs in the list below can be followed, when active, by a noun group acting as object, although 'recap', 'recapitulate', 'sum up' and 'summarize' are also used without an object following.

abridge	quote	regurgitate	retell
paraphrase	recap	rehash	summarize
parrot	recapitulate	restate	

The phrasal verb 'sum up' is used in the same way.

The article <u>quoted</u> Michael Jackson as saying, 'I think I'm the world's loneliest man.'
Lane was <u>quoted</u> as saying that Clear was 'a difficult person to work with'.
You can get sick to death of a friend <u>regurgitating</u> her partner's opinions.
I was asked to <u>recap</u> my testimony before Congress.
I'll just <u>recap</u> for people who might not know this.

2.37 There are a number of reporting verbs which refer to the progress of the language event – starting, continuing, interrupting, and stopping.

Function: the reporting signal

The major verbs of this kind are shown in the following list. They can all be used in direct quote structures. However, most are not normally used in indirect report structures.

| begin | end | interject | interrupt |
| continue | finish | interpolate | persist |

The following phrasal verbs can be used in the same way.

| chip in | get in | go on | put in |
| cut in | | | |

> *'Joe Thundercloud,' he begun, 'you are my friend. Don't ever forget that.'*
> *'Bob was up with her all night,' Benjie continued, as though she hadn't spoken.*
> *'Helen may have been drunk, but she knew what she was saying, Mark,' Jeanne persisted.*
> *He was jumping up and down as he shouted this news. 'And sometimes they call her Grandma,' put in Marcus in his equally loud voice.*
> *At that point Sam interrupted her, as if he had not been listening to what she had been saying. 'I travelled down with Martha this evening.'*

A small number of verbs belong to this group in meaning but are not used with a quote.

| hesitate | pause | stop |

The following phrasal verbs are used in the same way.

| break off | butt in | carry on |

> *Afterwards as owner and rider were having a lively discussion I butted in to inquire if the horse was for sale.*

2.38 There are some reporting verbs which you can use to show how what is being reported fitted in with the rest of what was said, often by the same speaker.

Here is a list of the major verbs of this type. Of the verbs in this list, 'add' can be used in direct quote structures, indirect report structures, or followed, when active, by a noun group acting as object; 'mention' can be used in indirect report structures, or followed, when active, by a noun group acting as object; 'digress' is used by itself; 'elaborate' is often followed by a prepositional phrase with 'on'; and 'qualify' and 'withdraw' are followed, when active, by a noun group acting as object.

| add | elaborate | qualify | withdraw |
| digress | mention | | |

The following phrasal verbs can also be used with a noun group acting as object.

| tag on | take back | touch on |

He paused, but when there was no comment, he <u>added</u>: 'The police have identified the dead man.'
He admitted there were some good poets and novelists around, but he <u>added</u> that he had read none of them.

drawing attention to the speaker's or writer's words

2.39 A small group of reporting verbs can be used to draw attention to the words used by the speaker or writer to describe or name something. These verbs frequently introduce a partial quote (see 1.56–1.60). With some the partial quote or the report of the words used is given in a prepositional phrase with 'as'; these are marked in the list below.

address (as)	define (as)	dub	nickname
brand	depict (as)	entitle	refer (as)
call	describe (as)	label	term
characterize (as)	designate (as)	name	

The stories have been <u>branded</u> racist by the 'Politically Correct'.
FISA <u>called</u> the risk 'dangerous'.
In 1961, she divorced Miller <u>describing</u> him as 'a better writer than a husband'.
This young entrepreneur has been so successful his hometown has <u>dubbed</u> him 'The King of Baton Rouge'.
The authorities <u>nicknamed</u> the building The Morgue, and the term stuck.
Crompton-Batt does <u>refer</u> to his staff as 'my girls'.

showing your attitude towards what you report

2.40 When you pass on information or opinions to other people, you are in a sense responsible for the truth of the information or the validity of the opinions. On the other hand, if you report the information or opinions, you are not directly reponsible.

For example, if you were to read in a newspaper this statement about recent changes in the British school system: 'Heads are being put in an impossible position', you would understand that the journalist disagreed with the changes. In the original article, however, the journalist wrote:

Jeff Holman, assistant secretary of the National Association of Head Teachers, said: 'Heads are being put in an impossible position.'

The effect is now very different. The journalist is reporting an opinion, not stating it as his or her own. If the Minister of Education decided to complain about the report, the journalist could reply that he or she was simply reporting what someone had said and is not responsible for the ideas expressed.

The fact that the ideas are reported also means that the journalist is free to agree or disagree with this statement. This particular report does not actually show the journalist's attitude towards the ideas.

2.41 Most reporting verbs do not in themselves show the reporter's attitude towards what the speaker says. For example, in the following report, the verb *asserted* does not indicate whether the reporter himself believes that *national boundaries* really are *a cliché* or not.

'National boundaries are a cliché,' asserted Ronald M. Freeman, head of European investment banking.

Here it would be possible for the reporter to continue with a comment of his own such as: 'But Freeman was clearly wrong'. The reporter could also report someone else who had a different opinion: 'But other bankers argued that national boundaries are important.'

However, there are a number of reporting verbs which you can use to show that you do think that what the speaker says is true.

In the next example, the reporter uses the reporting verb *acknowledged*, which signals that he believes that it is true that *Congress had no choice*.

Some Congressmen swallowed their anger and acknowledged that Congress had no choice.

In this case, it would seem odd if the reporter then expressed a different opinion: 'But in fact Congress did have a choice'.

The reporting verbs which show the reporter's attitude may show a positive attitude (what the speaker says is true) or a negative attitude (what the speaker says is not true or is open to doubt).

2.42 Here is a list of the major reporting verbs which you can use to indicate or strongly imply that you believe that what the speaker says is true (see also 2.57). All the verbs can be used in indirect report structures; those which are marked with an asterisk (*) can also be used in direct quote structures.

acknowledge*	disclose	indicate	reveal
admit*	divulge*	mention	
concede*	foretell	note*	
confess*	forewarn	recall*	

The following phrases and phrasal verbs can be used in the same way.

let on	let slip	make clear	point out*

Even the liberal Ford Foundation has acknowledged that family breakdown is a major cause of social problems.
'In retrospect,' Seiji admitted after the war, 'it could be said that I was in favour of military aggression.'
John Grant openly confesses that he is far better at setting crosswords than solving them.
Robert Birmingham also points out that forward planning can help avoid stressful pitfalls.
Keynes suggested that Beveridge should make clear that he was not advocating frequent adjustments in the level of benefits.

2.43 Note that when you use the negative forms of these reporting verbs, you normally believe that the message in the reported clause is still true.

In the first example below, Rebecca is in fact the man's wife; and in the second example, Jossi had really been trying to prevent the crime.

When the men there asked about his wife, he said that she was his sister.
He would not admit that Rebecca was his wife.
Jossi bit his lip and did not reveal that he had only been trying to prevent
the crime.

2.44 You can also use a reporting verb to indicate or strongly suggest that you believe that what the speaker says is untrue or at least open to doubt.

From the time he first began to speak, Ravi claimed that he had lived a
past life in another district of Kanauj where he had been murdered.

Here is a list of the major reporting verbs which can be used in this way.

allege	lie	misinform	purport
claim			

The phrasal verb 'make out' can also be used in the same way.

But it's absurd to make out that the USSR invaded so as to threaten the
Persian Gulf.
Mailed from Queenstown, the letter was typed and purported to come
from a black extremist.

The reporting verbs in the list below also indicate that you believe that what the speaker says is untrue. Unlike the verbs above they are not used in full report structures, but are followed by a noun group acting as object or are used by themselves.

bluff	exaggerate	fib	misinform
distort	fabricate	misquote	

'The money was only a fraction of what we have,' the colonel said. 'We
exaggerated its importance to keep you cost-conscious.'
'How old is that boy?' 'He claims to be seventeen or eighteen, says he's not
sure which. In either case, he's fibbing.'

2.45 The use of these reporting verbs is an important way of showing your opinion about what you are reporting.

In academic writing, for example, you are expected to evaluate the other writers that you quote or report, to indicate whether you agree with their ideas or not. If you choose a reporting verb such as 'state', you do not make your opinion clear, and you can later evaluate the other writer's ideas as right or wrong.

The strongest arguments for ethical objectivity, states Trueblood, are not
empirical.

If, on the other hand, you choose a reporting verb such as 'point out', you are showing that you agree with the writer's ideas.

> *Mollenkopf (1983, p.14) <u>points out</u> that Federal government intervention 'accelerated and directed the second transformation of American cities'.*

See Chapter 5 for more discussion of academic texts.

In other types of text, such as journalism or political speeches, the use of these verbs can also be a way of guiding or manipulating the audience. The journalist or speech-writer can subtly convey a particular view of who is right and who is wrong without drawing attention to this evaluation: they are more likely to report that people who share their political views 'point out' facts, whereas people who have opposite views are more likely to 'claim' things. This may be intended to have an effect on the audience, encouraging them to accept the journalist or speech-writer's view of who is right and who is wrong.

> *The report <u>points out</u> that human rights violations have continued and this year it has received further reports of torture.*
> *The official line deals with this problem by <u>claiming</u> that the United States is basically trying to do good in the world.*

See Chapter 5 for more discussion of newspaper reporting.

showing that you do not accept responsibility

2.46 If you want to make it clear that you are reporting someone else's opinion and that you do not accept responsibility for the ideas expressed, you can use a clause beginning with 'what'. The clause contains a reporting verb.

> *He had then written down <u>what he said was</u> the latest weather forecast.*

You could express this as 'He had then written something down. He said that it was the latest weather forecast'. This is a neutral report of what he said.

Alternatively, you could express it as 'He had then written down the latest weather forecast'. In this case, you are clearly accepting that this is in fact the latest weather forecast.

By using the 'what'-clause, you subtly add in a comment of your own, without having to use a separate sentence for your report structure (note that *what he said was the latest weather forecast* is the object of *written down*). The comment means something like 'This is what he said, but I do not know whether he was right or not'.

2.47 This type of comment structure often has the reporting verb 'say'. You can emphasize your attitude even more by using one of the negative verbs listed above, especially 'claim'.

> *I was looking at the scallops, or <u>what they claim are</u> scallops.*

They are demanding more than £100,000 compensation for what they allege was the 'catastrophic' effect the contamination has had on their lives.

When you use 'claim' in this way, it is often followed by a 'to'-infinitive.

The Times and the Daily Mail published what they claimed to be the inside story.
It is true that religious and political leaders have emerged from time to time with what they claimed to be a new model.

You can also use a passive form of 'say' followed by a 'to'-infinitive (compare 2.78).

I got myself a table at what was said to be the best restaurant in town.

See also 4.35 on the use of this structure with verbs expressing opinions.

showing your attitude through reporting adjuncts

2.48 There are other ways in which you can show your attitude towards a reported message. One important way is by using a reporting adjunct (see 1.67–1.74).

Many reporting adjuncts are neutral, in that they do not show whether or not you believe what you are reporting. You can use them to make it clear that you are reporting someone else's ideas; but you do not have to show your own opinion.

According to Mr Thomas, the addictive sense of achievement offered by gymnastics is unparalleled.
It had apparently been a large business with as many as eleven warehouses, but in my time no trace of it was left.

2.49 If, on the other hand, you use a reporting adjunct with 'as', you show that you definitely accept the truth of the reported message. In fact, in this case you are often presenting the other speaker or writer as agreeing with your ideas rather than the other way round.

As Anju points out, 'For most of us in this country, keeping your family involved in what you do is natural.'
The two cricketers deserve better, as Graham Gooch admitted.

You show this attitude even if you use a reporting verb in the reporting adjunct with 'as' which does not appear in the lists above.

As Montaigne wrote, 'It needs courage to be afraid.'
Indeed, as one of the engineers told Zuboff, 'There are operators who can run the paper machine with tremendous efficiency, but they cannot describe to you how they do it.'
Or, as Auden put it, there is only a limited number of ways of knocking a nail into a piece of wood.
The difficulty is, as the author himself states, that 'the ancient history of India is mostly legendary'.

Function: the reporting signal

Here is a list of some of the reporting verbs which appear relatively frequently in reporting adjuncts with 'as'. The verbs marked with an asterisk (*) are the ones which appear particularly frequently in this structure.

admit	hear	predict	state
argue	indicate	remark	suggest*
confess	inform	say*	tell
demonstrate	mention	show*	write
explain	note		

'Point out' and 'put it' are also frequently used in this structure.

2.50 You can also use other reporting adjuncts to show that you believe that the reported message is not true or is open to doubt.

During the journey to the police station he allegedly told officers: 'That Dunstan the solicitor is next. He will be dead in seven days.'

Here is a list of reporting adjuncts which can be used in this way.

allegedly   purportedly   supposedly

One of them stuck a needle into the animal's spine to draw off fluid from its brain. This was supposedly to discover something about sleep deprivation.

Newspaper reports of legal proceedings often use 'allegedly' to indicate that the things being reported have not been proven as facts. The journalist does not necessarily believe that the reported message is not true.

2.51 Reporting adjuncts with 'so' do not have the same meaning as adjuncts with 'as'. You can use a neutral reporting verb in a reporting adjunct with 'so' when you do not want to indicate whether you accept that the reported message is true or not. This is therefore similar to other reporting adjuncts such as 'according to' (see 2.48).

Camels, so everyone says, are tough, hardy creatures.
Life is a jolly affair, so they tell me, and we have to take it with smiles and laughter all the way.

You can also use a negative reporting verb such as 'claim' when you want to suggest that the reported message is not necessarily true.

Pope Joan was noted for her scholarship and, so some writers claimed, her experience in the occult sciences.

2.52 You can show very clearly that you do not believe or agree with what the speaker says by using 'or so' instead of just 'so'.

Now he is rich and one of the leading experts, or so he claims, on German-language books in Turkey.

Here is a list of the major reporting verbs appearing relatively frequently in reporting adjuncts with 'or so'.

argue   claim   say   tell

Once Elisabeth crept under a table and there caught a mouse, <u>or so she said</u>.
He died in prison. From pneumonia. <u>Or so they say.</u>
Derek is lovely, and a professor and famous, <u>or so he keeps telling me.</u>
They had decided not to have children for at least a year. There were – <u>or so they argued</u> – economic reasons.

Another reporting verb which appears relatively frequently in this structure is 'go' with a non-human subject (see 2.73).

They were the only ones left in his bag – <u>or so the story goes</u>!

2.53 In certain circumstances, a reporting adjunct with 'as' does not convey the positive attitude described above.

Opposition councillors argued that satisfactory compromises had not been achieved, <u>as the Conservatives claimed</u>, but rather that the council had capitulated to the developer's wishes.
It was she, and not her mother-in-law, <u>as she said</u>, who was jealous of her husband's love.

In the examples above, the adjunct appears with a negated report (*had not been achieved; not her mother-in-law*), and the reporter clearly does not agree with the speakers (*the Conservatives; she*).

If, <u>as Hemingway suggested</u>, 'courage is grace under pressure', then the trip proved once and for all that I was sadly lacking in courage.

In the example above, the reporting adjunct appears in a conditional clause starting with 'if', and the reporter's opinion of Hemingway's statement is not given.

In these cases, the reporting verb in the adjunct will be one of those in the negative list in 2.44 or a neutral verb such as 'suggest'.

showing the effect of what is said

2.54 There are a small number of reporting verbs which you can use when you want to report the effect of what the speaker says on someone else, rather than the actual words that the speaker uses. In the following example, the reporter does not say what *Tania* said, but the result is clear from the reported clause: *the doctor* came because of what *Tania* said.

Tania finally persuaded the doctor to come.

Here is a list of the major verbs which can be used when you want to report what happened as a result of a speaker's words.

convince	dissuade (from)	persuade	prevail (on/upon)

They had been rejoicing over the fact that they had <u>convinced</u> Congress to cut spending and taxes.
Sita did her best to <u>dissuade</u> him from attending any of the ceremonies.
Ventner insisted that the car body was all right, and <u>prevailed on</u> him to try it out with passengers on an actual trip.

Function: the reporting signal

2.55 There are some other reporting verbs which can also be used to report the effect of the speaker's words on someone else's actions if they are followed by a prepositional phrase, or a preposition and '-ing' clause, with 'into' or 'out of'. When they are followed by 'into', they mean roughly the same as 'persuade'. When they are followed by 'out of', they mean roughly the same as 'dissuade'.

Here is a list of the major verbs which can be used in this way.

cajole	nag	talk	wheedle
coax			

> *I'm only really here at this meeting because a friend of my husband's talked me into coming here.*
> *You talked me out of getting rid of Terry, you protected him from me.*
> *She was sent to Washington, and McKinley and Sherman were cajoled into receiving her.*

2.56 The above examples all report the action or behaviour that is the result of the speaker's words. If 'convince' and 'persuade' are followed by a 'that'-clause, on the other hand, they can be used to report the effect of the speaker's words on another person's beliefs and opinions.

> *He had seen President Grant and convinced him that there was a solution to the difficulty.*
> *Winston Spencer Churchill persuaded the British they were still the tops, they still knew how to do things.*

2.57 Certain other verbs are also used when you want to focus on the result of what someone says rather than on what they actually say. In this case, the results are not actions or opinions but facts. In the following example, you are not told what *Philip Klass* says in his article, but you are told the conclusion that is the result of what he says.

> *Philip Klass proves conclusively that this has happened not once, but several times.*

Here is a list of the major verbs which can be used in this way.

demonstrate	establish	prove	show

> *Heisenberg proved that we can never know everything with complete accuracy.*
> *Boxer established that this increase in oxygen radicals was caused by an enzyme deficiency.*
> *Pioneers in educational research showed that a child learns better and faster with this method of teaching.*
> *Olson demonstrated that, if children are given a problem to solve, their hypotheses become more specific and precise with age.*

These verbs are similar to the reporting verbs which show that you accept what the speaker says as true (see 2.42). If you say that someone has 'proved' or 'demonstrated' something, you normally mean that they have shown it to be true and you cannot therefore add a comment such as: 'but they are wrong'.

2.58 Note that these verbs need not refer to language events. You can prove something in many different ways, not only by talking or writing about it – for example, by an experiment. It is only from the context that you can decide whether the proof is through language; and in many cases it may not be clear.

Pythagoras had proved that the world of sound is governed by exact numbers.
Psychiatry has demonstrated and proved that an unfulfilled wish lives on in the unconscious.

This ambiguity is also true of 'persuade' and the other verbs listed in 2.54: you can 'persuade' someone to do something by using physical force, for example. However, when you use these verbs, you generally mean that the persuasion was carried out through language.

showing whether a report is of speech or of writing

2.59 The central types of language event in reports, as noted above, are speaking and writing. The choice of reporting verb is one of the main ways of showing that you are reporting speech or writing rather than, for example, thoughts.

'Thank you, Mrs Fuller,' I sighed.
'It's the cold hour, this, before the lights go up,' wrote Virginia Woolf in her diary.

2.60 Where the subject of the reporting verb is clearly a speaker or writer, the verb itself may be one that is used to report opinions, perceptions, and beliefs, but the report is understood to involve a spoken or written language event.

Jacobs thinks that there may be a hard core of phenomena still unexplained by contemporary science.
Halliday (1970:331) sees modality as 'a strand running prosodically through the clause'.
In this book the author explicitly committed himself to stepping outside the conventional preconceptions of modern social analysis.

This also happens sometimes when the subject is the written text.

The report believes that imprisonment creates at least as many problems as it solves.
The bulk of this chapter has concentrated on the single woman with children.

Function: the reporting signal

2.61   Most reporting verbs do not in themselves show whether the report is of speech or of writing. The wider context may make it clear whether the report is of speech (as in the first example below) or writing (as in the second example), or this may remain ambiguous (as in the third example).

The police are still <u>advising</u> people to stay off the roads.
Three months later, Channing received a last letter from him, <u>advising</u> her to seek a divorce on grounds of desertion.
The companies have for months been <u>advising</u> customers to purchase hard disks with the machines.

2.62   Most reporting verbs have this double function of referring to both speech and writing. However, there are some reporting verbs which are usually only used to refer to speaking.

The largest group are those which refer to the manner of speaking.

He can drive home, she <u>giggled</u>, he can drive home. I am staying here.

See 2.18–2.26 for a list of the major verbs of this type.

2.63   There are some language events which are normally accepted as spoken rather than written events. For example, a 'conversation' is a spoken language event, and the related verb 'converse' is restricted to speaking.

The restriction is not entirely predictable however: a 'talk' definitely involves speaking, but a speaker, writer, or written text can 'talk' about a topic. If you 'dictate' something, you say it aloud, but a 'dictation' can refer to the written text that is the result.

Here is a list of the major verbs which signal that the language event involved speaking. Most of the verbs in this group are not used in full report structures, although the ones marked with an asterisk (*) are sometimes used in a direct quote structure.

chat	heckle	phone	recite*
converse	lecture	pronounce*	telephone
dictate	natter	radio	utter

In addition, 'answer back' and 'read out' also indicate that the language event involved speaking. 'Read out' is sometimes used in a direct quote structure.

Within a few minutes of his arrival home with Rose, Henry had <u>telephoned</u>.
He <u>dictated</u> a note to his supporters in the Senate: 'I hope that all true friends of the Treaty will refuse to support the Lodge reservations.'
When each of them <u>pronounced</u> 'Till death do us part,' I had a sense of the gravity of this promise.
We <u>radioed</u> for food and water when nightfall came.

2.64 There is one way of signalling reports of speech which is restricted to very colloquial speech. The verb 'go' is fairly frequently used as a reporting verb in colloquial speech, roughly meaning 'say'. It is only used with direct quotes.

> *So he said, 'No we haven't had any dogs like that,' he went, 'we've never had any dogs like that.'*
> *And the barman looks at him, and he goes, 'We don't often get bears in here.'*

See also 2.73.

2.65 A fairly small number of verbs can only be used to refer to writing. Some of these, including the verb 'write' itself, refer to the method by which the message is produced or the instrument which is used. Of these, only 'write' is commonly used in full report structures, although the others may sometimes be used in direct quote structures.

inscribe	pencil	type	write
pen	print		

The phrasal verbs 'ink in' and 'key in' are also used in this way.

> *Another woman wrote, 'I have more respect for my mother than when we began this course, and I feel closer to her.'*
> *He wrote a name and a London telephone number.*
> *A memorable description of veteran Confederate soldiers on the march was penned with grudging admiration by one of the town's Unionists.*
> *He came in and picked up a publicity leaflet with 'PRIZES! PRIZES! PRIZES!' printed at the bottom.*

2.66 You can use a number of phrases consisting of a verb and the adverb 'down' to refer to writing. They are not normally used in full report structures.

jot down	put down	set down	write down
note down	scribble down	take down	

> *He took his notebook from his pocket and jotted down the address and number that she gave him.*
> *Never put anything down on paper which might be used in evidence against you at a later date.*

2.67 A few reporting verbs refer to the manner of writing. They are generally not used in full report structures, although they can sometimes be used with direct quotes. Here are the major ones.

jot	print	scrawl	scribble

The phrasal verb 'dash off' is used in the same way.

> *She scribbled a note to tell Mum she'd gone out and not to worry.*
> *One woman angrily scrawled, 'I am the mother of a very nice girl.'*
> *Beside was printed, in gothic letters, 'Castle (ruins of)'.*

2.68 A few reporting verbs refer to mechanical means by which the written message is conveyed. These are the major ones.

cable	telegraph	telex	wire
fax			

> *Alan had <u>wired</u>, 'No question of refusing. Received no orders.'*
> *She is reported to have <u>cabled</u> that there would be no invasion.*
> *A recipe for a curry from Malaysia can be <u>faxed</u> to London on the same day.*

2.69 A few other reporting verbs refer to the type of written text which is produced. They are generally not used in full report structures, although the ones marked with an asterisk (*) in the list can be used with direct quotes (often partial quotes).

annotate	document	sign
autograph	draft	subtitle*
caption*	entitle*	transcribe

> *The photograph was <u>captioned</u>: 'Darling! How many times must I tell you! Never ring me at work.'*
> *No reader would believe that this was a true story if it were not <u>subtitled</u> 'a non-fiction account of an American crime'.*
> *However, a case in which the winners of several horse-races were predicted has been <u>documented</u>.*
> *Calling for paper and pen, she <u>drafted</u> a letter.*

2.70 Apart from the choice of reporting verb, there are a number of other ways of making it clear in the reporting signal whether you are reporting writing or speaking.

> *<u>In that letter</u> he narrates an incident which happened in the prison yard.*
> *<u>The author</u> discusses possible interpretations of the evidence.*
> *<u>This chapter</u> will explain what you should eat.*

For the use of the text itself as 'writer' in the last example above, see 2.71.

The special conventions used for signalling reports in academic writing normally refer to written text.

> *As <u>Ravault (1980) points out</u>, this is not easy to do.*
> *'Division of labour,' <u>he explains</u>, 'is the principle upon which all government is founded' <u>(1836a, p.76).</u>*

See Chapter 5 on reports in academic writing.

Talking about the speaker

non-human speakers

2.71 In addition to the information carried by the reporting verb, you can use the reporting signal to give information about the speaker. In the majority of reports, the speaker is human. However, you can also refer to the written or spoken text itself as if it were the speaker, the subject of the reporting clause.

There are two signs, one proclaiming: 'This is the Birthplace of Bill Clinton, Next President of the USA'.

This chapter has suggested that hostel accommodation fails to equate with the housing preferences of lone migrant workers.

The book tells how he tried to dry his mother's tears with a handful of tissues.

The story tells of two young boys who enter a magical garden and shrink so small that they are able to go inside the castle.

And many of these chemicals are not safe, as Sophie's story tells.

His first book 'Death at an Early Age' documented the lives of poor children in Boston's public school system.

The paper says the man has kept Europe guessing as to his identity in numerous television and press interviews.

One report says a man was seen running from the house soon after the shooting.

2.72 When you report what was said on television or radio, you can use the spoken source of information in the same way: that is, as the subject of the reporting clause.

Hungarian radio says the river Danube has burst through a dam at two points just north of the capital.

The forecast says possible showers this evening.

2.73 There are two reporting verbs which normally appear with non-human rather than human subjects: 'go' and 'run', and a verb+object phrase 'have it'.

'Have it' and 'go' tend to be used with a fairly restricted range of subjects: the most common subjects of 'have it' are 'legend', 'story' and 'tradition'; and the most common subject of 'go' is 'story'.

'Run' is used with a wider range of subjects referring to types of text, but it usually occurs in a fixed pattern: 'X runs as follows'.

Local legend has it that he once sold the same piece of land to three different buyers.

One theory has it that it is cholesterol's tendency to repair damaged tissue that proves to be its undoing.

The story goes that he drowned after falling into a pond, dead drunk.

One evening, so the story goes, Hemingway took a very drunk Joyce home in a wheelbarrow.

Thus, the sequence of talk runs as follows: 'I was playing tennis at Lord's yesterday. This game's all right, but you know, after tennis, squash seems inferior.'

Note that the use of 'go' illustrated here is not colloquial, unlike the use mentioned in 2.64.

Function: the reporting signal

For more information on the use of 'have it' with human subjects in reporting adjuncts, see 1.71.

avoiding mentioning the speaker

2.74 If you do not want to mention the speaker, you can use the passive form of many reporting verbs. As with the use of the passive in general, you can do this for a number of reasons: if you specifically want to avoid mentioning the speaker; or if you do not know who the speaker is; or if it is not important who the speaker is; or because the speakers are people in general; or if you want to mention the hearer first in order to focus on that person rather than the speaker.

One common way in which you can avoid mentioning the speaker is by choosing one of the reporting verbs where you must or can mention the hearer (see 2.81–2.96), and making the hearer the subject of the clause, with the verb in the passive.

> *An international conference in London has been told that new evidence supports the view that the ozone layer has suffered substantial damage.*
> *Families are cautioned that 'sometimes stroke survivors lose the benefits of rehabilitative treatment because they don't realize they should have it.'*
> *Hart looked around himself in panic, for he'd been admonished not to move from his spot.*
> *They decide which couples should be dissuaded from adopting a baby.*

You can use the same kind of structure with reporting verbs where you must mention the target (see 2.28–2.32).

> *He had been praised at school so often for his initiative.*
> *I was reproached for not noticing anything.*

2.75 Another common way of avoiding mentioning the speaker is by using the passive form of certain reporting verbs with **introductory 'it'** as the subject (for more about introductory 'it', see 4.34). The message is given in a reported 'that'-clause. You use this structure especially when you are referring to what is said by an unspecified group of people, or by people in general; but you can also use it for the other reasons listed above.

> *It is commonly acknowledged that Roman Catholics, Anglicans and Free Church people do not join together for regular prayer for unity.*
> *In Zen Buddhism it is asserted that we already know everything we need to know in order to manage.*
> *From one of these came more sensational news about the animal. It was claimed that the platypus laid eggs.*
> *It has also been implied that she may have had a relationship with Maiya Tranchell-Hayes.*
> *It was alleged that Vassall's superiors did know that there was a spy in the Admiralty.*

Here is a list of the major reporting verbs which can be used in this way. Note that not all reporting verbs which can be followed by a 'that'-clause can appear in this structure. In particular, most verbs which can appear with the hearer as subject (see 2.74 above) cannot be used in this structure – this applies especially to 'tell'.

acknowledge	decree	note	reveal
admit	deny	observe	rule
agree	disclose	predict	say
allege	emphasize	promise	state
announce	explain	propose	stipulate
argue	guarantee	recommend	stress
assert	hint	record	suggest
claim	imply	remark	write
concede	maintain	report	
confirm	mention	request	

The phrasal verb 'point out' can be used in the same way.

The reporting verb 'rumour' can only be used in the passive (see also 2.78).

> *It was rumoured that he had once been an officer of the Cossacks who had been sentenced to life imprisonment.*

2.76 The structure described above includes a reported 'that'-clause. There are also a few reporting verbs which you can use with **introductory it** as subject and which are followed by a 'to'-infinitive clause.

> *It was forbidden to feed the dog or to leave milk out for the cat.*

Here is a list of the major verbs which are sometimes used in this way.

forbid	permit	propose	recommend

> *Is it permitted to have guests in the rooms?*
> *It was proposed to pull down Chartres Cathedral and build in its place a temple of wisdom.*
> *It is recommended to use this technique for various types of nerve problems as it affects the entire system and balances it.*

2.77 Note that you can only use these passive structures with 'it' when a 'that'-clause or 'to'-infinitive clause follows. You cannot use them if only a noun group follows. For example, it is not correct to say: 'It was reported a serious accident on the motorway'.

2.78 With certain reporting verbs you can use a special kind of passive structure where the reporting verb appears inside the reported message.

> *Conditions in the jail are said to be horrific.*

This could be paraphrased as: 'It is said that conditions in the jail are horrific'. Note that the form of the reporting verb is plural (*are said*) because of the plural subject (*conditions*).

In this structure, the reporting verb is always followed by a 'to'-infinitive. In many cases, the second verb is 'be', as in the example above, and it is often a perfect infinitive – an infinitive with 'have' – as in the next example.

> *Over one thousand million dollars is said to have been deposited with the bank.*

Here is a list of the major verbs which can be used in this structure. The verbs can all be used also in the passive structure with 'it' described in 2.75.

agree	claim	predict	rumour
allege	guarantee	report	say

> *Photos of her husband and the girl together were said to be one reason why the marriage ran into difficulty.*
> *In the last four years, Madonna is reported to have earned 57 million dollars.*
> *One-eighth of our warm air is claimed to be lost through the windows.*
> *Holt was rumoured to have sold his soul to the Devil at some earlier date.*
> *And this is the school where the kids are alleged to break windows all day long.*

2.79 Note that this kind of passive can also be used with reported verbs in sentences with 'there is' and 'there are'.

> *There are said to be differences between the political and military wings.*

The reporting verb in this example is in the plural form (*are said*) because of the plural noun group following (*differences*).

2.80 A number of verbs of feeling and opinion can also appear in these passive structures. See 4.35.

Talking about the hearer

mentioning the hearer

2.81 Although you normally need to mention the speaker in reports, you can often choose whether or not to refer to the hearer. The choice sometimes depends on the reporting verb you choose, and sometimes on the type of reported clause that follows the reporting verb.

2.82 With some reporting verbs, you normally mention the hearer whatever type of report structure they are used in. Here are the major verbs of this type.

adjure	convince	instruct	promise
admonish	dare	misinform	reassure
apprise	direct	notify	remind
assure	dissuade	persuade	request
beg	enjoin	plead	threaten
beseech	incite	pledge	vow
charge	inform	press	

The following phrasal verbs are used in the same way.

| call on | egg on | talk into | talk round |
| drum into | prevail upon | talk out of | tip off |

'You're very sure of yourself,' she admonished him, gently.
Traditionally, bosses are admonished that they should not be friendly with workers.
Film reviewers are often sternly admonished by Hollywood not to give away the ending.
The sources said the Bishop of Dili admonished the demonstrators for their actions.
The Judge sent the jury out of court and admonished the prosecutor.

See also 2.28 and 2.31 for reporting verbs where you normally mention the target.

not mentioning the hearer

2.83   With some reporting verbs you do not normally mention the hearer, whatever type of report structure they are used in. Here are the major verbs of this type.

add	contend	inquire	record
affirm	decline	maintain	refuse
allow	demand	object	reply
assert	deny	predict	retort
attest	dispute	profess	riposte
aver	forecast	propose	rule
avow	foretell	query	undertake
confirm	enquire	question	volunteer

The phrasal verb 'touch on' is used in the same way.

'They don't know what it takes to be successful,' asserted Mike Hyde.
Writer Simone de Beauvoir asserted that marriage is traditionally the destiny offered to women by society.
The statement asserted the rights of opposition groups to operate freely within the law.
The actors had volunteered to give an impromptu entertainment to while away the evening.
'I saw him come out of these woods, but I myself was on the hill opposite. I'll show you,' Miss Gray volunteered.

2.84 Note that, with the reporting verb 'answer', you do not normally mention the hearer when it is used in a full report structure, with a quote or 'that'-clause following. If you use it in other structures, you can choose whether or not to mention the hearer.

When asked by the Queen what this would cost, Walpole, according to a famous story, answered that the price would be three crowns – England, Ireland and Scotland.
Well, don't just sit there – answer me!

2.85 You normally do not mention the hearer with many of the reporting verbs which are mostly used in direct quote structures rather than indirect reporting structures (see 2.18–2.24).

Marshall bellowed: 'We're like two ducks cooked in the same oven.'
'Let me see,' she coos.

choosing whether to mention the hearer

2.86 With some reporting verbs, you normally mention the hearer if they are used in one type of report structure, but not necessarily if they are used in another type of report structure.

The most common of these verbs is 'tell'. When it is used with a quote or a reported clause, or by itself, the hearer is normally mentioned. Note that the hearer may be the subject of a passive verb, as in the last two examples below.

When she heard the girl was missing, she told her mum: 'I know where she is.'
He told me he would look for another job.
The doctor told him to go away and eat as much hot curry as he could.
Even so, she could have asked. Mrs Madrigal would have told her.
All of the men have been told that dark blue suits and red ties look best on television.
They wasted 20 minutes walking in the wrong direction, a public inquiry in Cardiff was told.

If, on the other hand, 'tell' is followed by a prepositional phrase or noun group summarising the message, you can choose whether or not to mention the hearer. The same is true when 'tell' is followed by a 'wh'-clause summarising the message (see 3.53).

In writing about her own garden, she tells about her successes and her failures.
I wrote to her and told her about the diet.
And what the movie does is it tells a lot of obvious jokes about Los Angeles.
Before his death, Black Elk told his story to the late John G. Neidhardt.
Ship's captain Kevin Murphy told how French trawlers risked disaster by sailing in the wrong shipping lanes.
Dr Storm told me how the trial was conducted.

2.87 Here is a list of the major reporting verbs which have the hearer mentioned as object when you use them with a 'to'-infinitive clause, but which you can also use in other report structures without mentioning the hearer.

advise	command	exhort	recommend
authorize	commission	forbid	tell
caution	counsel	implore	urge
challenge	encourage	invite	warn
coax	entreat	order	

Earlier, Mr Aitken had <u>challenged Esther to meet</u> him and discuss her campaign against bullying.
Also at the hearing, his lawyers <u>challenged an attempt</u> to subpoena his American Express bills.
He <u>ordered her to keep</u> silent.
He <u>ordered that</u> I be given access to a typewriter.
One of the teachers had <u>urged him to learn</u> some mathematics.
Valerius Maximus <u>urged that</u> the lover 'as a sick man, must be cured by change of air.'

2.88 Note that with the verb 'threaten', you do not mention the hearer if you use a 'to'-infinitive reported clause; you can choose whether or not to mention the hearer if you use a 'that'-reported clause; and you must mention the hearer if you use a prepositional phrase.

The station commander <u>threatened to arrest</u> me for 'disturbing the peace and using abusive language'.
A representative visited the BBC and <u>threatened that</u> cooperation in BBC enterprises would be ended unless the BBC abandoned the programme.
She had always <u>threatened him that</u> she would marry on her twenty-first birthday.
They <u>threatened the patients with</u> injections of painful drugs.

2.89 With a few reporting verbs which can be followed by a 'to'-infinitive clause, the meaning changes according to whether you mention the hearer or not (see 1.49–1.50). In the first example below, the hearer (*him*) is the understood subject of the reported clause (*say*); in the second, the speakers (*waitresses*) are the understood subject of the reported clause (*see if I had any money*).

I asked him to <u>say</u> that I'd been in the lab.
The smiling waitresses <u>asked to see</u> if I had any money.

Here is a list of the major verbs which can be used in this way. Note that, if you use 'plead', you use a prepositional phrase beginning with 'with' to mention the hearer (see 2.95).

ask	beg	plead

One verb, 'promise', can be used with or without a reference to the hearer when followed by a 'to'-infinitive clause without changing the meaning.

The woman <u>promised to stay</u> with her husband.
He <u>promised the minister to serve</u> his fellow man.

2.90 With some reporting verbs, if they are followed by a 'that'-clause you can either mention the hearer as the object of the reporting clause or not. Here are the major verbs of this type.

advise	caution	promise	warn
bet	fax	teach	wire
cable	guarantee	telegraph	write

Bob <u>cautioned us that</u> we should look at buying a number of smaller technology companies rather than a giant like Xerox.
Dr Spock <u>cautioned that</u> a lack of vitamins could result in reduced body size.

Note that 'write' is used in this way in American English. In British English, if you use 'write' and want to mention the reader you normally do so in a prepositional phrase beginning with 'to' – see 2.92.

2.91 You can use the verb 'ask' with or without a reference to the hearer when it is followed by a 'wh'-clause or a 'whether/if'-clause.

They <u>asked me</u> what the big stories of the day were.
If they <u>ask who</u> wants to speak to him, tell them it's a detective.
If you <u>ask a woman what</u> she is good at she will stop after two minutes, but if you <u>ask what</u> she is not good at she will talk for two hours.
He <u>asked me</u> again if he could have some money.
All turned and <u>asked if</u> I was hurt.

mentioning the hearer in a prepositional phrase

2.92 With many other reporting verbs, you can mention the hearer in a prepositional phrase beginning with 'to'. In all these cases, you can choose whether or not to mention the hearer.

'Excuse me,' he <u>said to them</u>. 'This man needs a drink.'
He <u>admitted to the King</u> that Churchill would probably do the job well.
Haig <u>claimed to his wife</u> that 'The Enemy's attack seems to be coming exactly against the points on our front which we expected.'
I <u>explained to Lucy</u> what it was that Nurse meant.
Melissa <u>brags to Andy</u> about visiting a psychiatrist.

Here is a list of the major verbs of this kind. Note that, unlike the verbs listed above, you do not use these verbs in the passive form with the hearer as subject.

acknowledge	describe	insist	reiterate
admit	dictate	intimate	remark
announce	disclose	joke	repeat
apologize	divulge	lament	report
boast	emphasize	lie	reveal
brag	exclaim	mention	say
certify	explain	moan	state
claim	expound	mumble	stress
comment	express	murmur	suggest
complain	grumble	mutter	testify
confess	hint	observe	vow
confide	indicate	proclaim	wail
declare	insinuate	protest	write

The following phrases and phrasal verbs are used in the same way.

call out	let slip	point out	send word
cry out			

2.93 With 'propose' and 'swear', you can also choose whether or not to mention the hearer in a prepositional phrase beginning with 'to' if you use a 'that'-clause. If you use a 'to'-infinitive clause, on the other hand, you do not normally mention the hearer.

Later, Franklin <u>swore to his attorney that</u> no records had ever been destroyed.
In 1977, a dean at Harvard <u>swore that</u> the university would never close, 'except for an act of God, like the end of the world, maybe.'
Then I, too, <u>swore to</u> uphold the Constitution of the United States.

2.94 With certain other verbs, the reverse is true: when you use them with a 'to'-infinitive clause, you mention the hearer in a prepositional phrase; but when you use them in other structures you can choose whether or not to mention the hearer. Here is a list of the major verbs of this kind, together with the prepositions used to mention the hearer.

appeal (to)	shout (to/at)	whisper (to)	yell (to/at)
call (on/for)			

'Cry out (to)' is used in the same way as these verbs.

Try to encourage it by <u>appealing to her to help</u> you in any way she can.
A Colonial Office circular <u>appealed for 'loyal co-operation'</u>.
He <u>appealed for help to the Normans</u>.
The mother appeared on television <u>appealing about her son</u>.

supporting or challenging the hearer

2.95 Some verbs can be used to report language events in a way which emphasizes that the speaker and hearer are both involved. In these cases, you can choose to mention the hearer in a prepositional phrase beginning with 'with'.

The vet <u>agreed with me</u> that a walk would help the wounds to drain.

Here is a list of the major verbs which can be used in this way. The verbs in this list that are marked with an asterisk (*) are **reciprocal verbs** – as well as saying, for example, 'I quarrelled with my sister', you can say 'My sister and I quarrelled.'

agree*	debate*	negotiate*	reason
argue*	disagree*	plead	remonstrate
commiserate	discuss*	quarrel*	wrangle*
concur*			

I've discussed the matter with my colleagues at our meeting this morning.
I <u>commiserated with him</u> over the recent news from the west where his favourite General St Clair had lost nearly a thousand men.
I <u>quarrelled</u> bitterly <u>with my sister.</u>

The phrasal verb 'thrash out' is used in this way and is reciprocal.

2.96 With a number of reporting verbs, you can mention the hearer in a prepositional phrase beginning with 'at'. You do this when you are describing a situation in which the hearer is being addressed in a forceful way or is being verbally attacked or criticized.

He opened his lungs and <u>bawled at me</u>: 'You stupid woman, you're obsessed by me.'

Here is a list of the major verbs which can be used in this way.

bark	grunt	rave	snarl
bawl	hiss	roar	sneer
bellow	holler	scoff	storm
carp	howl	scream	swear
curse	jeer	screech	thunder
gasp	moan	shout	wail
growl	nag	shriek	yell
grumble	rant	snap	

Don't be afraid to <u>shout</u> and <u>scream at them.</u>
'We've been made to look idiots,' he <u>snarled at Sergeant Yates.</u>
He had <u>sneered at her</u>, 'Go call your brother, maybe he'll beat me up.'
He had little sympathy with women who would <u>moan at him</u> from time to time that they found themselves living in a world without rules.

Note that you can use 'at' in this way to suggest some kind of verbal attack or aggressiveness even when the verb itself does not usually have this implication.

'Boring old fart,' he <u>muttered at the judge.</u>
It would be her who'd drive him to murder by <u>talking at him</u> nonstop.
Juries are often grateful to the Colonel for not <u>preaching at them.</u>

Where no aggression is meant, another preposition may be used to mention the hearer (see 2.92).

Other kinds of reporting signal

using reporting nouns

2.97 So far in this chapter, the focus has mainly been on reporting signals which include a reporting verb. However, much of what has been said about the different functions of reporting verbs is also true of reporting nouns. Most reporting nouns are related to reporting verbs and can be used in very similar ways. The type of reported clause that can follow any of the nouns is normally the same as the type that occurs with the related reporting verb, except that reporting nouns cannot be followed by '-ing' clauses.

Interestingly, one study <u>reported that</u> adolescents who perceive their parents as 'democratic' are likely to regard their parents as happy.
The Financial Times carries a <u>report that</u> Pravda is to go commercial.
He had <u>promised to</u> take his eldest son to a football match that Saturday.
He has made no firm <u>promises to</u> reform the prison system.

Note that reporting nouns are not very often followed by quotes (but see 2.101–2.107).

showing the speaker's purpose through the reporting noun

2.98 You can use a reporting noun to show the speaker's purpose (compare 2.10).

The confirmed 'food-aholic' may indignantly reject the <u>suggestion that his 'favorite' food or drink is bad for him.</u>
You made a <u>statement that half your staff are crazy</u> and I'm trying to verify it.

Here is a list of the major reporting nouns showing speaker purpose which can be followed by a reported 'that'-clause.

accusation	concession	insistence	proposition
acknowledgement	confession	intimation	protest
admission	confirmation	lament	reassurance
admonition	contention	message	recommendation
advice	criticism	news	remark
affirmation	declaration	notification	reminder
allegation	decree	objection	report
announcement	demand	observation	request
argument	denial	order	retort
assertion	disclosure	plea	revelation
assurance	edict	pledge	specification
bet	excuse	point	statement
boast	explanation	prayer	stipulation
caution	guarantee	prediction	suggestion
charge	hint	proclamation	testimony
claim	implication	promise	threat
comment	information	prophecy	vow
complaint	insinuation	proposal	warning

If general confidence is increased by this measure, it would be the first time that the morale of the other ranks had been improved by the announcement that the officers are going to retreat first.

A six-year old boy was dumped on the doorstep with a cursory explanation that he might stay for several weeks.

It was not two days since the Duchess had issued instructions that no more tickets were to be given away.

A characteristic formulation of this kind is the statement that 'Weber showed the interdependence of ideas as a social variable with other social variables' (Barber, 1956, p. 93).

2.99 Some of the above nouns are related to reporting verbs which show your attitude towards what the speaker says (compare 2.40). In this case, the reported noun shows the same attitude as the verb.

He wasn't prepared for her admission that she was cheating, deceiving him.

But perhaps her greatest joy came from John's acknowledgement that she was a good listener.

Claims have been made that high blood pressure can be lowered by yoga and other relaxation techniques but there is no convincing proof of this.

2.100 There are also reporting nouns which show the speaker's purpose and which are followed by a reported 'to'-infinitive clause (compare 2.13).

'Your request has been granted.' 'What request?' 'Your request to be excused from the conduct of this case.'

They have issued a new warning to foreigners to register with the authorities by the fifth of November.

Here is a list of the major nouns which can be used in this way.

advice	encouragement	order	refusal
appeal	exhortation	plea	reminder
call	instruction	pledge	request
challenge	invitation	promise	threat
claim	message	proposal	vow
command	offer	recommendation	warning

Tench had never lost his stoutness. At nine it had given him the bulk to back up his claim to be pack leader in the school yard.

We resolutely declined Hamlet's advice to hold a mirror up to nature.

After his wife died last December, he accepted an offer to practise law in Washington with a big corporate firm.

Blackmail operates by the threat to reveal facts of which a man is ashamed.

2.101 Note that the reporting noun 'question' is not normally followed by a reported 'that'-clause. However, it can be followed by a quote.

Posing the question, 'What is it that causes so much concern?', the Rotherhithe Community Planning Centre offered the following answer. In reply to a simple question 'Do you like housework?' middle-class women were far more likely to give a negative answer than working-class women.

It can also be followed by a reported 'wh'-clause in a prepositional phrase. The preposition is most often 'of', although 'as to' and 'about' can also be used.

This raises the <u>question of what determines the time-perspective of individuals and society as a whole.</u>
The breadth of Zhou's understanding is outlined in her answer to the <u>question as to why spiritual immortals should concern themselves with such things as making rain.</u>

showing the manner of speaking through the reporting noun

2.102 There are some reporting nouns which show the speaker's manner (compare 2.18) and which can be followed by a quote, often in a prepositional phrase beginning with 'of'. They are not normally followed by reported clauses.

She drew away suddenly with a <u>cry of 'Ugh, how he stinks'.</u>

Here is a list of the major nouns which can be used in this way.

bellow	cry	murmur	shriek
call	ejaculation	roar	whisper
chant	exclamation	scream	yell
chorus	howl	shout	

Much depended on the helmsman timing his <u>shout of 'Lee-oh!'</u> correctly.
This criterion may evoke an immediate <u>howl of 'how foolish'</u>, since who sees a doctor for no reason?
'Have any of you been made sick by him?' Another <u>roar of 'No'.</u>
In fact, many parents complained or joked about the persistent <u>chorus of 'Why? Why? Why?'</u> that their children raised at that age.

showing what was said through the reporting noun

2.103 There are reporting nouns which in themselves give an idea of what was actually said or written (compare 2.28). When you use the related reporting verb, you always mention the target. With the noun, you do not need to mention the target, but, if you do, you use a prepositional phrase – the most common preposition is given in the list below. You can usually also add more information about the message in a prepositional phrase or in an '-ing' clause introduced by a preposition: as with the verbs, the most common preposition is 'for'.

Some of these nouns can be followed by a reported 'that'-clause or even a quote. These are marked with an asterisk (*) in the list below.

abuse (of)	compliment (on)	libel (against)
accusation* (against)	condemnation (of)	mockery (of)
admonition* (of)	congratulations (to)	praise (of)
apology* (to)	criticism* (of)	rebuke* (to)
attack (on)	curse (on)	reproach* (to)
censure (of)	eulogy (of/about)	reproof (to/for)
charge* (against)	flattery (of)	ridicule (of)
commendation (of)	insult (to)	slander (against)
commiseration (with)	lampoon (on)	thanks (to)

I received a letter from her in reply to my congratulations on having been elevated to the peerage.

Good parents naturally expect something from their children in return: not spoken thanks for being born or being cared for, but considerateness and affection.

She made no apology for the fact that she was wearing her working clothes as she offered him a cup of tea.

How often has one heard the criticism that Method actors always play themselves?

The child needs to feel love at his back. He doesn't want to hear the accusation 'Where did you learn to do that?'

indicating how the message fits in through the reporting noun

2.104 Some reporting nouns indicate how what is reported fits in with the rest of the language event (compare 2.34). The following nouns can be followed by a reported 'that'-clause. The nouns marked with an asterisk (*) can also be followed by a quote.

agreement	quote*	response*
answer*	rejoinder*	retort*
denial	reply*	riposte*

Intensive questioning elicited the reluctant answer that he had had one or two minor seizures of a similar nature in the last few months.

His legal case rested on the denial that succession to the peerage meant disqualification from the House of Commons.

A representative of the firm gave the rather quaint reply that 'the structure of the company is so complex that it prevents analysis within the laid-down criteria'.

Often I have answered a mother's question, 'What shall I do about my child?' with the reply, 'Go and get yourself analyzed.'

One who tried to persuade a doubter that the Prime Minister would stop handbagging her colleagues met with the riposte: 'You told me that before last year's election.'

drawing attention to the speaker's words through the reporting noun

2.105 Some reporting nouns draw attention to the words used by the speaker to describe or name something (compare 2.39). The nouns can be followed by a prepositional phrase with 'as' giving a partial quote or a report of the words used.

> *The established definition of leisure as the opposite of work may need severe qualification.*
> *He gave the world Harold Wilson's definition of the Labour Party's organisation as 'a penny-farthing bicycle in an atomic age'.*

Here is a list of the most frequent nouns which can be used in this way.

characterization   definition   description

reporting non-specific language events

2.106 There are a number of reporting nouns which you can use when you report 'general' language events such as proverbs or mottos (that is, language events which do not involve a specific speaker or which are not described as having taken place at a specific time). Here are the major nouns of this kind. These nouns do not have a related reporting verb. They can introduce a quote (or partial quote), and most of them, apart from 'motto', 'proverb', 'riddle', and 'tag', can introduce a reported 'that'-clause.

adage	dictum	proverb	tag
aphorism	maxim	riddle	
cliché	motto	slogan	

> *The ancient Greek adage 'Know thyself' is true for all areas of life.*
> *This illustrates Rochefoucauld's maxim that 'If we had no faults of our own, we would not take so much pleasure in noticing those of others.'*
> *Many boys would go along with the dictum that the best food in England is breakfast three times a day.*
> *He won last month's presidential election on the slogan of 'honesty, work and technology'.*

labelling the language

2.107 Some nouns which refer to language having particular qualities can be used to introduce a quote or a partial quote. These include nouns such as 'word', which describe the amount of language used, those such as 'heading', which describe the relation of the quote to the rest of the language event, and those such as 'expletive', which reflect a social judgement about the language. Here are the major nouns of this kind.

colloquialism	heading	phrase	term
euphemism	idiom	rider	title
expletive	line	sentence	word

He wrote the <u>word 'exasperate'</u> on his computer.
This song was originally written and performed by South African Johnny Kongos, under the <u>title 'He's Going To Step On You Again'</u> – a record that came out in 1971.

mentioning the speaker and hearer with reporting nouns

2.108 In many cases, when you use a reporting noun you do not mention the speaker or hearer. If you do want to mention the speaker, you can use a possessive with the reporting noun.

I didn't give much thought to <u>her claim</u> that she was being followed.
<u>Mr Highhawk's suggestion</u> that the museum make models of the skeletons and rebury the originals was not practical.

You can also use an adjective or noun modifying the reporting noun. This is especially used with words referring to nationalities and institutions.

The opinions of the papers on how to take the <u>American announcement</u> that it was prepared for face-to-face talks show differing views.
Scuffles have broken out in central Hong Kong following a <u>government statement</u> that the Bank of Credit and Commerce International is to be liquidated.

You can also use a prepositional phrase beginning with 'by' or, less often, 'from'.

A gasp of astonishment greeted the <u>announcement by Mr Martin Jones</u> that he would not be calling any such evidence at all.
Ten suspected spies have been arrested this week following an <u>admission by Kuron</u> that he had passed secrets to East Berlin.
The American announcement follows a <u>warning from the Central Intelligence Agency</u> that the country had developed a considerable stockpile of weapons.

2.109 If you want to mention the hearer, you use a prepositional phrase beginning with 'to'.

Perhaps her own coldness had somehow given strength to the Count's <u>plea to Tim</u> to return.
Perhaps the most revealing insight provided by Mitterrand was his <u>confession to a journalist</u> that 'I have chosen a career which runs counter to a powerful strain in my character'.
I'm ready to swear that Charlie dropped a <u>hint to me</u> once that he'd been on the stage.

using reporting adjectives

2.110 There are two reporting adjectives which you can use to show the speaker's purpose (compare 2.10) and which can be followed by 'that'-clauses: 'adamant' and 'insistent'. The combination of 'be' and reporting adjective functions in a very similar way to a reporting verb.

> *The Foreign Minister <u>was insistent</u> that the purchase of political favour was incompatible with State-to-State relations.*
> *Marx <u>was adamant</u> that revealing the real state of affairs was dependent upon a thorough detailed analysis of actual social practices.*

2.111 You can use certain reporting adjectives to give an idea of what was actually said or written (compare 2.28). The major adjectives of this kind are given in the list below. The target can be mentioned in a prepositional phrase – the most common preposition is given in the list below. If you mention the target, you can also add more information about the message in a prepositional phrase or in an '-ing' clause following a preposition: as with the related reporting verbs, the most common prepositions are 'for' and 'as'.

abusive (to/towards) critical (of)
censorious (of) dismissive (of)
complimentary (about)

> *The left is <u>critical of</u> the Communist Party for choosing the second course.*
> *Singer is <u>dismissive of</u> the 'phraseology' of the 'dependency school'.*

Choosing different types of reporting signal

2.112 The focus in this chapter so far has mainly been on the information that can be given in different parts of the reporting signal.

This section looks at the reasons why you might choose different types of reporting signal. It also looks at why you might choose to put the reporting signal in different positions in relation to the quote or reported clause.

Remember that using any reporting signal, that is, using a report of any kind, has the effect of creating a distance between the reporter and the message, so that the reporter is not directly responsible for the message.

leaving out the reporting signal

2.113 If you want to emphasize what the speaker says rather than the fact that this is a report, you can choose not to have a separate reporting signal. In this case, you can have a direct quote on its own.

> *But Harry Penrose interrupted. 'We're riding this afternoon. Are you coming, Lady Geraldine?' She was grateful to Lady Penrith. 'I promised to play bridge with Lady Penrith.' 'Oh Lord, what a bore.' 'Well what about Miss Etchell?'*

Function: the reporting signal

The reporting signal is often left out in written narratives, such as novels. It can sometimes be left out in oral narratives (in this case, the quote is signalled by intonation – see 1.14).

One important effect of leaving out the reporting signal with quotes is to make the narrative more dramatic by presenting the speech as if it were happening now rather than being reported later.

2.114   Instead of a direct quote, you can also have an indirect quote with no separate reporting signal.

> *The voice of a girl with a foreign accent answered. Mrs Mallory was out. But as soon as I said my name she was less formal. Mrs Mallory was at the hospital, but she had said I might call. She was expecting me, a room was prepared.*

Like direct quotes, you use indirect quotes in this way in written narratives and, less frequently, in spoken narratives.

The main effect is also to make the narrative more dramatic; but in this case the reference features (e.g. the use of past tense in the underlined parts of the example above) show that the words are reported. You use this when you are telling the story from one person's point of view (*I* in the example) and you want to present the speech as if that person were hearing it now. The readers of the narrative are therefore encouraged to imagine that they are present at the original speech event but as that person rather than as themselves.

putting the reporting clause in different positions

2.115   If you decide to use a reporting clause as a reporting signal, you can put it in different positions in relation to the quote or reported clause (see 1.6 and 1.32).

The most common position for the reporting clause in an indirect reported structure is in front of the reported clause.

> *But he said he never carried out any of their orders.*

In this case, it is clear that you are first of all telling your hearer that someone said something. The focus is mainly on the fact that this is a report of someone else's words. After signalling this, you go on to tell your hearer what the person said, but in a way which relates that person's words to your reporting rather than to his or her speaking (see 3.77–3.98). The main effect is to make the reported language event part of your speaking. You integrate it into what you are saying rather than making it stand out dramatically. Your hearer is therefore encouraged to see the language event from your point of view as you report it.

2.116   In direct quote structures, you most often put the reporting clause after the quote.

> *'We'll wait out here until the doctor has seen him,' the miner said.*

The main focus here is on the speaker's words. The reporting signal is added at the end. It signals that this is a report, but in a way which makes the signal less important than the quote. This is often used in novels and newspaper reports. It gives extra importance to the writer's words, but incidentally reminds the reader that this is a report.

2.117 In the majority of cases, in full report structures the reporting clause follows a quote, but comes before a reported clause. However, you can vary this. You can put the reporting clause before the quote.

Somebody had to lighten things up, so <u>Mary Ann said</u>: 'Can't take him anywhere.'

This is the normal order in academic writing:

However, <u>Freeman (1983a, p.12) points out</u>: 'Unfortunately, individual freedom can be so exercised as to undermine not only the freedom of others but also their human dignity.'

In these cases, you start from the fact that you are reporting someone else's words, but then you quote those words exactly as the speaker said them. You therefore give equal weight to both parts of the report.

2.118 You can also put the reporting clause after the reported clause. This happens especially in newspaper reporting.

Members of the United Steelworkers ratified a four-year contract with Armco Inc., <u>the union said</u>.

In these cases, it is not clear that the first clause is a reported clause until the reporting clause appears at the end. If you leave out the reporting clause in the above example, the sentence looks like news given directly by the journalist. One effect of this is to make the readers adjust their view as they reach the end ('This is not the journalist herself writing, as I thought, but a report of what the union said'). As this adjustment does not occur until the end of the sentence, readers are perhaps more likely to accept the reported clause as objective fact.

2.119 You can also put the reporting clause in the middle of the quote or reported clause (see 1.8 and 1.34). Sometimes the reporting clause comes at a 'natural break' in the speaker's words – a point where the speaker's sentence could be grammatically complete.

'I have to be at a meeting in ten minutes,' <u>said Carl</u>, 'or I'll have enemies.'
He was better than Elvis Presley, <u>he said</u>, and about to prove it with a one-man show.

The main effect of this is similar to putting the reporting clause at the end. With a quote (as in the first example), the focus is more on the speaker's words. With a reported clause (as in the second example), the focus is equally balanced.

2.120 When the reporting clause does not come at a 'natural break', the effect is slightly different. This is more common in novels than in other kinds of text, but it is also used sometimes in spoken news reports.

> *'What I want to know is,'* said Sloane, *'if one particular way would be successful.'*
> *The roof,* he said, *had recently been reinforced and camouflaged.*

One effect of this is to highlight the part of the quote or reported clause which comes before the reporting clause (*What I want to know is; The roof*). The rest of the quote or reported clause is delayed by the reporting clause, so your reader is waiting for the grammatical structure to be completed. This makes the reporting clause seem like an interruption, which is less important than the message in the speaker's words. At the same time, however, the reporting clause is in a relatively unusual position, which draws attention to it. The general effect is therefore to make the reader notice the way the language is used and to emphasize both parts of the reporting structure equally.

using a reporting adjunct as reporting signal

2.121   Instead of a reported clause, you can use a reporting adjunct as the reporting signal.

> *According to the spokeswoman for the trade representative,* 'The president has not made a decision on this, and there is not a deadline.'
> *So let us first operate,* as Szilard suggests, *with one molecule, M.*
> *Vases* reputedly *brought back from Japan in 1890 were actually fired in Britain last week.*

Grammatically, if you use a reporting adjunct, it is the reported clause or quote which is the main clause. The reporting adjunct acts as a comment on the main clause. The effect of the comment depends on the kind of reporting adjunct.

2.122   If you use one of the neutral reporting adjuncts which mention the speaker ('according to', 'to quote', 'in the words of', etc.), the effect is similar to using a reporting clause. However, there is a slight difference.

> *According to a French spokesman,* a security initiative will be announced tomorrow.

If you change this so that you use a reporting verb, you might find: 'A French spokesman said that a security initiative will be announced tomorrow'. With the reporting adjunct, the words which tell you that this is a report ('according to') come right at the beginning, whereas in the other version the word which tells you that this is a report ('said') comes a little later, after the subject. The adjunct therefore emphasizes slightly more than the verb that this is a report. One effect of this is to distance the reporter from the report and emphasize that he or she is not responsible for what is said.

2.123 If you use one of the reporting adjuncts which do not indicate who the speaker is ('apparently', 'reportedly', and so on), the effect can be to make the adjunct less prominent.

He has reportedly instructed his family not to interfere.

Compare this with: 'It has been reported that he has instructed his family not to interfere'. You can use these adjuncts when you want to indicate that you are not responsible for the information that you are giving without drawing too much attention to this indication.

2.124 If you use an 'as'-clause as reporting adjunct, you present the speaker as agreeing with you – you treat what he or she says as a support for your own statement.

As dad put it: 'You have to face the truth.' Well, we faced the truth.

See also 2.49.

using a reporting noun as reporting signal

2.125 If you use a reporting noun as the reporting signal, you can use it with a general verb such as 'give' or 'make' in a way which is very similar to using a reporting verb.

The Danish paper makes the reasonable and widely accepted suggestion that changes in the sun's brightness can affect the temperature on earth.
The National Salvation Front won the elections by making extravagant promises that it will protect the voters from the hardships associated with market reform.
They should make a public announcement that they would give up violence as a means of achieving political objectives.
I believe he's made the statement that he lost 150,000 dollars.
I make no apology for making comparisons, I do it all the time.
The deputy Prime Minister has given a warning that the country's energy supplies will last only a short time in the face of economic sanctions.

One reason for using the reporting noun+verb structure instead of a reporting verb is that you can add more information by using adjectives to modify the reporting noun, as in the first three examples above.

2.126 Here is a list of the major reporting nouns used in this way with the verb 'make', and followed by a reported clause.

allegation	declaration	prediction	rule
announcement	demand	promise	statement
appeal	objection	proposal	stipulation
assertion	observation	proposition	suggestion
claim	offer	proviso	threat
comment	plea	recommendation	vow
complaint	pledge	remark	
condition	point	request	

The following reporting nouns are used in this way with the verb 'give',

followed by a reported clause or, in the case of 'advice' and 'information',
a prepositional phrase or preposition and '-ing' clause.

acknowledgement	hint	news	reminder
advice	information	permission	suggestion
assurance	instruction	pledge	undertaking
explanation	invitation	promise	warning
guarantee	order	reassurance	

Other verbs which can be used with reporting nouns in this way include
'put forward' (used especially with 'suggestion','recommendation' and
'argument') and 'issue' (which can be used with a number of reporting
nouns instead of 'make' when the speaker is making an official statement
or is an institution such as a government). There are also particular
combinations of verb+noun such as 'drop a hint' and 'set a condition'.

2.127   In many cases, the reporting noun is not used with one of these
general verbs as the equivalent of a reporting verb, but is used as a
noun in its own right.

*The Daily Telegraph says that the Chancellor's <u>acknowledgement</u> that
the cost of unity would be high was seen as a sign that he may be
changing his tone slightly.*
*His resignation follows his <u>admission</u> that during anti-government
demonstrations last year he used the words 'let the tanks come in'.*
*His visit came despite an earlier <u>announcement</u> that there would be no
ministerial visit until the occupation was over.*
*She sat calmly through the film despite the usherette's <u>protestations</u> that
she was under age.*
*Dr Sidis categorically rejected the <u>suggestion</u> that his son was naturally
gifted.*

2.128   There may be many reasons why you use a reporting noun
rather than a reporting verb, but two aspects are worth commenting
on.

One is that it is very easy with a reporting noun to avoid mentioning the
speaker. It is not clear in the following examples who is the speaker who
'stated' or 'suggested' what is reported.

*A very strong case can be made for the <u>statement</u> that science grows by its
maybe answers more than by its yes or no answers.*
*Yet now there is a <u>suggestion</u> that these purchasers will have to find a
25% down-payment.*

Avoiding mentioning the speaker in this way may be innocent, or it may
be a deliberate strategy by the reporter. The reporter may want to make
the report appear more general – this is probably the case in the first
example above. Or he or she may want to 'hide' the person responsible
for some reason – this is perhaps the case in the second example. The
effect can therefore be very similar to reporting verbs used in the passive
form with **introductory 'it'** as subject (see 2.75), especially when you use

the noun in a 'there is' structure. The second example above, then, is similar in effect to this sentence:

It has been suggested that smaller tenants don't have the resources to fight rent increases.

2.129 Another aspect of using a reporting noun rather than a reporting verb is that it treats the report as a fact. Compare these two examples, one using the verb 'state', the other using the noun 'statement'.

The author states that initially the quality of life will increase as the energy availability increases.
They are also calling on the President to withdraw his statement that the demonstrators were hooligans and no better than animals.

In the first example, the reporter's main purpose is to report what *the author* says – this is what the sentence is 'about'. The reporter is making a claim about events (that *the author* states something) which in principle is open to question (the author could answer 'But I don't state that').

In the second example, on the other hand, the reporter's main purpose is to talk about the other people's reactions. A complete report is given of the President's words, but the sentence is not 'about' his words. What the President said is treated as an already established fact. (This may be because the President's words have already been reported earlier in the text.) In any case, in this report it is not open to question that the President said these words.

Although these considerations may seem quite subtle, in any communication you and your hearer will treat some things as established facts and other things as new propositions. You negotiate and change what is fact and what is new as you go on with the communication.

The choice of expressing your ideas through a verb or through nominalisation allows you to indicate whether something is, at that moment, treated as a fact or as something new. For example, you may choose to express an idea using a verb. As the communication continues you may refer to the same idea again, using a nominalisation. In this way you indicate that what was a new proposal is now, for you and your hearer, an established fact.

Choose a verb or a nominalisation as the reporting signal, then, is one important way of conducting negotiation between speakers, thus creating successful communication.

3 Function: the message

3.1 Chapter Two looked at the functions of the reporting signal. This chapter looks at what is reported – the message. Like Chapter Two, it deals with 'central' types of reporting: those which report what someone has said or written. The terms 'speakers' and 'hearers' again include 'writers' and 'readers' unless otherwise indicated.

3.2 There are basically three ways of reporting what someone has said or written.

● You can report the **words** of the message in a **quote**:

'In all of popular culture,' he declared, 'there is no one more fascinating than Carmen.'

● Or you can use a reported clause to report the **meaning** of the message in a **paraphrase**:

He had murmured that he was convinced he was going to die.

● Or you can use a 'wh'-clause, a prepositional phrase, or a noun group to report the **general idea** of the message in a **summary**:

Malcolm was on the phone complaining about money.

● There is also a fourth way: you can deliberately choose not to give information about the message.

He looked a little sheepish when he answered.

However, this is not part of 'central' reporting and will not be focussed on.

Reporting the words of the message

using quotes

3.3 If you want to report the actual words that the speaker used, you use a quote.

'What's going on?' demanded Bunbury. 'And who for heaven's sake is this chap?'
His intercom buzzed. 'Mr Demiris is on line two for you.'

3.4 You can also use a quote even if you do not report the actual words that were spoken. You may have forgotten exactly what was said, or you may not even know what was said; but you are still reporting what the speaker said as if you were using their own words. Note the way the reporter admits that he is not quoting Tessa Blackstone's exact words in the following example.

Tessa Blackstone was on the radio today, and she said something like 'Well I believe it's that people were so embarrassed that they wouldn't dare tell anyone that they were going to vote Conservative.'

You use inexact quotes especially in conversation, where being completely accurate is less important than keeping your listener's interest. Using a quote generally makes the report more dramatic. It also suggests that you are reporting the words that the speaker might have used to express their message (even if they did not actually use those particular words), and that therefore you are giving a more faithful report than if you use a reported clause.

3.5 Sometimes the reporter uses a quote even when it is quite clear that the speaker did not say the quoted words. This happens especially in headlines in 'popular' newspapers. For example, here is the headline that was used in one newspaper for a speech made by Queen Elizabeth II. The words are clearly meant to be a quote of her words (the writer uses 'us', for example).

PLEASE BE KIND TO US

The newspaper prints the exact text of the speech on another page. The text shows that the Queen did not use the words 'quoted' in the headline. She did, however, say that if people want to criticize her and her family they should do it with 'a touch of gentleness, good humour and understanding'. The headline writer has altered this so that it is shorter and more dramatic and catches the eye of people who might buy the newspaper.

The full text of this newspaper report can be seen in exercise 15, page 201.

3.6 At the other extreme, in some contexts such as academic writing you are expected to quote the writer's exact words, even including the original punctuation. If you change the quote in any way, you are expected to show this. For example, if you leave out part of the quote you show this by a series of dots, usually three.

Adorno et al. chose instead the term 'ethnocentrism', which connoted 'provincialism' or cultural narrowness, 'a tendency...to be rigid in acceptance of the culturally "alike".'

If you want to add something to the original quote, perhaps to make the meaning clearer, you put it in square brackets.

Mollenkopf (1983, p.14) points out that Federal government intervention 'accelerated and directed the second [post-industrial] transformation of American cities'.

3.7 If you want to emphasize that you are quoting something exactly as it is in the original, even though it looks like a mistake, you put (sic) after the doubtful word or phrase.

A week later came a reply: 'Dear Sir, Mr Weiss died a week ago after a lot of couging (sic). Yrs sinc. E. Ladbroke, landlady'.
In an art lesson once the female teacher said: 'Today we are going to draw aeroplanes. The ladies (sic) may like to draw birds instead.'

Function: the message

3.8 Here is a list of the major reporting verbs used with quotes.

add	confess	moan	say
admit	continue	mumble	scream
advise	cry	murmur	screech
agree	declare	muse	shout
announce	demand	mutter	shriek
answer	end	object	sigh
ask	enquire	observe	sob
assert	enthuse	offer	stammer
assure	exclaim	order	state
beg	explain	plead	storm
begin	finish	proclaim	suggest
bellow	gasp	promise	tell
boast	go	protest	thunder
cable	groan	rasp	urge
call	growl	remark	wail
chorus	grumble	repeat	warn
claim	hiss	reply	whine
command	howl	report	whisper
comment	inquire	respond	write
complain	insist	retort	yell
conclude	jeer	roar	

The following phrasal verbs are used in the same way.

burst out	go on	put in
carry on	point out	throw in

See also the fuller lists of verbs, phrasal verbs, and phrases describing the manner of speaking in 2.18–2.24.

using partial quotes

3.9 You can also use a partial quote (see 1.56) in your report. A partial quote can be used to make the quoted words more prominent. It suggests that this part of the message is particularly important or striking in some way and is therefore worth giving in the speaker's original words.

There was a ripple of laughter when he asserted that Germany now had 'unusually' successful relations with Britain.
Mr Hurd predicted that Dr Boutros Ghali was going to be a 'very effective' secretary-general.
The Revenue replied that 'the Board of Inland Revenue is unable to supply exact figures' for years prior to this date.
The presidency has been described as 'an irrelevant bore'.

3.10 A partial quote can also be used to give your listener or reader an idea of the original speaker's style.

A hoarse voice told the policeman that Antoine Argoud, 'nicely tied up', was in a van parked behind the CID building.
Mr Kinnock told the Prime Minister that her 'tantrum tactics' in Rome would not stop the process of change.

The house was 'small', she noted in her journal, 'but is to be put in good order.'

Reporting different speech acts

3.11 When you are reporting, you can show what the speaker's purpose or intention in speaking was. Utterances with different purposes or effects are known as different **speech acts**.

Three speech acts which are often carried out by means of particular grammatical structures are: giving information (usually in **statements**), asking for information (usually in **questions**), and giving instructions (usually in **commands**). There are many other speech acts which are not carried out by means of particular grammatical structures but by a variety of structures (often involving modal verbs); these include offering to do something, making suggestions, giving advice, and making requests.

3.12 You can show the kind of speech act partly through your choice of reporting verb (especially those listed in 2.10 as showing the speaker's purpose).

'But why?' I queried.
It has also been announced that Italy has recognized Russia as an independent state.

If you choose to use a quote, the quote itself often shows the speech act, and you do not need to show it through the reporting verb. The examples below show a quoted statement, question, command and suggestion, all with the reporting verb 'said'.

'She likes you,' he said.
'What do you want?' the manageress said when the kid entered the office.
'Get out of here,' Carlyle said.
'Let's drive!' you said.

However, the quote does not always show clearly what the speaker's intention is. You can indicate or emphasize the speech act through the reporting verb.

'We wouldn't get in the way,' Suzanne promised. 'We'd just stand quietly in a corner.'

3.13 If you choose to use an indirect report structure, the type of reported clause that you use can also indicate the speech act.

For example, after the reporting verb 'ask', you can use a 'wh'-clause to report a 'wh'-question:

Our reporter asked the President what he thought was behind the unrest.

or a 'whether/if'-clause to report a 'yes/no'-question:

I began to ask women if they could describe the things they do to make themselves feel safer.

or a 'to'-infinitive clause to report a command:

The police were <u>asking us to disperse</u>. They were <u>asking everybody to disperse</u>.

or a 'that'-clause to report a request:

He simply <u>asked that you make contact with him</u>.

The next three sections focus on the ways in which you can use different kinds of reported clauses to report different kinds of speech acts.

Reporting statements

using 'that'-clauses

3.14 The usual way of reporting a statement that a speaker has made is in a 'that'-clause (see 1.28–1.31).

He protested <u>that he didn't get enough time to practise target shooting</u>.
Excited voices were shouting <u>that the street was blocked by soldiers</u>.
A spokesman acknowledged <u>that there was room for improvement</u>.
Several representatives of the creditors predicted <u>that the process would take weeks</u>.

But notice that 'that'-clauses can also be used to report other kinds of speech act – see 3.44 below.

3.15 Here is a list of reporting verbs that can be used with a 'that'-clause reporting a statement.

acknowledge	concede	maintain	repeat
add	confess	mention	reply
admit	confide	moan	report
affirm	confirm	mumble	respond
agree	declare	murmur	retort
allege	deny	mutter	reveal
announce	disclose	note	say
answer	dispute	notify	scream
argue	divulge	object	shout
assert	emphasize	observe	sob
assure	exclaim	predict	state
bellow	explain	proclaim	stress
bet	forecast	promise	swear
boast	foretell	prophesy	tell
brag	grumble	protest	testify
caution	guarantee	reassure	wail
certify	inform	record	warn
claim	insist	reiterate	whisper
comment	joke	remark	write
complain	lament	remind	yell

The following phrases and phrasal verbs are used in the same way.

blurt out	let slip	point out
call out	make out	shout out

See also 3.49.

using 'to'-infinitive clauses

3.16 With the verb 'claim', you can report a statement using a 'that'-clause or a 'to'-infinitive clause.

They claim it was their territory until men built the house here.
He was the sort of man who would always claim to be in control of a situation.
Several people claimed to have seen someone shoot Mark Sanderson.

The last example above could be rewritten as 'Several people claimed that they had seen someone shoot Mark Sanderson'.

Note that a 'to'-infinitive clause can only be used in this way when the understood subject of the verb in the reported clause is the same as the subject of the reporting verb. In the last example above, *Several people* is both the subject of *claimed* and the understood subject of *to have seen*. In the first example, however, there are two different subjects: *They* and *it*.

See also 2.78 for other cases where a 'to'-infinitive clause is used to report a statement.

using '-ing' clauses

3.17 You can report a statement using an '-ing' clause with a small number of reporting verbs (see 1.55).

He admitted stealing a heart-shaped box, an oval-shaped box and a letter opener.
He acknowledged having a social relationship with her.
Two biologists at the University of Wurzburg in Germany have reported seeing frogs changing sex before their very eyes.

The first example above could be rephrased as: 'He admitted that he had stolen a heart-shaped box'.

Here is a list of the major verbs which can be used in this way.

acknowledge	deny	mention
admit	describe	report

using a main clause with a reporting adjunct

3.18 A reporting adjunct is normally used to report statements rather than any other kind of speech act. (See 1.67–1.74)

Charleston is historic and aristocratic, as your reporter said, but not haughty, as he suggested.
According to the advertising agency, the average American watches 30 hours of television each week.

Reporting questions

reporting 'yes/no' questions

3.19   There are two main kinds of question, and so there are two main ways of reporting questions.

One type of question is a 'yes/no' question. If you want to report this kind of question in an indirect report structure, you use a clause beginning with 'if' or 'whether' (see 1.45–1.46).

When it was time to go he asked if we were staying in Ostend and queried whether we had any life jackets on our boat.
He wanted to ask him if he had seen the baby, if he could tell him how she looked, what she was like.
It is up to the convenor to inquire whether the group agrees with their vision.

'if' and 'whether'

3.20   You can use both 'if' and 'whether' in reporting 'yes/no' questions.

I went over and asked him if he would like another drink.
When she asked whether I would like a whiskey I accepted eagerly.
Ask if you are free to go or whether you are being restrained.

Except in certain circumstances, which are explained below, 'if' is used more often than 'whether' in reporting questions.

3.21   In particular, 'if' is used when you are reporting requests and offers.

Just then I found them. He asked if he might have a look.
The Foreign Secretary asked if I would let him know what areas I was proposing to discuss.

3.22   When speakers ask a 'yes/no' question they may expect one answer rather than the other. If you want to suggest that the speaker expects a particular answer ('yes' or 'no'), you are more likely to use 'if'.

Our reporter asked an expert if baby corn comes from exactly the same plant as the better-known full-sized kind. 'Yes, that's right.'

On the other hand, the speaker may not expect a particular answer. If you want to suggest this, you are more likely to use 'whether'.

When asked whether they thought there were risks for women who go out in this area after dark, over a third of respondents believed it fairly safe.

3.23 'Whether' is used more often than 'if' in reports of 'yes/no' questions which include the phrase 'or not'. If you use 'whether ... or not', you emphasize that the speaker does not know whether the answer to the question will be 'yes' or 'no'.

Once the programme has come on and he has queried <u>whether</u> it is on at the right time <u>or not</u>, he loses interest in television.

The victor is never asked afterwards <u>whether or not</u> he told the truth.

Neither Russell Targ nor Dr Puthoff bothered to ask <u>whether or not</u> a normal explanation could account for the effects.

Notice that the phrase 'or not' can come immediately after 'whether' or at the end of the reported clause. It is possible to use 'if' instead of 'whether' when 'or not' comes at the end, but 'if' is much less common than 'whether' in this case.

3.24 Some 'yes/no' questions mention two alternatives separated by 'or'. These questions, like 'whether ... or not' questions, emphasize that the speaker does not expect one answer rather than the other. Not surprisingly, then, if you report one of these questions you usually use 'whether' rather than 'if'.

She asks sharply <u>whether</u> it is of men's images of women <u>or</u> women's images of women that I am writing.

I was once asked <u>whether</u> it was more difficult to learn a new move, <u>or</u> forget an old one.

Potential investors were asked <u>whether they want protection or whether they would prefer an extra £1 million</u> to strengthen the cash flow of the company.

3.25 When speakers ask a negative 'yes/no' question, they usually expect the answer to be 'no'. If you report a negative 'yes/no' question, you are more likely to use 'whether' rather than 'if'.

You ask <u>whether there isn't</u> a more 'natural' way of preventing this disease.

He asked his son whether he was really happy and <u>whether he did not wish</u> to have someone to whom he could turn for sympathy and true affection.

I asked him <u>if he had not been</u> terrified.

3.26 If you want to indicate that a speaker is using a question as a way of implying a negative opinion, you can use the reporting verb 'question' followed by 'whether'.

The standards of some candidates were so bad that examiners <u>questioned whether they should have been entered</u> for A-levels.

And the newspapers and the academics all <u>questioned whether there really was a Mafia.</u>

In the first example above it is clear that the examiners thought that the candidates should *not* have been entered for A-levels. In the second example it is clear that the newspapers and the academics thought that the Mafia did *not* exist.

Function: the message

reporting 'wh'-questions

3.27 The second type of question is a 'wh'-question. If you want to report this kind of question in an indirect report structure, you use a clause beginning with a 'wh'-word (see 1.39–1.44).

He came in and asked <u>where she was</u>.
She hadn't asked him <u>why he was taking her to a medical research laboratory rather than to a normal hospital</u>.
I asked him <u>how long he had known all this</u>, <u>how he had found out</u>.
At least half a dozen other members approached me with similar expressions of goodwill – never once asking me <u>where I was from</u>, <u>what I was doing here</u>, or any other pointed queries.
When anyone queried <u>where the vehicle was</u> he told them he had it out on special loan.
When her aunt questioned <u>why she had been crying night after night</u>, Annabelle sobbed that she was ugly and none of the boys liked her.

3.28 When the rest of the question is clear from the context, you can report the question by just using the 'wh'-word. This is more common in spoken and informal English, and happens especially with 'why'.

His mother is crying. He asks <u>why</u>. 'Because your father isn't here,' she says.
The girl, he thought, had been transferred to another building. When I asked <u>where</u>, he explained that patient information was private.

3.29 There are only a few verbs which are used to report questions (both 'yes/no' and 'wh'-questions). These are the major ones.

ask	inquire	question
enquire	query	

Many other reporting verbs can be followed by 'wh'-clauses, but these are used to give a summary of a statement rather than a paraphrase of a question – see 3.53 below. See also 4.29 on reporting uncertain thoughts. For information on how to report questions asking for advice, see 3.42.

using 'wh'-clauses to report exclamations

3.30 A speaker can indicate that he or she is making a judgement about the degree to which a quality exists or the extent to which something is done or felt. This is sometimes called an **exclamation,** especially if the sentence also implies surprise, disappointment, pleasure, or displeasure. It is often written with an exclamation mark. A variety of grammatical forms can be used. In the first example below, the quality and its extent is referred to in an adjective group. In the second example, the quality of 'pleasantness' is referred to in a noun group. In the third example, the extent to which the speaker *cares* is expressed in an adverb group.

It is all terribly distressing.
What a pleasant welcome!
I care very much about doing things the right way!

3.31 You report exclamations and similar judgements about qualities using 'wh'-clauses beginning with 'how' or 'what'. 'How' is followed by an adjective or adverb; 'what' is followed by a noun group.

He complained how 'difficult it is to have efficiency in the I.A. with such slow promotion'.
Everyone, including Mrs Bingham, remarked how much she resembled Marie Antoinette.
Sharpe tried to throw it off by saying how terrible the retreat to Corunna had been.
She said how lucky I was that I could save money in that way.
He congratulated me warmly and said how much he was looking forward to meeting her.
Tony had said what an unexpected pleasure it was.

Here is a list of the major reporting verbs which you can use with a 'wh'-clause to report exclamations and similar judgements about qualities.

acknowledge	complain	inform	say
admit	confess	insist	stress
announce	confirm	mention	tell
assure	emphasize	observe	testify
boast	exclaim	remark	
comment	explain	remind	

The phrasal verb 'point out' is also used in this way.

3.32 This kind of report is normally used in informal contexts such as ordinary conversation. With some of the verbs, in more formal contexts you can report a similar judgement by using a 'wh'-clause in a prepositional phrase.

They occasionally commented on how good her work was.
She reminded me of how generous she and Doyle had been to Joe and me over the past months.

Here is a list of the verbs from the list above which can be used in this way. The preposition that you use is given in brackets.

assure (of)	confess (to)	remind (of)
boast (of)	inform (of)	tell (of)
comment (on)	insist (on)	
complain (about/of)	remark (on)	

Reporting orders, requests, advice, promises, suggestions, and offers

3.33   There is a range of speech acts which are broadly concerned with your own or other people's future behaviour. For example, if you promise something, you say what you will do in the future; if you give a command, you say what someone else will do (assuming they obey you). The 'future' may be distant or immediate – in the example below, the child carries out the command to spell the word immediately.

'Spell the word spot.' 'S-P-O-T.'

The important thing is that the action that you are talking about has not yet taken place when you talk.

3.34   When you report most speech acts referring to future behaviour, there are two main types of structure that you can use: 'to'-infinitive clauses and 'that'-clauses with modals (or the subjunctive). However, reporting suggestions does not fit completely into the same pattern – in particular, the verb 'suggest' is not followed by a 'to'-infinitive clause, and suggestions, unlike the other speech acts dealt with here, can be reported using an '-ing' clause.

using 'to'-infinitive clauses

3.35   If you want to report the speaker influencing (or trying to influence) the hearer's future actions, by means of a command, request, suggestion, or piece of advice, you can use a 'to'-infinitive clause. For example, the following sentence is reporting the speaker saying something like 'Lie down on your back!'.

Inside were four men, one of whom ordered <u>him to lie down on his back</u>.

The hearer, who is expected to carry out the order, is mentioned as the object of the reporting verb (*ordered him*). The hearer can also be mentioned as the subject of a passive form of the reporting verb (see 2.74).

It is a poisonous substance and <u>growers are recommended to ensure</u> that no 'unprotected persons' enter the field for at least one day after spraying.

With some reporting verbs, the hearer is mentioned in a prepositional phrase; but it is still the hearer who is expected to carry out the action mentioned in the reported clause.

The policemen shouted <u>at us to get out</u>.

3.36   Here is a list of the major verbs that can be used with a 'to'-infinitive clause to report a command, request, or other speech act referring to the future actions of the hearer. The hearer must be mentioned. With the verbs where the hearer is mentioned in a prepositional phrase, the preposition is given in brackets in the list.

Orders, requests, advice, promises, suggestions, and offers.

admonish	command	incite	request
advise	counsel	instruct	shout (at/to)
appeal (to)	direct	invite	tell
ask	encourage	nag	urge
beg	enjoin	order	warn
beseech	entreat	plead (with)	whisper (to)
call (on)	exhort	press	yell (at/to)
challenge	forbid	recommend	
coax	implore	remind	

Friends approached him advising him to come out in print with a criticism of Akhmatova.

Sarah boiled, rinsed and starched the laundry, calling on the child to help carry water.

Rose challenged him to come on stage and explain his opinions away to 25,000 people.

Doctors have told Benny to slim down drastically.

The phrasal verb 'egg on' is used in the same way.

3.37 Note that if the verb in the reported 'to'-infinitive clause is in the passive form, the person who is actually to carry out the action is not normally mentioned. This occurs especially with the reporting verb 'order'.

The officers ordered her to be shot.
The king ordered him to be sold as a slave.

3.38 You can also report speech acts such as commands, advice, and suggestions by using a 'to'-infinitive clause with the reporting verb 'say'. In this case, you do not normally mention the hearer even though the hearer is the one who will carry out the order or suggestion. This is used in informal speech or writing.

Flo said not to bother with the leaving party, because she's not going yet.

3.39 When you report the effect of what the speaker says on other people (see 2.54), the effect is obviously in the future when the speaker begins speaking, and so you use a 'to'-infinitive clause with some of the reporting verbs.

The Colonel persuaded her to sell the stock.
For the 1959 election he was persuaded to change his mind.

The major verbs which can be used with a 'to'-infinitive clause to report the effect of what the speaker says are 'convince' and 'persuade'.
The phrasal verbs 'prevail on' and 'prevail upon' can also be used in this way.

3.40 If you give an order, you are trying to influence another person's future behaviour. If, on the other hand, you give a promise or ask for permission to do something you are talking about your own future behaviour. You can use a 'to'-infinitive clause when you report

a promise, an offer, or a request to do something. The hearer is not usually mentioned (except if you use 'promise' – see 2.89).
Here is a list of the major words used in this way.

agree	guarantee	promise	undertake
ask	offer	propose	volunteer
beg	plead	swear	vow
demand	pledge	threaten	

You're the first guest who has ever asked to eat with us.
Devorchak had sworn to win a medal a day just to prove to himself that he could do it.
The landlords threatened to break the rioters' bones.

reporting requests without mentioning the hearer

3.41   You can report a request which is to be carried out by someone other than the speaker or hearer by using a 'to'-infinitive clause with certain verbs. In this case, the understood subject of the reported clause (the person who is to act) is mentioned in a prepositional phrase beginning with 'for'.

I asked for a vet to come and shoot the injured deer.
He ran outside and called for his oldest son to get some coffee for the honoured guests.
The politicians begged for someone – anyone – to come forward and negotiate.

If the verb in the clause reporting the request is in the passive form, you also mention the subject of this verb (the thing that is to be done) in a prepositional phrase beginning with 'for'.

He asked for three other offences to be taken into account.
Mrs Davenport rang and asked for Emily to be sent.
The campaign in Britain from 1951 onwards called for action to be taken against the unions.

Here is a list of the major reporting verbs which can be used in this way.

appeal	beg	plead
ask	call	

reporting a question asking for advice

3.42   If you want to report a question in which the speaker asks for advice or instructions, you can use a 'to'-infinitive clause following a 'wh'-word (see 1.48). In this case, the speaker is asking about what they should do. The reporting verb is nearly always 'ask', and the most common 'wh'-words are 'what' and 'how'.

I realized I couldn't just sit in this man's office for ever. So I asked him what to do.

The women of her tribe had asked him many things, but none of them had ever <u>asked how to make fire</u>.

Note that 'why' is not used in this kind of reported question since 'why' questions are not used to ask for advice.

3.43   If you use this kind of clause after 'ask', you can mention the hearer, but the understood subject of the reported clause is still the same as the subject of the reporting clause.

A soldier in the next room wearing earphones <u>asked his officer how to spell the names</u>.
She called up the vet to <u>ask him what to do with the animals</u>.

See also 3.60 on using a 'to'-infinitive clause following a 'wh'-word to give a summary of a speech act such as an order or a suggestion.

using 'that'-clauses

3.44   When you use 'to'-infinitive clauses in reports, you are normally talking about what the speaker or hearer will do. If you want to report an order or suggestion which relates to someone or something else, you can use a 'that'-clause with a modal. The modal is usually 'should'.

In many cases, as the examples below show, the verb in the reported clause is in the passive form and the person who is expected to carry out the action is not mentioned.

He also suggested <u>that someone should sleep in the offices every night</u>.
The ministers recommended <u>that this should receive urgent attention at next week's meeting of EC heads of government</u>.
The prime minister has requested <u>that parliament should be recalled</u>.
The order stipulates <u>that supplies should be provided through the United Nations</u>.
The judge ordered <u>that the man should be deported</u>.

The 'that'-clauses in most of the above examples could not be replaced with 'to'-infinitive clauses. The exception is the last example with *ordered*, which could be expressed as: 'The judge ordered the man to be deported' (see 3.37).

3.45   Occasionally, a 'that'-clause with 'should' is used to report an order or a suggestion, even if it is the hearer who might be expected to carry out the action. This happens especially with 'suggest'.

Monty then suggested <u>that Jeremy should walk down to the village with us</u>. Jeremy refused.
The magazine recommends <u>that people should avoid vehicles featuring the ultra-drive</u>.

However, except with 'suggest', it is commoner in these cases to use the subjunctive – see 3.47.

3.46 Note that 'suggest' is not used with a 'to'-infinitive clause even when the reported suggestion is addressed directly to the hearer. As the above examples show, it can be followed by a 'that'-clause. See also 3.51 on using '-ing' clauses in reported suggestions.

3.47 In more formal contexts, you can also leave out the modal in 'that'-clauses of this type. In this case, the verb remains in the base form, as though the modal were still there – that is, it does not change to the past tense, or add '-s' in the third person singular form of the present tense, or use 'do' to form the negative. This is sometimes called the **subjunctive**.

On the day of my arrival I had to request that the grubby bathroom <u>be cleaned</u> again.
The poorer patient paid cash when money was available and, if not, asked that the fee <u>be charged</u> to account.
Dr Goldstein's going to be a little longer than she thought. But she asked that you <u>stay</u>, if possible.
The committee has recommended that the student in question <u>not be allowed</u> to resubmit the assignment.
Meanwhile he ordered that his daughters <u>transfer</u> to the attics and his mother <u>move</u> down to their rooms.

3.48 As noted above (3.45) you can also use this kind of clause to report an order, etc. even if it is clearly the hearer who is expected to carry out the action.

Helen admitted that she rarely wears much make-up in the evening. Judith Pallan recommended she <u>try</u> a light beige foundation.

In this case, there is little difference between a 'that'-clause and a 'to'-infinitive clause. The example above could be expressed: 'Judith Pallan recommended her to try a light beige foundation'.

3.49 Here is a list of the major verbs which can be followed by a 'that'-clause containing the modal 'should' or the subjunctive in reports of speech acts such as orders or suggestions.

advise	demand	propose	suggest
agree	direct	recommend	urge
ask	insist	request	warn
beg	order	rule	
command	ordain	specify	
decree	plead	stipulate	

using 'that'-clauses to report the speaker's future actions

3.50 You can also use a 'that'-clause with a modal to report what someone says they are going to do.

The modal is usually 'would' or, less frequently, 'will'. In this case, unlike the structures described in 3.44–3.49 above, the modal in the 'that'-clause cannot be left out to form the subjunctive. All the reporting verbs which can be used in this way can also be followed by a 'to'-infinitive clause.

You promised me you'd take care of her.
I promised to keep an eye on him.
Avi swore that he would do everything in his power to help us.
He swore to tell the truth, the whole truth and nothing but the truth.

Here is a list of the major reporting verbs which can be used in this way.

agree	pledge	swear	vow
guarantee	promise	threaten	

using '-ing' clauses

3.51 With a small number of verbs, you can also report a suggestion by using an '-ing' clause. In this case, you do not mention the hearer.

Barry suggested going to another coffee house.
She recommends encouraging the others to reminisce about their past lives.
He also proposed building a middle-priced housing development along the lake.

Here is a list of the reporting verbs which can be used in this way.

advise	propose	recommend	suggest

Summarizing messages

3.52 If you use a 'that'-clause to report what someone says, you are giving a paraphrase of the original meaning. However, you can also report a summary of the general idea of what is said. If you use a summary, you can simply report the speaker's purpose in speaking.

I'm going to give you some advice that will help your golf game.

Or you can include an indication of the content of what the speaker said.

Experts predicted years of stagnation for the world's banking industry.
Meares talked about the spiritual growth he had witnessed in his patients.

summarizing statements

3.53 One way in which you can report a summary of what is said is by using a 'wh'-clause.

I explained where I thought we were.
I have no hesitation in repeating what was said.

In court last January she told his attorney <u>why she needed the doctor's assistance.</u>
It tells you <u>how much longer you can stay in the sun.</u>
The contract stipulates <u>what facilities may be used by the crew.</u>

3.54 Note that these 'wh'-clauses are not reporting questions, although they are identical in form to 'wh'-clauses which are used to report questions (compare 3.27).
Here is an example of a reported question.

He came straight to us, <u>to ask us what we were up to.</u>

The question might have been 'What are you doing?', or 'What are you up to?' Compare this example of a summary, which is *not* an example of a reported question.

I told him <u>what had happened.</u>

This reports not a question but a story or an account of a series of events.

3.55 With certain reporting verbs, you are more likely to use a 'wh'-clause to summarize the message if the language event is 'negated' – if you are reporting what was *not* said.

He <u>wouldn't say</u> where he'd been.
She <u>didn't say</u> whether she required an explanation or not.
It was <u>hard to say</u> whether my contempt for Michael Stryker was greater than my pity.
They say he's ill himself, they <u>don't say</u> if he's mad, too.

3.56 As well as being negative, as in the examples above, the reporting clause may be interrogative, or may contain a modal. These report possible language events rather than actual ones.

<u>Did he say</u> where he'd seen her?
<u>Could you please confirm</u> in writing whether you wish to accept this offer.
He wondered when they <u>would say</u> whether he'd got it or not.

As some of the examples above show, clauses beginning with 'whether' and, less frequently, 'if' can be used in these possible and negated cases, although they are rarely used in summarizing actual language events.

3.57 If the rest of the message is clear from the context, you can just use the 'wh'-word as a summary. This is more common is spoken and informal English, and happens especially with 'why'.

'What's it for, Charlie?' 'Does it matter?' 'Yes it does. You ask for a contact, you <u>tell me why.</u>'
She asked why he was so silent all the time, but he <u>couldn't say why.</u>

3.58 In many cases, 'wh'-clauses giving summaries are referring to something that has already been mentioned or explained. In the following example, the reason why the journalist *wouldn't be going to the next race* is that he had been *made redundant*.

The journalist was made redundant by the magazine he was working for. He rang Senna and said he wouldn't be going to the next race and explained why.

In other cases, the summary prepares for a fuller report which follows. The example below was spoken by a radio reporter introducing a recording of *Dr Storm* describing the trial.

On the line from Copenhagen, Dr Storm told me how the trial was conducted.

In some cases, giving a summary avoids the need to go into unnecessary detail. In the example below, a reported description of *how steam engines worked* would probably be rather long.

He explained how steam engines worked.

If the language event is negated – if the reporter reports what someone did not say rather than what they did – there is clearly no actual language to report; so it makes more sense to use a summary of the kind of information that was missing than to use a reported clause giving a paraphrase.

He didn't say whether he'd wait or not.

3.59 Here is a list of the major verbs which can be followed by a 'wh'-clause reporting a summary of a message. The verbs marked with an asterisk (*) are more likely to be used to report negated language events.

acknowledge	disclose	indicate	report
add*	discuss	list	reveal
admit	divulge*	mention*	say*
announce	emphasize	outline	specify
chronicle	enumerate	predict	state
confess	explain	proclaim	stipulate
confirm*	forecast	record	suggest*
declare	foretell	recount	summarize
describe	formulate	relate	tell
dictate	hint	repeat	whisper

The following phrases and phrasal verbs are used in the same way.

let know	let slip	make it clear	point out

summarizing orders, suggestions, and advice

3.60 When you want to give a summary of an order, a suggestion, or a piece of advice, you can use a 'to'-infinitive clause following a 'wh'-word. Note that the hearer must normally be mentioned.

And it's 'high season' too for the 'advice' industry, which tells people what to do – and what not to do – on holiday.

An undercover British police unit worked alongside the Italians, advising them who to watch and how to deploy their forces.
The Heinz Good Beach Guide tells you where to go to find the cleanest beaches in Britain.

Here is a list of the major verbs that can be used in this way.

advise	teach	warn
remind	tell	

Compare this use of 'to'-infinitive clauses following a 'wh'-word with the use of the same structure to report questions asking for advice (3.42).

using 'so' to avoid repeating something

3.61 A different way in which you can summarize a statement is by using 'so'.

'We're going south.' 'Why?' 'Because I've said so.'

You use 'so' when you want to avoid repeating something that has just been said. In the example above, the speaker could say *'Because I've said that we're going south'*.

You use 'so' in this way with two reporting verbs: 'say' and 'tell'.

'I don't think John likes what I'm doing.' 'Has he said so?' 'No, I just sense it.'
He'd like to know you better. He likes you – he said so.
She knows that you and I adore each other. I have told her so.
He had always been told she was very clever: she had told him so herself often enough.

3.62 Note the difference between using a 'wh'-clause and 'so' to summarize statements.

When someone uses a 'wh'-clause as a summary (see 3.53), you cannot normally tell what the original speaker actually said. When someone uses 'so', on the other hand, you can normally tell exactly what the speaker said.

Compare these two summaries.

She simply smiled and nodded and said what everyone else was saying.
June was the worst month, everyone had said so.

In the first case, the report does not tell you what *everyone else was saying,* whereas in the second, you know that everyone had said that *June was the worst month.*

using prepositional phrases as summaries

3.63 Another way in which you can summarize what the speaker says is by using a prepositional phrase (see 1.93–1.96).

He complained about the delay.

One of the most common prepositions used to introduce summaries is 'about'. Here is a list of the major reporting verbs which can be used with a prepositional phrase with 'about', or with an '-ing' clause introduced by 'about', to give a summary of a message. With some of these verbs you must normally mention the hearer; these verbs are marked with an asterisk (*) in the list. With the others you do not normally mention the hearer, except with 'ask' and 'warn', when you can choose whether to do so or not.

agree	contact*	joke	shout
argue	enquire	lie	speak
ask	enthuse	moan	talk
boast	exclaim	muse	tell*
brag	explain	mutter	waffle
caution*	gabble	prattle	warn
chat	gossip	protest	whine
chatter	groan	rave	write
complain	grumble	remind*	
consult*	inquire	reminisce	

The following phrases and phrasal verbs are used in the same way.

carry on	hold forth	prattle on
go on	keep on	

Hill had invited the crew over to Nine West that evening to <u>talk about joining forces</u>.
Lendl <u>spoke about his growing love affair with Wimbledon</u> and how he has gradually come to terms with the eccentricities of British life.
There's a man in Birmingham who's been <u>complaining about a consignment of shoes</u> he's lost.
He cursed for a while, <u>muttering about low-grade plugs and cables without waterproofing</u>.
Gerald persuasively <u>wrote about the push of humanity toward a higher form of consciousness</u>.

3.64 Other reporting verbs can be used with 'of'. With the verbs marked with an asterisk (*) you must mention the hearer.

assure*	inform*	reassure*	talk	write
complain	notify*	remind*	tell	
convince*	persuade*	speak	warn	

He has even <u>talked of allowing people to buy their own homes</u>.
Yesterday correspondents in the capital <u>spoke of frightened people venturing out onto streets deserted after a night of terror</u> as government soldiers killed and looted at random.

3.65 Other reporting verbs can be used with 'on'. With the verbs marked with an asterisk (*) you must mention the hearer.

agree	congratulate*	remark
advise*	consult*	report
comment	insist	write

The Financial Times, in its editorial, <u>comments on the statement by the British Chancellor of the Exchequer.</u>
Edna had <u>insisted on their leaving early.</u>

The phrasal verb 'hold forth' is used in the same way.

3.66 Other reporting verbs can be used with 'to'.

| admit | allude | confess | object |
| agree | assent | consent | refer |

The phrasal verb 'own up' is used in the same way.

Nora <u>admitted to her suspicions about Jim</u> because of the night the cows escaped.
The real reason was that people <u>objected to money being given to workers</u> but not to industrialists.

3.67 Other reporting verbs can be used with 'for'.

apologize	clamour	plead	scold*
appeal	criticize*	praise*	thank*
beg	invite*	pray	vouch

He <u>apologized for disturbing their Sunday dinner.</u>
I <u>thanked him for vacating his room.</u>
On the date of his execution, his mother <u>begged for an audience with the governor.</u>

The phrasal verb 'tell off' is used in the same way. See also 2.29–2.32 for more verbs which can be used with 'for'.

3.68 There are a few other prepositions which are used with small numbers of reporting verbs to give a summary of the message. For example, a speaker may 'hint at' something or 'protest against' something.

The farmers' weather forecast has already <u>hinted at snow showers in the north.</u>
Bo Lundberg <u>protested against all supersonic aircraft</u> at the Montreal Conference in 1961.

3.69 One effect of using a prepositional phrase in reports is to move the emphasis away from the content of the message and to focus more on the language event as an event. In the following example, the focus is on the fact that the economy caused discontent.

People were <u>grumbling about a sick economy</u> as they celebrated the bicentennial.

Compare this with a report which contains a 'that'-clause, where there is more emphasis on what people said.

Life is full of the promise of spring. Yet the French are <u>grumbling that they have too much time off</u> to enjoy all this.

using noun groups as summaries

3.70 You can use a verb together with one of the nouns referring to language events, such as 'answer' or 'invitation', to give a summary of what the speaker says (see 1.97–1.98).

They <u>extended an invitation</u> to other former states of the Soviet Union to participate in the alliance.
Government officials are repeatedly <u>issuing denials</u> of reported plans to alter the course of the elections.
Things might have been very different if I hadn't <u>answered that tricky question</u> about the nurse's visa.
She <u>repeated urgent advice</u> that all people outside the disaster area should stay where they were.

3.71 In some of these verb+noun combinations, the noun refers to the language event and the verb adds little further information. The noun therefore carries most of the meaning. The noun is often modified by an adjective (e.g. 'He has delivered a formal protest'). The following verb+noun combinations are used in this way.

ask + question
deliver + message/speech/lecture/warning/judgement/denunciation
give + hint/talk/speech/warning
issue + statement/warning/decree/appeal/order/ultimatum
make + statement/joke/complaint/offer/appeal/apology/proposal/request/
  speech
offer + suggestion/explanation/prayer
pose + question
recite + prayer/list/poem/litany/monologue
relate + story
speak + words/oration/message
tell + story/tale/joke/lie/anecdote
utter + word/prayer/apology/warning/prophecy

The supervisors joined in group discussions, <u>posed questions</u> and helped students deal with a variety of individual pupil difficulties.

3.72 In addition, there are some verbs which are often used with summarising noun groups to give more information about the language event, such as how it was performed or how it fitted into the rest of a conversation, or what the speaker's purpose was. Here is a list of verbs that can be used in this way. Each verb can be used with a variety of summarising noun groups.

Function: the message

add	fire	note	suggest
begin	mumble	pronounce	whisper
call	murmur	scribble	write
continue	mutter	shout	

Here are some phrases and phrasal verbs which are used in the same way.

call out	put forward	reel off
let slip	read out	shout out

> *They had taken a look at me in hospital and murmured a few condolences before announcing that there was nothing wrong.*
> *The genial taxi driver assumed they were tourists and reeled off a list of historic places they must not fail to visit.*

3.73 With some verb+noun combinations, the noun refers to a previous language event which the language event being summarized responds to in some way. Here is a list of the major verbs that are used in this way.

answer	deny	pass on	refuse
contradict	dismiss	quote	repeat
copy	echo	read	report
decline	explain	recap	retell

The phrasal verb 'pass on' is also used in this way.

> *I declined his offer of coffee and dessert.*
> *Mr Turner denied a suggestion that he is seeking revenge on the company for his redundancy.*

3.74 With other verb+noun combinations, the noun refers to a future language event which the language being summarised elicits. Here are the major verbs used in this way.

ask (for)	demand	invite	request

> *Tom's boss demanded a pledge of loyalty from him.*

3.75 With many verbs you can give a summary of what is said in a noun group even when the noun itself does not refer to a language event. In this case, it is the verb which refers to a language event, while the noun group tells you what is talked about.

> *Baker admitted assault at Birmingham Crown Court.*
> *The statement asserted the rights of opposition groups to operate freely within the law.*
> *The officer claimed ignorance of this secret order.*
> *Many traders forecast a continuation of the market's recent trend.*

In many cases, it would be possible to rephrase these summaries using a reported clause. For example, the last sentence above could be expressed: 'Many traders forecast that the market's recent trend would continue.'

3.76 Here is a list of reporting verbs which can be used in this way.

acknowledge	describe	offer	reaffirm
admit	discuss	order	recommend
affirm	emphasize	outline	record
announce	exaggerate	permit	report
assert	explain	pledge	request
call for	express	point out	reveal
claim	forecast	praise	signal
communicate	foretell	predict	specify
condemn	guarantee	proclaim	stress
confirm	highlight	promise	suggest
criticize	make clear	propose	teach
declare	mention	query	threaten
demand	note	question	urge

Relating the report to your time of speaking

3.77 When you quote a speaker's words, you repeat them as they were spoken in the original context. In the example below, *I* in the quote clearly refers to the speaker (whereas *me* in the reporting clause refers to the reporter).

   'By this time I was getting very tired,' he told me.

When you use an indirect report structure, on the other hand, you report what the speaker says in a way which is appropriate from your point of view at the time when you report it. If the reporter had chosen to use an indirect reported clause in the example above, he might have written 'He told me he was getting very tired'.

This section looks at how you make the message fit in to your report when you use an indirect reported clause, and how the message then differs from the original words.

3.78 In any language event, some parts can only be understood in relation to the context. For example, you might hear the following sentence:

   I'll give you a ring tomorrow.

In order to understand who 'I' refers to, you need to know who is saying 'I'. In order to understand which day is meant by 'tomorrow', you need to know when the speaker is speaking. The parts of a language event which can refer to different things according to the context are called **reference features**.

Reference features relate especially to who is speaking, who they are speaking to, when they are speaking and where they are speaking.

This section looks at the differences between the reported message and the original words which are related to the change of context. Typically, as reporter, you are speaking at a different time and in a different place from the original speaker; and you are a different person. The reference features in your report relate to you rather than to the original speaker.

Referring to time in indirect reported clauses

3.79 One of the most important reference features is **tense.** A primary function of tense in English is to show your view of how an event or state which you are talking about relates to the time when you are talking.

The tense that you use for your reporting verb influences to some extent the choice of tenses that you can use for the verb in the reported clause. However, you mainly choose the tense of the verb in the reported clause according to what you feel is appropriate at the time when you are speaking.

using past tenses in the reported clause

3.80 When you report what a speaker has said, you are reporting a language event which happened in the past; and what the speaker was talking about is now also in the past. Therefore the reporting verb and the verb in the reported clause are usually both in a past tense.

I discussed it with my sons and they said they wanted to see me happy.
Earlier, a judge said there was confusion over whether the photographs even existed.
Others nearby said they were now afraid to go out at night.
A military spokesman said six RAF helicopters were taking part in the rescue.
Last year he said he wanted to negotiate in good faith. Now we know that wasn't the case.
'This sounds like nonsense to me. Do you understand it?' My mother said she did.

3.81 If the speaker was speaking about something which was already in the past when they spoke, you can simply use a past tense in the reported clause.

A spokesman said police were stoned by angry residents as they drove away from the camp.
David Orr said the U.S. didn't begin screening this pipeline until Friday.
He said they all eventually ended up on the resort island of Contadora.
An opposition group said it carried out the attack.

If you want to emphasize that the situation was already in the past when the speaker spoke, you can use the past perfect tense.

A White House spokesman said there had been no deals to obtain his release.

A spokesman for the president said student representatives had failed to turn up for a meeting.
The People's Party said he had been the victim of a dirty tricks campaign in the run-up to the election.
He said the idea had not even been raised during his visit to the United States.

In these two groups of examples, it would be possible to use either the past tense or the past perfect tense in any of the reported clauses. In fact, many reporters use the two tenses in consecutive clauses referring to the same event. This demonstrates that the two tenses are interchangeable in this way.

A newspaper article said she had asked for a £6,000 fee to attend a charity event. The article said a function was cancelled because the fee was considered to be too high.
Another passenger said he had 'looked death in the face and knew I had won'. Eyewitness Patrick Silver said the plane somersaulted three or four times before hitting the water.

choosing past or present tense in the reported clause

3.82 Sometimes what the speaker said in the past may still be true when you report it. In this case, you can choose whether to use a present tense or a past tense in the reported clause.

At present the rebels are moving on foot. They said their current headquarters was about twenty miles from the border.
Today he said he was too busy to follow up on speculation.
Yeltsin, for his part, said he is willing to try.
Only 42% said they disinfect their dishcloth more than once a week.
The FDA said it is in the process of reviewing the country's top-selling drugs.
The Foreign Minister said there are signs the two alliances are dropping their old enmities.
Stempel said the company is doing cost estimates.

Notice how, in the following example, the use of the present tense in the first part of the report suggests that *government policy* is a permanent situation, whereas the use of the past tense in the second part suggests that the country's need for income is a temporary (and undesirable) exception to this policy.

A Foreign Ministry spokesman said government policy is not to sell arms to sensitive areas. But he said his country needed the income to convert arms factories to non-military production.

If you change the tense in the first sentence from present 'is' to past 'was', and the tense in the second sentence from past 'needed' to present 'needs', the emphasis also changes – in this case the report suggests that the need for income plays a more important role than the stated policy.

Note that you can emphasize even more strongly the fact that the situation still exists by using a present tense for the reporting verb as well as for the verb in the reported clause – see 3.85 below.

3.83   There is a similar choice between present perfect and past perfect tenses in the reported clause. If you want to emphasize the fact that the situation which started in the past is still true or relevant when you report it, you use the present perfect.

His resignation comes only hours after the Home Secretary <u>told</u> Tory representatives that he <u>has swept</u> drunken louts off the streets.
In August the shareholders' annual meeting <u>was told</u> that the pace of improvement <u>has slowed</u>.

If you do not particularly want to emphasize that the situation is still true or relevant, or if the situation is in fact no longer true, you use the past perfect.

A federal air traffic controller <u>said</u> he <u>had received</u> no such orders until now.
Speaking to reporters in Mississippi today, Sununu <u>said</u> he <u>had told</u> the president he would leave.
Yesterday he <u>told</u> reporters that a deadline of the fifteenth of January <u>had been agreed</u>.
'Have you started on that yet?' I <u>told</u> her I <u>had</u> not.

using a reporting verb in a present tense

3.84   So far in this section, the reporting verb has been in the past tense. Sometimes, however, the reporting verb is in the present tense. There are a number of reasons why you may use a reporting verb in the present tense. Most of the reasons are the same as for ordinary uses of a present tense: for example, because you are making a general statement about what many people say.

Every director <u>tells</u> me that facing the employee shareholders is an anxious moment.

There are some cases, however, which apply particularly to reporting verbs. If you are reporting something that is written down, you always have the option of using a present tense for the reporting verb, no matter when the text was written.

Matt's report <u>says</u> they had game licences.
The author <u>claims</u> that he based this on the recollections of Brother Hermannus.
Rothman (1960, p.21) <u>asks</u> why the present distribution of power should be regarded as any more stable than in the past.

This is clearly related to the general option of using a present tense to report the content of certain kinds of written text. For example, when you retell the story of a novel or play, you normally use a present tense.

This occurs just after Pandarus finally does invite Criseyde to his house.
When Criseyde asks whether Troilus will be there, Pandarus says that he
will not be.

3.85 You can also use a present tense for the reporting verb to report
what someone said in the past if you want to emphasize strongly that
what they said is still true and relevant as you report it.

Miss Woods has been round the house with the police and she says there's
nothing missing.
The shopkeeper says he won't be able to carry on if the population drops
any further.
It helps that your friend's handy with a pistol. She tells me she actually
got in some target practice in the woods yesterday morning.

3.86 If you use a reporting verb in the present tense, you still use a
tense in the reported clause which is appropriate at the time when you
are speaking. For example, if you report what a written text says, you
can use a present tense for the reporting verb; but, if the text is about
something that is no longer true, you use a past tense for the verb in
the reported clause.

The early Arts Council reports make clear that the exhibition was
intended to show that artists produce works of great beauty.
The Daily Express comments that it was a pity that the concert was so
bad.

3.87 If, on the other hand, you use a reporting verb in the present
tense when telling a story, to make the story seem vivid or because
you are retelling a written story, you treat the whole report as if it
were about the present. This means that you use a present tense in the
reported clause if the situation is true or relevant at the time when the
speaker speaks. Note that the present perfect counts as one of the
present tenses in this sense.

When they are in the presence of this Prince, he asks them if they are
willing to obey his commands.
The agent calls him repeatedly again. Jafar finally returns the calls. The
agent tells him a company has been found for the export deal.
And Father William tells him it is because he has led a good life.

3.88 It was mentioned above (3.82) that, if what the speaker said in
the past is still true when you report it, you can choose whether to use
a present tense or a past tense in the reported clause. However, this
choice is in fact only open to you when you use a past tense for the
reporting verb. If you use a present tense for the reporting verb to talk
about a language event in the past, you must use a present tense in the
reported clause if the situation still exists.The following example means
that they still have the plantation when you report her words.

She tells me they have a plantation on that island.

If you changed this to 'She tells me they *had* a plantation', it would mean that they no longer have the plantation at the time when you report her words (and at the time when she speaks). If you changed it to 'She told me they had a plantation', on the other hand, this could refer to three different situations: they no longer had the plantation when she spoke; or they still had it when she spoke, but not when you report her words; or they still have it when you report her words, but you do not particularly want to emphasize this.

See also 3.109–3.112.

Other reference features in reported clauses

3.89 As mentioned in 3.78, parts of a language event can refer to different things according to the context – who is speaking to whom, and where and when they are speaking. These are called reference features. One of the clearest examples of reference features are the personal pronouns – the people referred to by the pronouns 'I' and 'you' clearly change regularly through a conversation according to who is speaking.

> *'How can I give you a massage if you keep getting up?' said the masseur.*
> *'Maurizio,' Forstmann said, 'I know you have problems. But I have bigger problems.'*

Apart from verb tenses, discussed above, the main reference features concern the people and things involved in the language event, the time, and the place.

When you use an indirect report structure, you relate the reference features in both the reporting clause and the reported clause to the context in which you are speaking. This section looks in more detail at the ways in which you do this.

referring to people and things

3.90 When you report what a speaker says, you refer to people and things in a way that is appropriate for you. This concerns especially your choice of pronouns (such as 'I', 'me', 'mine', 'myself') and possessive determiners (such as 'my', 'your'). To illustrate how this works, here is a footballer reporting a conversation between himself and his manager John Lyall.

> *When John Lyall came in 1990 he told me some clubs had enquired about me and also told me he had turned them down.*

If it is John Lyall who is reporting this conversation, he might say '*I told him some clubs had enquired about him*'. If he is reminding the footballer himself about the conversation, he might say '*I told you some clubs had enquired about you*'.

Similarly, if the footballer is reminding John Lyall of the conversation, he might say '*You* told *me* some clubs had enquired about *me*'.

3.91 Note that making the reference appropriate may mean choosing a noun group ('some clubs') rather than a pronoun ('you'). If the footballer is talking to some people from the other clubs mentioned, he might say 'He told me *you* had enquired about me'.

If the footballer has not yet mentioned John Lyall in this case, he might say '*John Lyall/John/The manager/My boss* told me you had enquired about me'. Obviously there are many ways in which the footballer could refer to John Lyall (whether or not he is using a report structure). His choice depends partly on how much he thinks the listener knows. If he thinks the listener knows a lot about the situation, he may say 'John' or even just 'he'. If he thinks the listener does not know much about the situation, he can give more information: for example, 'John Lyall, the manager of the team I played for at that time'.

3.92 The demonstratives 'this', 'that', 'these' and 'those' are reference features, because understanding what they refer to often depends on the context of speaking. The *officials* in the following example may actually have said something like 'We welcome *this* appeal'.

> *Officials for Oxfam and Save the Children have told the BBC that they welcome the appeal by the government to the international community.*

In the context in which the officials were speaking, it would be clear which appeal they were referring to. In the report, on the other hand, the reporter adds extra information to make it clear to the listeners.

In other cases, it is clear at the time of reporting what 'this' and 'that' refer to, and you can then use them in your report.

> *Earlier this month asylum seekers broke into foreign embassies in the hope of safe passage out of the country. The authorities said this was out of the question.*
> *He said he was prepared to lose the money because that was part of the cost of doing business.*

In expressions referring to times (see below), you often use 'that' rather than 'this' in reported clauses.

referring to places

3.93 The place in which you are reporting may be different from the place where the speaker spoke. In this case, the **adjuncts of place** that you use are related to your location rather than to the original speaker's location. In the first example below, the report implies that the speaker probably said 'Crike isn't here'.

> *He rang the number on the card Crike had given him, only to be told that Crike wasn't there.*
> *The watchman shouted that the tramp had not been there that night.*

referring to times

3.94 As with people and places, you make references to time appropriate to when you report what someone else said.

Many **adjuncts of time** in English change their reference according to the context. The majority of these take the time of speaking as the point of reference. For example, 'last year' refers to the year before the year in which you are speaking. Thus, if 'this year' is 1994, 'last year' obviously refers to 1993.

However, there are also many adjuncts of time which take as their point of reference a different time (in the past or, less frequently, in the future). These are called **shifted** adjuncts of time. If you start by referring to a year in the past, you can use that year as a point of reference and relate the time of other events to that year. If, for example, you start talking in 1994 about what happened in 1984 ('ten years ago') and then want to refer to 1983 you do not say 'last year'. Instead you can refer to it as 'the year before' or 'the previous year'.

> *A few years ago she decided to visit Finland: friends of hers had toured the country in their car the previous year and had praised it highly.*

3.95 When you report what someone said in the past, you normally use these shifted adjuncts in the reported clause.

> *After a pause he added that his horses could not travel to the Bosque just then.*
> *The Count had written to say that he hoped he might see her for a moment that evening.*
> *A brief letter from John said that an American biologist might work with him during the following year.*
> *Uncle Sam was asleep; I said that I would return the next day.*
> *'Charlie, you must come again soon.' I said that I would come next week.*
> *I said that I would see her in the morning.*
> *He said you must have gone to the pub the previous evening.*

3.96 Here is a list of shifted time adjuncts, matched with their **unshifted** equivalents (the ones which take the present as the point of reference).

unshifted	shifted
now	then
today	that day
this morning/evening/week/month/year	that morning/evening/week/month/year
yesterday	the day before *or* the previous day
last week/month/year	the week/month/year before *or* the previous week/month/year
a week/month/year ago	a week/month/year ago *or* a week/month/year before

recently	recently *or* shortly before
tomorrow	(the) next day *or* the following day *or* the day after
tomorrow morning	in the morning *or* the following morning
next week/month/year	(the) next week/month/year *or* the following week/month/year *or* the week/month/year after
soon	soon *or* shortly after

3.97   Note that some time adjuncts can be used in both shifted and unshifted contexts: for example, 'recently' and 'soon' in the list above. 'The other day' may mean 'a few days before today' or 'a few days before the day in the past that I am speaking about'. All time adjuncts which begin with 'in' meaning 'after' (e.g. 'in a week' or 'in two day's time') can be used in shifted and unshifted contexts.

They said they would expect me in the bar <u>in about fifteen minutes.</u>
A German astrologer predicted in July 1923 that the Prince might <u>soon</u> 'expose himself to personal danger'.

There are other time adjuncts which refer to specific times (e.g. 'at six o'clock', 'on 4th April', 'in 1990'). These are not related to the time of speaking, and therefore they do not change in the way described above.

3.98   In some cases, you can use an 'unshifted' time adjunct even if the reporting verb is in the past tense.

You can do this when the time adjunct is still appropriate for the time when you speak.

Officials admitted police used excessive force in dispersing protesters <u>this month.</u>
You said I could come and see you <u>this morning.</u>
The Irish Foreign Minister said that the European Community would re-examine its policy at a meeting in Dublin <u>next week.</u>

You can also do it in some cases when the context makes it clear that the time to which the adjunct refers is in the past. This happens especially with 'now'.

Our father said we must be beyond the cottage by <u>now.</u>
Vera did not refuse him; but she said that she would not give him any answer <u>now.</u>
A federal air traffic controller said he had received no such orders until <u>now.</u>

Messages following reporting nouns

3.99   So far in this chapter, most of the examples of different aspects of the message have had reporting verbs in the signal. However, much of what has been said is also true when you use reporting nouns in the signal.

reporting different speech acts

3.100 Many of the reporting verbs listed in 3.14–3.51 have related reporting nouns. In general, you can use the same kind of clause to report different speech acts after the noun as you can after the verb. However, reporting nouns are not followed by '-ing' clauses even if the related verb can be. Also, some reporting nouns behave differently to the related verb: for example, the nouns 'accusation' and 'criticism' can be followed by a 'that'-clause reporting a statement, but the verbs 'accuse' and 'criticize' cannot. And there are a few nouns, such as 'news', which are not related to verbs but which can be used with a 'that'-clause to report statements.

3.101 You can report statements in 'that'-clauses following reporting nouns which are mostly related to the verbs listed in 3.15.

> *There was a general <u>acknowledgement that there wasn't much news about</u>.*
> *The fat lady behind the counter sold him one with the <u>comment that this was the last copy</u>.*
> *Widely reported is his <u>forecast that unemployment will continue to rise</u>.*
> *Of course Lloyd George wanted to be prime minister; there is no need to take seriously his <u>protestations that he did not</u>.*
> *The decision was made after <u>advice that radioactive material could leak into the air in the event of an accident</u>.*

Here is a list of the major reporting nouns which can be followed by a 'that'-clause reporting a statement.

accusation	claim	insistence	reassurance
acknowledgement	comment	lament	remark
admission	complaint	news	reminder
advice	concession	notification	reply
affirmation	confession	objection	report
allegation	confirmation	observation	response
announcement	criticism	point	revelation
answer	declaration	prediction	statement
argument	disclosure	proclamation	testimony
assertion	explanation	promise	warning
assurance	forecast	prophecy	
boast	guarantee	protest	
caution	information	protestation	

3.102 You can use a 'to'-infinitive clause to report a statement after the reporting noun 'claim' (compare 3.16).

> *It is impossible to check Antigua's <u>claim to have 365 beaches</u>, one for every day of the year.*
> *In this, Pincher upheld Meehan's <u>claim to have warned Mr Saunders that the Communists were interested in Blake</u>.*

3.103   You can report questions in 'wh-'clauses following a few reporting nouns, particularly 'question' (compare 3.29).

Since for the most part particle physicists know what they are doing, the question why they are doing it is not one which they pose.

However, you more commonly use a noun followed by 'of' before the 'wh'-clause (see 2.101).

Throughout his life Rowntree returned to the question of what constituted poverty.
We are not able to answer the age-old question of how the mind is attached to the body.
Some maintain that it is not a question of whether, but when reserves of minerals and fuels will run out.
If the question of when language arose is difficult enough, the issues of how and why are even more puzzling.

3.104   You can report orders, requests, advice, promises and so on in a 'to'-infinitive clause following reporting nouns related to the verbs listed in 3.36 and 3.40.

This will require promises to provide patent and copyright protection.
The United States says that it has received a favourable response from its allies to its request for them to send more troops and weapons.
This is the most explicit warning yet to Britain not to abandon the principle of 'convergence' with the Basic Law.

3.105   You can report orders, requests, advice and so on in a 'that'-clause with a modal or subjunctive following reporting nouns related to the verbs listed in 3.49–3.50.

In his diary he quoted approvingly Wilson's suggestion that the congressman should 'go to hell'.
He concluded with the suggestion that his son accept 'my motto: Everything for the French people.'

3.106   Here is a list of the major reporting nouns that can be used to report speech acts concerned with your own or other people's future behaviour. Note that the noun which corresponds to 'swear' (in the sense of 'give a solemn promise') is 'oath'; and that the noun 'request' here corresponds to the two verbs 'request' and 'ask'.

advice	encouragement	permission	ruling
agreement	entreaty	plea	stipulation
appeal	guarantee	pledge	suggestion
call	incitement	promise	threat
challenge	insistence	proposal	undertaking
command	instruction	recommendation	vow
decree	invitation	refusal	warning
demand	oath	reminder	
directions	offer	request	
directive	order	rule	

reference features in reported clauses following reporting nouns

3.107 The ways in which you deal with reference features in reported clauses following reporting nouns are basically the same as in full report structures (see 3.77–3.98). The most important point again is that you make the report appropriate to your own time of speaking.

The only difference is that the reporting noun itself does not show explicitly when the language event happened. In the majority of cases, the verb of the clause in which the reporting noun appears makes clear what time you are referring to.

> *The jury had also been impressed by his own admission that he had never revealed his activities during the war.*
> *All I wanted was an admission that she was there.*
> *He also complained about the Police Commissioner's recent statement that all news conferences would now be vetted by the police.*
> *A spokeswoman said the Department is disturbed by the Ministry's admission that it financed part of the action.*
> *With the admission that he is now a warrior and not a lover, Troiolo's sufferings are finally over.*
> *We are made uncomfortable by his statement that he will pursue 'things unattempted yet in prose or rhyme'.*
> *The development of new methods had raised the question whether the Church should now relax her teaching on this matter.*

3.108 As with full report structures (see 3.82), you may be reporting something which the speaker said in the past but which is still true when you report it. In this case, you can use a present tense in the reported clause if you want to emphasize that the situation still exists.

> *That American-made receiver was included in a display of audio equipment with the admission that the Americans are far ahead in this field.*

Using modals in reported clauses

3.109 **Modal verbs** are often used in reports of suggestions, tentative statements, and statements about obligation. They can be used whether or not a modal was used in the original language event.

> *On Earth Day, 1970, it was suggested that people might place two or three bricks in the water tanks of their toilets and thus cut down on the amount of water they used.*
> *After the rehearsal he said he might have a part for me in a new play next year.*
> *So we demanded 50 shillings a week and said we would strike if we didn't get it.*

I said I <u>had</u> to go and see my mother.

3.110 Some modal verbs have 'past' and 'non-past' forms. 'Might',
'could', 'would', and 'should' are sometimes said to be the 'past' forms
of 'may', 'can', 'will', and 'shall'. These 'past' forms can be used to show
that you are reporting an attitude that was held in the past. The modal
'must' has no 'past' form, but 'had to' is sometimes used to show that
an obligation was held in the past.

They told Mattie if they were lucky they <u>might</u> also see some rare birds.
They said that Society <u>had to</u> be destroyed.

3.111 On the other hand, the 'past' forms have meanings of their own
and it may simply be these meanings that are being reported. For
example, 'would' is often used to show that a situation is hypothetical,
'should' is used to show obligation, and 'might' and 'could' are
sometimes used instead of 'may' because they are more tentative; these
forms can be used in reports without themselves referring to past time.

Mr Pollack had said it <u>would</u> be a crime if she wasted her talent.
And late last night a spokesman said accounts of Mr Jenkin's resentment
<u>should</u> not be exaggerated.
Adela Pickering points out that some women <u>could</u> be playing a martyr
role with this behaviour.

3.112 If you report a suggestion or statement that refers to a
situation that is still true at the time when the report takes place, you
may choose to emphasize this by using the 'non-past' form of the
modal.

He could not predict the students' actions but said we <u>may</u> know more
tomorrow.
The ex-husband said in court that he <u>may</u> not be able to afford the travel
expenses.
A spokesman for the company said that the strength <u>will</u> come from the
re-marketing of its computer portfolio.

4 Other uses of report structures

4.1 When you use a reporting structure, you make a link between two pieces of information; for example, the fact that somebody said something and what they said. You can use the same kinds of structure to make links between other kinds of information, for example, the fact that you understand something and what it is that you understand. This chapter focuses on a varied range of ways in which you can use report structures apart from reporting what someone actually said or wrote.

Some of these uses – for example reporting the thoughts passing through someone's mind – may involve a previous language event, while others do not – for example reporting what someone sees.

In general the functions described in this chapter use the same kinds of structures as the 'central' reporting functions described in Chapters Two and Three, and many of the comments made in those chapters about the central functions also apply to these functions.

Reporting thoughts and perceptions

4.2 As well as reporting what people say, you can report what they think. You can report many kinds of thoughts – beliefs, knowledge, feelings, intentions, decisions, hopes, wishes, regrets – and also perceptions, such as seeing and hearing. In some cases, it is fairly clear that you are reporting language in someone's mind.

   'This is my destiny,' she thought exultantly.

In other cases, it is fairly clear that you are not reporting language.

   You could see now that he might make a boxer.

In the majority of cases, however, it is unclear whether you are reporting language or not.

   I had hoped that Jeremy might talk to me, cheer me up.

In this last example, the person might be reporting words that passed through her mind – something like 'I hope Jeremy will talk to me' or 'Perhaps Jeremy may talk to me'; or she might simply be reporting a vague feeling of hope which was not originally expressed in words. The reason for including such examples as reports is that they are reported *as if* the words passed through the person's mind.

In this chapter, the person whose thoughts are being reported is called the **senser**.

reporting the words of thoughts

4.3 In narratives, such as stories, novels, or jokes, you often report what someone thinks in a way that presents the thoughts as words actually passing through the person's mind. The most common way of doing this is by using a direct quote structure. Sometimes you use inverted commas around the quote.

He had that sinking feeling in his stomach. 'Oh, my God,' he said to himself. 'I'm in deep trouble.'

'Perhaps he's going to write a novel,' he said, while he thought to himself, 'God help the students in his English class.'

Colouring his hair was something he had thought of doing for years.'Brown,' he thought, 'a mousy brown.'

In the majority of cases, you do not use inverted commas around the quote.

Hastening homeward, Scylla thought, <u>Shall we have to leave, to travel, just as the rains begin?</u>

No one else, he thought to himself now a little sadly, <u>would care at all.</u>

<u>Not, I reflected, that she would solve my problems for me.</u>

When I was young, something in me wondered, <u>What will happen to all that beauty?</u>

And Tim thought, <u>she is thinking about Guy.</u>

4.4 Another very common way in which you signal that you are reporting the words that passed through the senser's mind is by using a **reflexive pronoun** referring to the senser in the reporting clause. You can do this by using a direct quote, with or without inverted commas.

'That's it,' he <u>said to himself.</u> 'I'm going to kill him.'

They're crazy, she <u>told herself</u> again and again, or they're trying to drive me crazy.

She <u>thought to herself,</u> How he talks! She couldn't imagine English people talking like that.

One day, I <u>promised myself,</u> I'll think up some privileges for myself.

Shall I, I <u>asked myself</u> in the first day's shooting, remonstrate when shouted at to keep quiet?

You can also use an indirect report structure.

She trembled violently but <u>told herself</u> it was the result of the last two anxiety-ridden days.

As she was removing her Persian vase she had <u>said to herself</u> that she was afraid Alan might break it.

He did not press her for further details, although he <u>admitted to himself</u> that he was curious.

Lynch <u>asked himself</u> if he would have found the situation funny at Frank's age, but the answer was no.

Note that 'think to oneself' is normally used in a direct quote structure rather than an indirect report structure.

4.5 In principle you can use a reflexive pronoun with any reporting verb where you can mention the hearer (see 2.81). However, not all of these reports are reports of thoughts. In some cases, they mean that the speaker spoke aloud but quietly – for example, if you report that someone 'muttered to herself' you mean that she spoke quietly and did not expect anyone else to hear her or reply to her.

Here is a list of the major reporting verbs which are used with reflexive pronouns to report the words passing through a senser's mind. With many of these verbs you use the reflexive pronoun in a prepositional phrase with 'to'; these are marked with an asterisk (*) in the list below.

acknowledge*	exclaim*	remind	think*
admit*	persuade	repeat*	vow*
ask	promise	say*	warn
confess*	remark*	tell	

4.6 You can use an indirect report structure without a reflexive pronoun to report the words passing through someone's mind or to show that the information in the reported clause is someone's opinion (which may or may not have been put into words). It is not always clear which of these is meant.

He'd thought a couple of months earlier <u>that Catchpole was coming along nicely</u>.
They decided <u>that teaching a sign language might be more fruitful</u>.
Hurtle thought <u>that if he were ever to draw Mr Spargo he would do him with a pair of horns</u>.

In most cases, this kind of report will be interpreted as reporting the senser's opinion, rather than the words they thought (see 4.12 below). Of the examples above, only the third appears to be reporting the words that the senser (*Hurtle*) thought.

One way in which you can make it clearer that you are in fact reporting the words that the senser thought is by placing the reporting clause in the middle of the reported clause or at the end.

It made her look like a troubled schoolgirl, <u>Helen thought</u>.
It was indeed, <u>he thought</u>, a perfect marriage of Nature and Civilization.
The nicest thing about New York, <u>Daniel decided</u>, after being there five minutes, was that you were invisible.

4.7 When you put the reporting clause in the middle or at the end, you often use an indirect quote (see 1.61–1.66). This happens especially with reported questions with the reporting verb 'wonder'. In the first example below, the report implies that the senser thought something like 'Why did I agree to stop here?' Note that the reference features (tense and pronouns) in the reported clause are relevant to the time of reporting, but that the clause is interrogative in form.

Why, <u>he wondered</u>, had he agreed to stop at this particular place?
When the moment came, <u>he wondered</u>, how much would he have time to know?

You can also put the reporting clause in the middle or at the end with reported thoughts that are not questions.

> *They were very nice, <u>she thought</u>, but it was a strain and there was no use pretending to herself.*
> *The defeat seemed to make all the sacrifices of the previous years futile and, heaven knew, <u>he thought</u>, there had been sacrifices indeed.*

There is very little difference between an example of an indirect quote like this and examples of indirect report structures with the reporting clause in the middle or at the end (see 4.6). The indirect quote simply sounds closer to the original words that the senser thought.

For more on how writers exploit these different ways of reporting the words of thoughts, see Chapter Five.

4.8 As noted above, many verbs used to report thoughts do not indicate clearly whether the reported words actually passed through the senser's mind. However, there are certain reporting verbs which in themselves normally imply strongly that they did.

> *Stephanie <u>reflected</u> that this poem was the poem she most cared for.*
> *Thomas gloomily <u>speculated</u> that he might be the next one to get into Mrs Simpson's bad books.*

Here is a list of the major reporting verbs that you can use in this way.

conclude	deduce	pray	reflect
conjecture	muse	reason	speculate

4.9 All the reporting verbs in the list above can also be used to report what a speaker said. If the verbs are used in direct quote structures, this normally implies that the words were spoken aloud. If you use these reporting verbs, you are indicating that the speaker spoke in a thoughtful way or after thinking carefully.

> *'To think,' Teddy <u>mused</u> sadly, 'that my little brother would turn out to be a Tory.'*
> *'You have definitely got a point, maybe it could have been productive to address our women as women,' he <u>reflected</u>.*

You can emphasize that the words were spoken by using the adverb 'aloud'.

> *'If we're mad enough to climb up to this chapel,' he <u>reasoned aloud</u>, 'the most you can expect is half an hour's rambling conversation with a crazy monk.'*

If, on the other hand, the verbs are used in indirect report structures or with indirect quotes, it often implies that the reported words were thought.

> *I <u>reflected</u> that whatever was going to happen now there could be no escape from it.*

He felt happier in his own car; better an ancient dented Aston, he reasoned, than a brand new Datsun.

However, if it is obvious that the reporter could make the report only if the words were made public – that is, spoken or written – then we must assume that speech or writing is being reported. In the first example below, the journalist could know what the *observers speculated* only if he or she heard them or read what they wrote.

Some observers speculated that the general also wanted to show that the most powerful army in the world can still act with confidence.
Greely concluded that he had received a better education than he would have in four years of college.

4.10 If you want to report something that is actually said, but from the point of view of the hearer rather than the speaker, you can use the reporting verb 'hear'.

Machiavelli was astounded when he heard that the Duke had accepted the captain's invitation.
I have heard that he is an exceedingly severe, quarrelsome individual.

Reporting ideas

4.11 There are many verbs that you can use in indirect report structures when you want to report people's ideas without necessarily implying that the words in the reported clause passed through the senser's mind.

In terms of their meaning, the verbs can be divided into four main groups.

● reporting opinions
● reporting mental operations
● reporting feelings
● reporting the process of finding out facts

A number of the verbs appear in more than one group, indicating that they can be used in slightly different ways.

reporting opinions

4.12 An important group of verbs are those which you use when you want to report someone's opinion. The most common verb in this group is 'think'.

She thought I was joking.
Because of the cold, she thought it would have been better to have waited until the spring.
He thought he knew who was giving the party, but he was wrong.

Here is a list of the major verbs which you can use to report people's opinions.

assume	expect	presume	think
believe	feel	reckon	understand
consider	hold	suppose	
doubt	know	suspect	

The phrases 'take it for granted' and 'take it' are used in the same way.

She believed that any emotions openly expressed must be false emotions.
Everyone took it for granted that it was a good thing. But was it?
Mary and he hadn't had children. He supposed that in a way it wasn't a bad thing.
I always suspected that Frank was not his real name.
I've always understood that she didn't want another child.
They felt that the charges against us were silly and would be dropped. They were right.
We were young. We never doubted that one day we would be parents.

See also 4.46 on using reporting verbs to express your own opinions.

4.13 With some of these verbs, you can report someone's opinion using a 'to'-infinitive clause. The first example below could be paraphrased as 'He believed that the Wise Man was guilty'.

Henderson does not record the name of the Wise Man; but he firmly believed him to have been guilty of a heartless and cruel fraud.
Marianne knew that the old woman felt herself to be perfectly capable of bringing the boy up herself.
I must get out of the corner without revealing that I knew her to be an agent.
He had gone to the doctors, although not with the question she had supposed him to be asking.
He fidgeted with something under his tunic; Cameron suspected it to be a pistol.

In many cases, the second verb is 'be'. Note that this structure is less frequently used than the structure with a 'that'-clause. Here is a list of the major verbs which you can use in this way.

assume	feel	presume	suspect	understand
believe	hold	reckon	take	
consider	know	suppose	think	

This structure has a corresponding passive reporting structure, which is more frequently used – see 4.35 below.

reporting mental operations

4.14 Another group is used to report mental operations, that is, thought processes such as coming to a decision.

125

After consultations with the Lord Advocate he had <u>decided</u> that there was no further action he could take.

When she married Murdo she <u>expected</u> that there would be money coming into the house regularly.

Here is a list of the major verbs that you can use when you want to report mental operations using a reported 'that'-clause. Note that 'mean' as it is used here is equivalent to 'want to say'. 'Conceive' as it is used here usually appears with 'can' or 'could' in negative or interrogative sentences.

accept	deduce	figure	infer	remember
assume	dream	foresee	judge	resolve
calculate	envisage	forget	mean	speculate
comprehend	estimate	gather	presume	suppose
conceive	expect	guess	recall	think
decide	fancy	imagine	reckon	wonder

The phrase 'make up your mind' (or 'make your mind up') is used in the same way.

The youth suddenly stood up, and said: 'Oh, come on.' I think he probably <u>meant</u> that they should leave the pub.

I could not <u>conceive</u> that anyone should shoot so accurately, even with telescopic sights.

The women were carrying on their own conversation, in low tones; I <u>gathered</u> that they were not expected to take part in male conversation.

I noticed a man on the far side of the leaves. I <u>supposed</u> that Jeremy had persuaded one of the local farm-workers to do a few hours' work in his garden.

The verbs listed in 4.8 are closely related to the verbs in this list because they also refer to mental operations.

4.15   You can use some of the verbs in this group to report someone's thoughts about their future behaviour. In this case you use a 'to'-infinitive reported clause (compare 3.35–3.41).

Eventually he <u>decided to do a course for trained nannies</u>, but the colleges would not take males.

Upon my return to Cambridge I had <u>expected to hear from the States about my fellowship</u>, but there was no official communication to greet me.

By then I was sure that Harold <u>meant to propose to me</u> and I knew I should say yes.

Here is a list of the major verbs that you can use in this way. Note that 'mean' as it is used here is roughly equivalent to 'intend'.

decide	forget	plan
determine	intend	remember
expect	mean	resolve

The phrase 'make up your mind' (or 'make your mind up') is used in the same way.

See also 4.21.

4.16 Note that with 'remember' and 'forget' there is a difference between using these words followed by a 'that'-clause and using them followed by a 'to'-infinitive clause. The differences are related to which comes first: the mental operation (remembering, forgetting) or the action mentioned in the reported clause.

In this example, the senser left the briefcase under the table first, and later remembered doing this.

Halfway down the stairs I remembered that I had left the briefcase under the table.

In the next example, on the other hand, the senser remembered what he was supposed to do, and afterwards did it. As usual, the 'to'-infinitive clause refers to an action which is still in the future when the action of the verb 'remembered' happens.

The following morning he remembered to finish Caldicott's letter.

In the next example, the senser made an arrangement to see the secretary first, and later forgot that he had done this.

I even forgot that I had arranged to see the secretary of the pistol-club.

In the next example, the senser forgot what she was supposed to do – which means of course that she didn't do it. The forgetting therefore clearly happened first.

'I quite forgot to give you the parcel this morning,' she said.

Note that with 'remember' you can use an '-ing' clause instead of a 'that'-clause. In this case also the remembering comes after the action described in the reported clause.

Back at school he remembered sitting and waiting for his turn to stand up and read aloud in class.
He remembered his father describing the way Colonel Moxon-Greife always got drunk.

'Forget' is also occasionally followed by an '-ing' clause, usually when 'forget' is made negative in some way.

A fire engine had hit the water main and I'll never forget seeing firemen holding their hoses with no water coming out.
How can he ever forget killing a whole family like that?

reporting feelings

4.17 Another group of verbs is used to report the senser's feelings.

She hoped that she could get him out of the house before her father came back.
I wished that she could have stayed longer.
The snow was settling and I feared that it would be over the top of some of the smaller children's shoes.

Other uses of report structures

Note that you can also report the senser's feelings by using an adjective followed by a reported clause. In fact, you have a much wider choice of adjectives for this purpose than verbs. See 4.38.

4.18 In many cases, you use these verbs to report feelings about unreal situations (situations that did not exist or situations that do not yet exist, or situations that you are not sure about). Therefore the 'that'-clause following these verbs often includes a modal or a past perfect tense. In this way, they are similar to conditional clauses referring to possible situations.

> *Later that night, when the temperature dropped below freezing, I wished that I had made myself a fire.*
> *He hoped that they might let him return there for a while.*
> *She always dreaded that her mother would telephone while he was there.*

However, 'regret' is different: if you report that someone regretted a situation, you mean that the situation definitely existed, but the senser wished that it did not. The following example means that the senser asked for very little but wished that he had asked for more.

> *He regretted that he had asked for so little.*

4.19 Here is a list of the major verbs which can be used with a 'that'-clause to report the senser's feelings.

Note that when 'mind' is used in reporting feelings it is normally used in negative or interrogative sentences. Also, 'mind' and 'prefer' can be used with 'that'-clauses but are more often used with other kinds of reported clause (see 4.20 and 4.22).

dread	hope	prefer	wish
fear	mind	regret	worry

4.20 You can use several of these verbs with a reported '-ing' clause instead of a 'that'-clause.

> *She didn't mind getting her hair wet in the rain.*
> *Fanny dreaded seeing Thomas again.*
> *She preferred being compelled into her decisions.*
> *For an instant I almost regretted not having accepted Lyon's arrangement.*
> *She didn't mind him giving her a few tips about riding motorbikes.*

Here is a list of the major verbs which can be used in this way. 'Mind' and 'dread' are in fact more often used with an '-ing' clause than with other kinds of reported clause.

dread	mind	prefer	regret

4.21 You can use some of the verbs in this group to report a senser's feelings about their possible future behaviour. In this case you use a 'to'-infinitive reported clause (compare 4.15 above).

She hoped to leave that evening for her sister's in Scotland, and resented any delay.
At first the husband had not wished to allow his wife to come near the hospital.

Here is a list of the major verbs which can be used in this way.

desire	long	wish
hope	want	

4.22 You can also use 'prefer' with a 'to'-infinitive clause to report someone's feelings about their usual behaviour or about their possible future behaviour. If you are reporting their feelings about their usual behaviour, you use 'prefer' or 'preferred'.

She preferred to bathe in mineral water, the bubblier the better.
The children said they preferred to see wild animals in safari parks where they could move around.

If you are reporting their feelings about their possible future behaviour, you usually use 'would prefer' or 'would have preferred'.

It was already rather late and I personally would have preferred to come home to bed.
Helen would have preferred to spend their money immediately.

'Prefer' is used with a 'to'-infinitive clause much more often than with other types of reported clause.

4.23 With some of the verbs listed in 4.14 and 4.19, you can report the senser's thoughts or feelings about someone or something else's future behaviour. This person or thing is mentioned as the object of the verb.

She always expected all her friends to know her voice as soon as they heard it.
He pointed at her as if he meant her to stand up and answer questions.
I wished him to push my mother-in-law in her wheel chair for half an hour.
They preferred him to find things out for himself.
She went in to make another cup of coffee and longed for the telephone to ring.

Here is a list of verbs which can be used in this way. Note that with 'long' you mention the someone or something else in a prepositional phrase with 'for'.

expect	mean	wish
intend	prefer	
long	want	

Some of these verbs can also be used in a corresponding passive structure – see 4.34.

reporting the process of finding out facts

4.24   There is a group of verbs which you can use when you want to report someone finding out, working out, or knowing a fact.

I found out afterwards that she was in fact quite popular.
A 1963 study found that only one child in three was malnourished in families with one or two children.
Isobel noticed that Griffiths had dark glasses on and that Meehan was wearing a peaked cap.
As soon as I saw him, I realized that I'd seen him before.

Here is a list of the major verbs which can be used in this way.

ascertain	know	observe	see
discover	learn	perceive	sense
find	note	realize	spot
intuit	notice	recognize	understand

The following phrasal verbs are used in the same way.

find out	make out	work out

4.25   The verbs in this group have an important feature in common. They show that you have a positive attitude towards the information that is in the reported clause – that is, you accept that what the senser finds out is in fact true.

It was a long time before Alan realized that he was alone.

In this example, the reporter indicates that *Alan* was in fact alone. It would be very odd for the reporter to contradict Alan by adding 'But in fact there was someone else in the room'.

Compare 2.41–2.43.

4.26   Many of the verbs in this group are often used to report summaries of the thought in 'wh'-clauses (compare 3.53–3.59). This also happens with verbs in the other groups which show that what the senser thinks is actually true – 'regret', 'remember', and 'forget'.

It took me nine months before I realized what had happened to me.
'Coming!' he cried when he realized who it was.
Pascal had realized how a calculating machine could tackle the task of 'carrying'.
You must find out in which particular corner of Westminster, Whitehall or the local authority planning department they reside.
Both clearly regretted what they had done.

4.27   If you want to represent a mental exclamation (compare 3.30), you can use 'realize' followed by a clause beginning with 'how' or, less frequently, 'what'. The first example below implies that, if the senser put his thoughts into words, he might have thought something like 'It's really cold in this cell!'

Then I realized <u>how cold it was in that cell</u>.
He realized <u>how expertly his departure had been organized</u>.
I hadn't realized <u>what a difference dyed hair could make to a face</u>.

You can also use some of the other verbs from the list above, such as 'see' and 'understand', but these are less frequently used in this way than 'realize'.

4.28 There are also a few verbs which you can use in a particular reporting structure with 'it' as the subject to report the senser finding something out. Notice that the 'it' in this structure is an **introductory 'it'**; that is, it does not refer back to anything that has been said before, but refers forward to the 'that'-clause.

<u>It occurred to me</u> that Shapiro might all the same be keeping an eye on me.
All of a sudden <u>it struck me</u> that unless somebody was prepared to do something, I couldn't go on.
<u>It dawned on him</u> that this was what being in love was all about.

Here is a list of the major verbs which are used in this structure. The senser is always mentioned, either as the object of the clause ('it struck me'), or as a possessive ('it crossed my mind'), or in a prepositional phrase ('it dawned on me'). If a prepositional phrase is used, the preposition is given in brackets.

dawn (on)	hit	occur (to)	strike

The phrases 'cross your mind' and 'come home to you' are used in the same way.

You can also use certain reporting adjectives to report someone finding out or knowing something. See 4.42.

reporting uncertainty

4.29 If you want to report that someone is unsure about something, you can use certain verbs with 'wh'-clauses. The most common verb in this case is 'wonder'.

I wondered <u>what David was thinking</u>.
Frederica wondered <u>why she had failed to notice what was there to be seen</u>.
And we all wondered <u>who they were</u>.
Tension filled the atmosphere as we all wondered <u>when and how Colleen would get her own back</u>.

You can also use a clause beginning with 'if' or 'whether'.

I wondered <u>whether I would find a camera in my cell</u>.
The grocer laughed, of course, but wondered <u>whether he wasn't being made to laugh at himself</u>.

I wondered whether or not I'd stumbled into some government establishment.
Life would be very different without them, and I wondered if he had thought of this.
He wondered if they would stop for breakfast.

4.30 There are other verbs which you can use to report that someone is unsure about facts, but these are used in a negative or interrogative clause, or in a clause with a modal.

They still haven't decided what these areas are.
You sat beside him at dinner. Can you remember what you ate?
He couldn't remember if she had come outside with him.
They did not know what each was going to say before the words were uttered.
He didn't know why he'd been invited either.

Here is a list of the major verbs which you can use in this way.

decide	remember	understand
know	see	

4.31 If you want to report that someone is unsure about their own future behaviour, you can use 'wonder' with a 'to'-infinitive clause following a 'wh'-word (including 'whether', but not 'if').

He wondered what to do about the number of injured men who had found their way to his little group.
I wondered how far to go with Smithy.
After the play, the Colonel wondered whether or not to pay his respects to Kemble.
He wondered whether to wait, or go at once to Nance's place.

If you want to emphasize that the senser thought about the arguments for and against a particular course of action, you can use 'debate' instead of 'wonder'.

He debated whether to add a query but decided against it.

You can also use the verbs listed above to emphasize that it was difficult for the senser to reach a decision. Again, these are used in a negative or interrogative clause, or in a clause with a modal.

I really didn't know what to do.
Mrs Healing couldn't decide whether to let the hedges grow high, or whether to keep them low.

Compare 3.42 about reporting questions asking for advice.

4.32 Instead of a 'to'-infinitive clause following a 'wh'-word, you can use a 'wh'-clause containing 'should'.

I wondered whether I should call for help.
She wondered whether she should go and try to help the man.

4.33 If you want to report that the senser is unsure about something, but that they think it is probably not true, you can use 'doubt' followed by a clause starting with 'whether' or 'if'. In the first example below, the senser thought that he would probably not be able to walk to the bedroom.

> *He felt so weak that he doubted <u>whether he would be able to walk as far as the bedroom</u>.*
> *I certainly doubted <u>if I could point to the place on a map</u>.*

These reports are very close in meaning to 'doubt' followed by a 'that'-clause (see 4.12), but there is a slight difference. In the example below, the senser was almost certain that it would not *have much effect*.

> *She doubted <u>that it would have much effect</u>.*

If you say 'She doubted *if it would have much effect*', you indicate that the senser still thought that it would not have much effect, but was a little less certain about this.

Note that if the reporting clause is negative, you use a 'that'-clause, because you are reporting that the senser was certain ('not to doubt' means the same as 'to be certain').

> *I <u>never doubted</u> that he was mine, that we would be together in the end.*

not mentioning the senser

4.34 As with reporting verbs referring to speaking and writing, you can avoid mentioning the senser by using the passive form of many verbs referring to thinking.

One common way in which you can avoid mentioning the senser is by using the passive form with 'it' as the subject (compare 2.75). The idea is reported in a 'that'-clause. You use this structure especially when you are referring to the opinions of an unspecified group of people, or of people in general. As in 4.28, the 'it' in this structure is an **introductory 'it'** and refers forwards rather than backwards.

> *Now <u>it has been decided</u> that cleaner cars are wanted, less polluting cars will be produced.*
> *<u>It was realized</u> that high-status products need not be recognizably of better quality.*
> *Until the 1940s <u>it was believed</u> that most cosmic rays came from outside the solar system.*
> *It's never been proved that he was in the porcelain business, but <u>it's generally supposed</u> that he must have been some relation of the owner of the Bow factory.*
> *He continued to live in his room in the flat, but now <u>it was understood</u> that he had a whole life outside.*
> *Yet <u>it can hardly be doubted</u> that there is snow there from time to time.*

Other uses of report structures

Here is a list of the major verbs that can be used in this way.

accept	conjecture	estimate	know	suppose
agree	consider	expect	presume	suspect
assume	decide	feel	realize	think
believe	deduce	forget	reason	understand
calculate	doubt	hypothesize	reckon	
conclude	envisage	infer	remember	

The phrase 'take something for granted' is used in the same way.

4.35 With some of these verbs you can use a special kind of passive structure where the reporting verb appears inside the reported idea (compare 2.78).

In this structure, the verb is followed by a 'to'-infinitive clause. Often, the second verb is 'be' and it may be an infinitive with 'have'.

Our national alternatives <u>are believed to be</u> 'to win or not to win'.
The city <u>is believed to have been</u> the first major urban centre of its type in the New World.

Most of the verbs which can be used in this structure are from the group which are used to report opinions. Unlike reporting verbs referring to speech and writing (except 'claim'), most of these verbs have a corresponding structure in the active form (see 4.13).

Here is a list of the major verbs which can be used in this way.

assume	fear	judge	suspect
believe	feel	know	take
consider	find	presume	think
discover	hold	reckon	understand
estimate	imagine	suppose	

The benefits <u>are felt to be</u> something which the worker receives as of right.
In the Middle Ages it <u>was thought to have marked</u> the point at which the chariots turned in their races round the hippodrome.
Non-smoking wives of heavy smokers <u>were found to be</u> at a higher risk of getting lung cancer than similar women whose husbands did not smoke.
In Massachusetts food prices <u>have been reckoned to be</u> 10-15% above the national average.

This kind of passive can also be used in a structure with 'there' as subject.

<u>There are thought to be</u> about three times as many species of insect as of all other kinds of animal put together.

4.36 Note that you can use 'supposed to' in this passive structure with roughly the same meaning as 'believed to'.

There is no evidence that this man <u>was supposed to be</u> a witch.

However, in the great majority of cases, you use 'supposed to' when you mean that a situation ought to exist but does not actually exist.

I saw tears in her eyes. 'Karin, <u>it's supposed to be</u> a cheerful business.'

You also use 'supposed to' when you want to say that there are rules or expectations about what a situation should or should not be.

Women are not supposed to be aggressive or as physically vigorous as men.

4.37 When you want to make it clear that you are reporting what people believe, and that you do not guarantee that their opinion is correct, you can use a clause beginning with 'what' (compare 2.46). In the majority of cases, you use the passive form of the verb followed by a 'to'-infinitive; the second verb is 'be'.

They had obtained a High Court order forbidding the sale of what is believed to be the first recording ever made by the musicians who later became the Beatles.
He suggests that Britain has made the blunder of going straight for what was thought to be the ultimate solution.
'And there was what was supposed to be a double suicide,' said Mrs Oliver.

The verbs which most frequently appear in this kind of comment are 'think' and 'believe', although most of the verbs listed in 4.35 can be used in this way. You can also use active forms of the verbs.

At Scarborough he learned what he felt to be an important lesson.

reporting feelings using adjectives

4.38 Instead of a verb, there are many adjectives that you can use if you want to report a senser's feelings. In this case, you normally use the adjective after a link verb, usually 'be'. You mention the cause of the feeling in the 'that'-clause.

For a moment, he had been afraid that Mitchell might die on the telephone.
Everybody was sad that she had to return to America.
She was proud that he had won a prize.
I was hopeful that this would be the first of many assignments.
Hours later they arrive and the mother is furious that they are so late.
François felt rather sad that he had no music to go with it.

Here is a list of the major adjectives describing feelings that you can use in this way followed by a 'that'-clause.

afraid	delighted	infuriated	scared
alarmed	disgusted	irritated	shocked
amazed	frightened	optimistic	sorry
angry	furious	overjoyed	surprised
anxious	grateful	pleased	terrified
appalled	happy	proud	thankful
ashamed	heartbroken	puzzled	thrilled
astonished	hopeful	relieved	unhappy
astounded	horrified	sad	upset
concerned	indignant	satisfied	worried

4.39 With some of these adjectives, you can also report the situation which causes the feeling in a 'to'-infinitive clause. Often the verb in the 'to'-infinitive clause is a verb of thinking or perception.

Children are proud to think that they can be really useful.
She was sad to see her so alone.

Here is a list of adjectives which you can use in this way.

delighted	pleased	sad	thrilled
happy	proud	shocked	
overjoyed	relieved	sorry	

4.40 If the senser's feeling is about a future situation, you can report it using some of the adjectives followed by a 'to'-infinitive clause.

Although food was scarce they were afraid to go back north.

Here is a list of the major adjectives which you can use in this way.

afraid	frightened	willing
anxious	keen	
ashamed	scared	

4.41 If you want to report someone's feeling when they have taken a firm decision to do something, you can use 'determined' with a 'that'-clause or a 'to'-infinitive clause. When the decision relates to someone else's behaviour, you usually use a 'that'-clause.

She was determined that her husband should be the happiest man in the kingdom.

When the decision relates to the senser's own behaviour, you usually use a 'to'-infinitive clause.

I was determined to ignore the sun.

reporting what someone knows using adjectives

4.42 You can report what someone knows or is sure about in a 'that'-clause following certain adjectives.

Newman was convinced that if he could only track Alexis's last movements he would be closer to the truth.
He must have been aware that I was watching him.
Virtually everyone in the Committee had been positive that we would win.

Here is a list of the major adjectives which you can use in this way.

aware	conscious	positive
certain	convinced	sure

reporting uncertainty using adjectives

4.43 When you want to report that someone is uncertain about a situation, you can use 'unsure', 'uncertain', or 'doubtful' followed by a 'wh'-clause.

Both are unsure what is wanted of them.
Mother was uncertain how to amuse us.
Some people are doubtful whether plastic should be recycled.

using reporting nouns

4.44 As with reports of speech and writing, you can report thoughts, ideas, and feelings using reporting nouns. In general, the nouns are related to reporting verbs. Some are related to the adjectives listed above.

He could not shake off the belief that Aram was still alive and well.

There are many nouns which are used in this way. Here are some of the major ones. The nouns can all be used with a 'that'-clause.

assumption	decision	hope	resolution
awareness	deduction	hypothesis	sense
belief	discovery	inference	speculation
calculation	doubt	judgement	suspicion
certainty	dread	knowledge	theory
concept	dream	opinion	thought
conclusion	expectation	prayer	understanding
conjecture	fear	realization	wish
consciousness	feeling	recognition	worry
conviction	guess	regret	

This is not really an argument why it could not happen, but rather the expression of a wish that it never will!
His decision that his own documents and letters should be destroyed does not suggest they contained much that would present him in a good light.
I had a vague sense that I was already halfway to hypnotising myself.
These thoughts were checked by the realization that he had lost his way.
The sorrow that they felt for their comrade's death was tempered by the thought that at least he had died happy.
This develops into an awareness that the individual's aspirations cannot be isolated from the society around him.

4.45 'Decision' and 'wish' can also be used with a 'to'-infinitive clause.

Her decision to come back and teach in this mediocre place was to do with Bill.
My wish for an adventure with Yvette was a wish to be removed from the life I had.

The noun 'doubt' can be used with a clause beginning with 'whether' or 'if'. The usual pattern in which this occurs is 'there is doubt'.

Now there is grave <u>doubt if it can struggle through the latest disaster</u>.
There is considerable <u>doubt whether the oil industry will be able to</u>
<u>sustain this rate of growth</u>.

Using reporting verbs to express your own opinion

saying what you think

4.46　You often use reporting verbs to talk about your own opinion.
The verb is normally in the simple present tense. The most common
verb is 'think'. 'I think' sometimes comes before a 'that'-clause without
'that'. It is also sometimes used as an interpolation in the middle of, or
at the end of, the clause that expresses the opinion.

'<u>I think</u> she's down in the kitchen,' says the wife.
OK, Sabine. <u>I think</u> I've got the message. But <u>I think</u> you've got one little
detail wrong.
<u>I think</u> I'm in love with both of you.
<u>I think</u> Mum may not be coming back for a few days yet.
<u>I think</u> if they really make up their minds about it I may have to buy them
myself.
'Everything is just about ready, <u>I think</u>, honey,' the woman said.
They trusted – Uncle Woodrow <u>I think</u> his name was.

4.47　This use of 'I think' is not really reporting. Its main function is
to signal that you are expressing your own opinion. You may want to
signal this because you are not completely sure about the information
you are giving. This is illustrated in the following example when the
speaker corrects herself by changing from 'I think' to 'I'm sure'.

<u>I think</u> he was a bit shorter than you are. In fact, <u>I'm sure</u> he was.

Or it may simply be that you do not want to sound too definite because
you know that other people may disagree with your opinion.

Movies came on; the radio came on; recorded music came on, and people
began to have other outlets for their entertainment, and a band all of a
sudden was old-fashioned, and they were interested in these newfangled
things. And now <u>I think</u> maybe it's exactly those kinds of things that
people are wanting to escape.

4.48　There are a number of other verbs which are used in a similar
way to show your opinion or your attitude towards what you are
saying.

<u>I believe</u> some of those lakes are over a hundred feet deep.
Someone said that Miller's land might be picked on. Hundred Acre Field,
<u>I believe</u>.
'I had an accident.' 'With a lamp post, <u>I suppose</u>. I knew you'd been
drinking.'

'Take Mrs Parry home.' 'I expect her husband will come for her.'
I suspect that Dawn had more intelligence than she showed.
Oh well. I daresay we'll hear about it in the end.
Oh dear, I hope nobody gets hurt.
'My mother's sick in the hospital.' 'Oh, that's terrible! Nothing serious,
I hope?'

Here is a list of the major verbs that you can use in this way.

believe	feel	reckon	think
daresay	hope	suppose	
expect	imagine	suspect	

Note that the verb 'daresay' can also be written 'dare say'.

saying that you are uncertain

4.49 If you want to emphasize that you are a little uncertain about
your opinion, you can use 'I should think' or 'I would think'. You can
also use 'I would/should say' for this purpose.

He would answer as if he was merely expressing an opinion – 'I should
think you would have to go to East Berlin.'
I would think she'd probably jump at the opportunity.
The town is, I would say, about 75% supportive of the plan.
It's her mind that's suffering now, not her body; physically she's
absolutely fit again, I should say.

If you want to make your opinion even more tentative, you can use the
modal forms with 'have': 'I would/should have thought' or 'I would/
should have said'. 'Would' in these cases is much more common than
'should'.

I would have thought your writing came easily to you, that's the
impression you give.
As far as I'm concerned, I should have thought that was a matter for
congratulation rather than enquiry.
He was the best senior NCO in the battalion, I would have said.
'She's growing up now.' 'I should have said she sprang out of her mother
fully grown.'

4.50 If you want to suggest a possible idea without saying that you
think it is necessarily true, you can use 'I wonder' followed by a clause
beginning with 'whether' or 'if'. The first example below could be
paraphrased as 'I think that might not really be the reason'.

I wonder whether that's really the reason she died.
It would be interesting to provoke some kind of reaction in Dr Marlowe.
I wonder if I could do it.

If you want to tell your listener that you are thinking about a particular
question, you can use 'I wonder' followed by a 'wh'-clause. Note that a

question mark is often used although the sentence is grammatically a statement.

I wonder what's the matter with Hilary?
I wonder how they would get on with the village folk?

showing that you disagree

4.51 If you want to show that you now have a different opinion from the one that you had in the past, or that your opinion is different from someone else's, you can use 'I thought'.

'I'm sorry, I thought the remark would amuse you.' 'It doesn't.'
'You see, I'm also the Colonel's biographer.' 'I thought,' said Mr. Wright rather sharply, 'that Matthew L. Davis was the biographer.'

expressing negative opinions

4.52 If you want to express an opinion that something is not the case, you can use 'I doubt' followed by a 'that'-clause. In this example, the speaker thinks that they will not send her in 'your' direction.

I doubt that they will send me in your direction.

If you want to make your negative opinion slightly less certain, you can use a clause starting with 'whether' or 'if'. This is more common than using a 'that'-clause.

I can't explain it. I doubt if anyone can.
I doubt if she had even read the play when she agreed to appear in it.
'Do you mean he can see us and we can't see him?' 'I doubt whether he can see us either.'
'Finished it?' 'No, I doubt whether I ever shall now.'

You could also express these negative opinions by using 'I don't think/believe' followed by a 'that'-clause – see 4.57.

4.53 If you want to express surprise or disapproval at someone's behaviour, you can use 'you would think' or 'you would have thought'. You imply that their behaviour appears inappropriate in the real situation. In the first example below, the speaker means that the man was behaving as if he was seeing the shop for the first time, but in fact he had seen it before.

You would have thought from his expression that he was seeing the shop for the first time.
First Saturdays were trade days, even in May when you would think people would be too busy getting land planted.

You can also use 'anyone would think' or 'anyone would have thought'.

'What's the matter with him?' said the girl. 'Anyone would think I had said something beastly.'

announcing future plans

4.54 You often use 'I think' when you make up your mind about your future plans. In this case you usually announce your plans using 'I'll'.

I think I'll go to bed.
I think I'll watch the news for a while and then go and shower and change.

'I think' and 'I'll' together signal that you are making up your mind as you speak. After you have made up your mind, of course, you are more likely to talk about your plans using 'going to' or the present continuous.

4.55 If you want to announce your future plans in a tentative way, you can use the past tense equivalent of this structure: 'I thought I'd...'. This allows for the possibility that your listener may disagree with your plans.

'What are your plans for now?' 'What? Oh. I thought I'd do some shopping in the village.'

4.56 If you think that it is likely but not certain that the plans or future events you are announcing will actually happen, you use 'I expect'.

'Where will you have lunch?' 'Oh, I expect I'll pick up a sandwich somewhere.'
I think I'll just go to the ladies' room. I expect I'll be all right.

If you are not very happy about your future plans, you announce them using 'I suppose I'll...'. You often use 'have to' in the reported clause to emphasize that you are not going to carry out the plans willingly.

'I suppose I'll have to move out,' he said. 'It's so unfair, the man always has to leave.'

negatives in reporting clauses

4.57 The fact that verbs such as 'think', 'expect', 'suppose', and 'believe' are not really reporting verbs in these cases means that they behave slightly differently from 'real' reporting verbs.

When you want to say that, in your opinion, something is not true or is not the case, you very often make 'think' negative rather than the verb in the 'that'-clause. The first example below means roughly the same as 'In my opinion I can't do it'.

But I don't think I can do it. You have to be very strong for games.
I don't think weddings are nearly as pretty as they used to be in our day.
I don't think I know of any duets for piano and trumpet.

You can also do this with a few other verbs.

In the forty years I have been sitting around in dressing-rooms I don't believe I have ever sat in a new armchair.
Well, I don't expect you'll remember me very well.

Other uses of report structures

I don't suppose he'll be pleased to see you this evening.

Here is a list of the major verbs which you can use in this way. The verbs marked with an asterisk (*) are usually followed by a 'to'-infinitive clause rather than a 'that'-clause.

believe	imagine	suppose	wish*
expect*	intend*	think	
feel	reckon	want*	

4.58 With all the verbs listed above, you can in fact make the verb negative when you are talking about your own or other people's opinions and intentions. The verb can be in any tense.

You don't think he was pushed, then?
We didn't think it was the same man.
It could be just a coincidence, of course, but I didn't think it was.
I shouldn't have thought Charlie Chaplin was very ordinary, and I'm sure darling Hamo isn't.
I didn't feel that his sickness was any great menace to me.
Are you sure you don't want to come with us?
The women waited on men hand and foot. They didn't expect them to do anything.

reporting clauses in 'wh'-questions

4.59 The section above describes how the negative can be 'moved' from the reported clause to the reporting clause when you are talking about people's opinions. In a similar way, an interrogative form can be 'moved' from the reported clause to the reporting clause in 'wh'-questions.

When you ask a 'wh'-question, you can ask for a definite answer (e.g. 'Where did he go?'). Alternatively, you can ask for your listener's opinion by using a reporting clause inside the 'wh'-question.

Where do you think he went?

Note that it is the reporting clause which is interrogative, not the verb in the 'wh'-question.

The reporting clause follows immediately after the 'wh'-word.

Why do you think I'm a member of the board?
Who do you think took the manuscript?
What do you think I should tell the General?
How long do you think the rain will go on?

You can also use other reporting verbs in this way, especially 'suppose', 'reckon', and 'believe'.

What do you suppose the cause is?

4.60 If you are angry with someone, you can ask them this kind of question about themselves. This normally means that you want them to stop doing what they are doing. Sometimes you stress that you are angry by using an emphatic phrase like 'on earth' after the 'wh'-word. The reporting verb is always 'think'.

Where <u>do you think</u> you're going?
Who <u>do you think</u> you are, talking to me like that?
What on earth <u>do you think</u> you're doing Mr Carr?

using 'so' and 'not'

4.61 When you give your opinion in reply to what someone else has just said, you can avoid repeating what they said by using 'so' after verbs like 'think'.

'Can you get me back, driver?' 'I think <u>so</u>,' the man said.
'And are you on speaking terms with them now?' 'I suppose <u>so</u>.'
'I hope very much you will be coming on Saturday.' 'I hope <u>so</u> too.'
'Is it available to rent?' I asked. 'I believe <u>so</u>, though we could enquire.'

Here is a list of verbs that are often used with 'so'.

believe	imagine	think
expect	reckon	
hope	suppose	

4.62 If you want to give a negative opinion, you can do it in two ways. You can make the reporting verb negative (see 4.57 above) and use 'so'.

'Is she sore at me for not coming home to dinner?' 'No, <u>I don't think so</u>.'
'Could it possibly be a plot?' '<u>I don't believe so</u>,' said Sir Sydney.

Or you can use 'not' after a positive reporting verb.

'You haven't lost the ticket, have you?' '<u>I hope not</u>.'
'It doesn't often happen,' Castle said. 'No, <u>I suppose not</u>.'
'She doesn't want a real investigation, does she?' '<u>I think not</u>,' said Poirot.

Note that with 'hope' you only use the second option: you don't say 'I don't hope so'.

With 'think', the second option sounds more formal than the first: it is more common to say 'I don't think so' than 'I think not'.

4.63 As well as using 'so' and 'not' to reply to someone else, you can use them with these verbs – especially 'think' – in a variety of other ways to avoid repeating something that has already been said or written.

'She married Tim to get away from her parents.' '<u>Do you really think so</u>?'
'This takes your mind off the words, I reckon.' 'I'm sorry to hear that <u>you think so</u>,' said Mr Annett.
He's called it Bumpkins, which is rather sweet of him, <u>don't you think so</u>, Anthea?
Is there such a thing, sir, as ancient history? <u>The Irish don't think so</u>.

Other uses of report structures

'She's a new woman.' 'I'm glad <u>you think so</u>.'
'The documents were probably a disappointment to them at the time.' 'A
disappointment, yes, <u>I suppose so</u>.'
We have debated quite a lot whether teachers should be in the group, and
on the whole <u>we think not</u>.

See also 3.61 on the use of 'so' with 'say' and 'tell'.

using tag questions

4.64   When you use a **tag question** after 'I think', you take the tag
from the 'that'-clause, not from 'I think'. In the first example below, it
would be odd to say 'I think you're an artist, *don't I?*'.

I think <u>you're an artist, aren't you?</u>
I don't suppose <u>you remember the other house, do you?</u>
I was skiving, I think <u>that's the slang term for it, isn't it?</u>
The lady's German, I believe, <u>isn't she</u>, or Danish?

You use a tag question in general because you want to give your listener
an opportunity to agree with you. In the examples above, the speakers
don't want the listeners to agree that this is what they think. They want
their listeners to agree with the ideas that they are suggesting.

4.65   You can also check whether your listener has the same opinion
by using the tag 'don't you?'. In this case, the stress is on 'you' rather
than on 'don't'.

Well, I think it's a success, <u>don't you?</u>
Yes, well, I think it's what we've been looking for, <u>don't you?</u>

Using reporting verbs to be polite

4.66   When you want to be polite in English, you often express
yourself in an indirect way. For example, 'I want some tea' is a direct
statement and, in many situations, it would sound impolite. On the
other hand, if you say 'Could I have some tea?', you are expressing
what you want in an indirect and therefore more polite way (a
question is less direct than a statement; and the use of the conditional
form 'could' makes the request even more indirect).

It was mentioned above (2.40) that reporting in general distances you
from what you are reporting. You can use this feature of reporting when
you want to be polite, because it makes what you say less direct.

avoiding upsetting other people

4.67   If you want to say something which you think might make your
listener upset or angry – for example, if you want to contradict what
they have just said – you can 'soften' what you say and make it less
impolite by using an expression such as 'I think' or 'I believe'.

'You'll be able to take him home tomorrow.' 'No,' he said. 'I think his mother will be happier if I take him home today.'

'Where did he go?' 'I'm not sure, Madame. I think he said he had an appointment.'

I think, on the whole, you'd probably feel more at home in Flint Street.

'I think I'll have another whiskey if you don't mind,' said Professor Baxendale.

I would agree wholeheartedly with the second half of your judgment, not with the first. I suspect that Davies embroidered quite a few of the episodes he describes.

Not all historians would agree with this position, but I feel that a good case can be made out for its support.

I wanted to consult her about something and I believe a telephone call was made and she said she could spare me a short time.

Here is a list of the major verbs which you can use to soften what you say in this way.

believe	feel	suspect	think

4.68   You can also make the reporting clause into a negative question apparently asking about your listener's opinion – as mentioned above, a question is less direct than a statement. In this case, the verb is normally 'think'.

But don't you think mothers often feel a bit lost when their sons get married.

'Well, Alan, those are rather the sort of things mothers want to know, don't you think?' 'Well, yes, I suppose so.'

making polite requests and suggestions

4.69   When you want to make a polite request or suggestion, you can use 'I suppose'. In this case, you make either the reporting clause or the reported clause negative. Note that the sentence often has a question mark even though it is grammatically a statement, because of its function as a request.

'I don't suppose you're prepared to make a full confession now?' he asked without much hope.

I suppose you couldn't just stay up an hour or two longer.

I suppose you couldn't hold on to the top of that screen behind you?

When you want to suggest an idea in a cautious and polite way, you can use 'you don't suppose'.

You don't suppose he'll get lost out there?

4.70   You can also make a polite request by using 'I wonder' followed by a clause beginning with 'if' or, less frequently, 'whether'. As with 'suppose', the reported request often contains 'could'; and the sentence often has a question mark.

I said 'I wonder if I could borrow your bucket'.
I'm so sorry to disturb you, but I wonder if I could camp in one of your fields?
Excuse me, I wonder whether you can help me?

4.71 To make your request or suggestion more tentative, you can use a past tense, either past simple or past continuous. This happens especially with 'think' and 'wonder'.

I was thinking maybe you could take on an assistant, kind of.
I was wondering, Mrs Castle, if we could have a talk.
I was wondering if you could help me with Ted.
I just wondered if you wanted to go out tonight.

Indicating your own purpose

4.72 Another way in which you can use reporting verbs for functions other than reporting is in signalling your own purpose in speaking or writing. You use one of the verbs which show the speaker's purpose (see 2.10). The verb is normally in the present simple tense, and the subject is 'I'.

I promise I won't keep you a minute longer.

This makes the function of what you are saying clear to your listener or reader. For example, if you say 'I'll take it', you might mean this as a promise, a warning, or a bet. You can show clearly which of these you mean by using the appropriate reporting verb: 'I promise I'll take it', 'I warn you I'll take it', 'I bet I'll take it'.

This often makes your statement stronger as well: 'I demand that you do it' is more forceful than 'Do it'.

When you use reporting verbs in this way they are called **performative verbs,** because you perform the function by saying them. If, for example, you say 'I promise', you are actually making a promise by saying this.

In very formal contexts, such as legal documents or court proceedings, the performative function of these verbs can be made clearer by using 'hereby'.

I hereby sentence you to three years' imprisonment.

4.73 Here is a list of the major verbs which can be used with a 'that'-clause as performative verbs.

accept	confirm	notify	report
acknowledge	declare	order	state
admit	decree	pledge	submit
advise	demand	pray	suggest
agree	deny	predict	swear
assure	disagree	proclaim	tell
bet	guarantee	promise	testify
certify	insist	propose	vow
concede	maintain	recommend	warn

Well, I admit I didn't make it difficult for him, I guess.
'I bet he's braver than Errol Flynn,' said Tom. 'I bet he's got a drawer full of medals back home.'
I guarantee nobody will know about you.
I suggest that you start with fruit instead of cereal.
If you do not give it back, I warn you that you are going to die.
I won't make a fuss, I promise.

4.74 Some reporting verbs can also be used as performative verbs, but they are followed by a 'to'-infinitive clause.

I beg you to reconsider, Willie.
I forbid you to go downstairs!

Here is a list of the major verbs which can be used in this way.

appeal	forbid	order	refuse
beg	implore	permit	request
challenge	instruct	pledge	urge
command	invite	promise	warn

4.75 Certain other reporting verbs are used as performative verbs but normally with a modal verb. The most common modal is 'would'. 'Must' and 'should' are also fairly frequently used; and 'may', 'can', and 'could' are used in questions.

I would add that for Mr Gerran the effects would be ruinous.
I would emphasize that the river is changing daily.
I would remind you that you have a contract.
Can I just point out that we've only got until Thursday to decide this?

Here is a list of verbs which you can use in this way. They are followed by a 'that'-clause.

add	claim	emphasize	remark	stress
admit	comment	inform	remind	
answer	confess	mention	reply	
argue	contend	observe	say	

The phrasal verb 'point out' is used in the same way.

4.76 Some verbs are used as performative verbs without a reported clause following. Some may be followed by a noun group or prepositional phrase. Some are sufficient on their own. For example, if you say 'I protest', you perform the function of protesting. What you are protesting about will be clear from the context. In the example below, the speaker has just received a gun which has been very skilfully made by a specialist.

'Good,' he said. 'Very good. I congratulate you. A beautiful piece of work.'

Here is a list of the major verbs which can be used in this way.

accept	confess	forbid	pronounce
accuse	congratulate	forgive	protest
agree	consent	name	renounce
baptize	declare	nominate	resign
challenge	dedicate	object	sentence

People's names should not be targets for mockery, but I forgive you for smiling.

If one single Member of Parliament stands up and says 'I object', then the whole process comes to an abrupt halt.

This is the crime of which I accuse my country and my countrymen.

May I congratulate you again on your excellent performance.

Other uses of report structures

4.77 Many of the functions discussed in this chapter are only partially related to central types of reporting; but they all have in common the fact that they relate to language in some way.

The words and structures used in reporting can also be used in many other ways. Some of these ways occur very frequently and have an important role to play in expressing meanings. However, they are not directly related to reporting, and therefore they are not dealt with in this book. Some of the ways are briefly mentioned here, as an indication of the variety of uses to which report structures can be put.

other uses of reporting verbs

4.78 A number of reporting verbs can be used metaphorically to describe how people interpret what is happening around them. In the first example below, *promises* means something like 'seems likely'.

Europe promises to be the next major battleground in the automobile industry.

Swirling snow threatened to block the road.

Their success with new and freer markets challenged Russia to change in order to keep pace.

In this case, the joke served a more important role. It immediately told Bruce we had heard his message.

The book took a little over two years to complete, and that it did not end in divorce says much for Lee's patience.

4.79 As mentioned in 2.58, the reporting verbs which are used to signal the effect of what is said are very often used to describe situations which do not actually involve language. This is also true of some reporting verbs referring to mental operations. For example, although you can 'check' something by asking a question, you often check something by looking at it instead.

These verbs have in common that they refer to actions which establish facts. This can be done through language; but it can also be done through physical actions or situations.

The pattern of life at Hunter's Drift <u>determined</u> that most of the 'goodbyes' had to be said at dawn.
The autopsy <u>showed</u> that Reece's death had been caused by head injuries.
I always have to go back and <u>check</u> that I've shut the kitchen door properly.

using reporting structures to comment on facts

4.80 The structures often associated with reporting can be used, not to report what someone has said or thought, but to present a fact and comment on it. These structures allow you to present the comment first and then the fact.

A few of the many ways in which this happens are illustrated below. One example use is given for each of the three main types of reported clause.

4.81 One of the ways you can comment on a fact is to use a 'that'-clause following a clause with 'it' as subject and with an adjective as the complement of the clause. In this structure, the 'it' is **introductory**, that is, it does not refer to something that has been said before, but it refers forwards to the 'that'-clause.

<u>It is strange that</u> it hasn't been noticed before.
<u>It was interesting that</u> people often did not notice for a long time that the music had stopped.
<u>It soon became noticeable that</u> the promises were made less and less frequently as time went by.
In the circumstances <u>it is hardly surprising that</u> the Sixties also turned out to be the great age of flying saucers.
<u>It was considered odd that</u> she still lived at home and seemed much younger than her age.

4.82 You can also comment on a fact using a 'to'-infinitive clause. A clause of this kind often follows a clause of the pattern 'it+linking verb+adjective', as in the first example below. It can also follow a clause of the pattern 'find or make+it+adjective or noun', as in the other example below.

<u>It was not possible to</u> avoid the babies completely, though.
We talked of politics mainly, but <u>I found it difficult to</u> concentrate.

4.83 If you want to comment on something which has not yet been decided or has not yet been made clear, you can use a 'wh'-clause or a clause beginning with 'whether' (but not a clause beginning with 'if'), following clauses of various other patterns, illustrated by the examples below.

<u>It does not matter whether</u> a child is a meat eater or not.
<u>Why does it make any difference what</u> this man Broum did in the war?
<u>It was of no importance where</u> we went or <u>what</u> we did.

5 Use

Introduction

So far this book has focused on individual structures and functions in reporting. However, in order to understand reporting fully, you need to look at the ways in which it is used in communication. You need to consider the places where reporting is used (and where it could be used but is not), the reasons why people use reporting, the kind of reporting they choose, and so on.

In any particular kind of communication (conversation, novels, lectures, and so on) you are more likely to use reporting in certain ways than in others. For example, people telling friends stories about what has happened to them tend to concentrate on what they themselves said and thought, whereas journalists writing news stories, in British newspapers, rarely report what they said themselves, even when they are reporting an interview in which they asked questions.

This chapter takes a number of longer stretches of communication, both spoken and written, and looks at the ways in which reporting is used in them. No single spoken or written text, of course, can provide a complete survey of all the relevant features; but the texts have been chosen as far as possible to give a representative sample of typical features of reporting in use.

The texts come from four different contexts in which reporting plays an important role: journalism, conversation, novels, and academic writing. In each case, the starting point for the analysis is an outline of the context. The aim of this is to set out the general expectations that the reporter and their reader or listener probably share about the ways in which reporting is typically used in that context. This gives the framework within which reporters make their choices.

The framework helps the reader or listener to recognize and interpret the reporting more easily. This aspect is perhaps clearest in academic writing, which has very specific conventions for dealing with reporting which are unlike those used in other contexts – see the final analysis. The framework also helps the reader or listener to judge whether a particular piece of reporting is typical or unusual in that context. An unusual use of reporting – for example a journalist reporting his or her own questions in a news story – is likely to have an effect on the reader's or listener's reaction to the text precisely because it is unusual.

After the outline of the context, there is an analysis of the text itself which identifies the different types of report used, looks at how the general expectations are met (or perhaps not met), and discusses the effect of the particular choices that the reporter made in producing the text.

In these analyses, 'report' is used in a very wide sense. It is used for any reference to another language event. This language event may be real (spoken, written, or thought) or imaginary (for example, what people in general might say if they were asked). The report may consist of a full report structure (for example, with a reporting clause and a quote), or of a word referring to someone using language (for example, 'They *talked* for an hour'). As mentioned in the introduction to this book, you can understand why one kind of report has been chosen only if you look at all the choices that could have been made.

Journalism

context

The main expectation that a reader brings to a newspaper report on current affairs is that it will give a reasonably objective 'true' picture of the event and of the evidence, reactions, and opinions of the people involved.

There are usually two groups of people whose information and opinions may be given in news stories: 'important' people (such as politicians, entertainers, and experts) and 'ordinary' people (such as someone whose car has been stolen or someone who has won a lot of money in a competition). These two groups of people may appear in the newspaper article as participants in the event, as witnesses to the event, or as commentators on the event. The last two cases will, of course, involve reporting.

For example, a government minister (an 'important' person) may visit another country (the event), may describe the visit (as a witness), and say why the visit is important (as a commentator). Organizations (governments, trade unions, companies, and so on) make up one group of 'important' people. Organizations may be presented as saying or thinking things as an institution ('The Ministry has denied the rumour'), or they may be represented by a spokesperson speaking on their behalf.

In the 'ordinary' person category, a child may survive a fall from the window of a 4th-floor flat (the event), the neighbours may describe what they saw (as witnesses), and the parents may criticize the dangerous design of the flats (as commentators). News stories which primarily concern 'ordinary' people are often called 'human interest stories'.

In some cases, journalists may be present at the event and therefore able to describe it at first hand (for example, a visit by a government minister, which will have been announced in advance); but often they are not present, and rely on the accounts of other people. In such cases, they can present their description as second-hand through the use of reporting structures ('The neighbours said they saw the child fall') or as first-hand by avoiding the use of reporting structures ('The child fell').

Whatever the source of information about the event, the journalist typically reports the opinions of people connected with the event. In most cases, the journalist's own speech and opinions are not explicitly reported in the text. Of course, the journalist can choose to some extent whose opinions are reported and how they are reported, and this often suggests a particular attitude towards the events even if the journalist does not comment explicitly.

As this brief outline indicates, from the point of view of reporting structures, the reader of a news story expects to find 'important' or 'ordinary' people as speakers giving their account of events and their opinions on them. The journalist is usually expected to make clear the source of the information and opinions in the text, although this will not always happen. The journalist will normally not appear in the text as hearer or reader or as speaker or writer.

background to the texts

The examples of journalism that are analysed below are texts from two different newspapers about the same event: a one-day strike by the railway workers in Britain. The rail strike was supported by a smaller strike by coal miners. The day before the strike, the newspapers and television reported many people predicting that the strike would cause serious traffic problems, because everyone who normally went to work by train would have to travel by road. In fact, many people decided to stay at home, and traffic was more or less normal. The decision to hold the strike on a Friday was presented in most of the newspapers the following day as a tactical mistake by the railway workers' union.

In this text and the others in this chapter, the paragraphs are numbered (1, 2, 3, etc.) and each report is indicated by a letter (a, b, c, etc.). Note that because a report may be embedded inside another, one report does not necessarily end when another one begins. For example, in paragraph 8 of this text, report (k) is embedded in report (j), and both continue to the end of the sentence.

(a) MORE ACTION THREATENED AS RAIL STRIKE EMPTIES STREETS

Keith Harper, Labour Editor

1 (b) FURTHER strikes in the coal and rail industries were threatened last night by union leaders on a day when many people beat the 24-hour British Rail stoppage by staying at home.

2 (c) Jimmy Knapp, leader of the Rail, Maritime and Transport Union, said his executive would be meeting on Monday to discuss tactics, although another stoppage is unlikely next week. By then, leaders of the train drivers' union, Aslef, will have received its ballot results.

3 While 13 of British Coal's 50 pits produced coal yesterday, most of them in Nottinghamshire, heartland of the Union of Democratic Mineworkers, (d) Arthur Scargill, the miners' leader, told a rally of 2,000 people in Barnsley that this was the first of a series of strikes.

4 (e) Kevan Hunt, BC's industrial relations director, described the strike as futile.

5 BC's punishment was to stop collecting union dues for the National Union of Mineworkers. It means that the NUM will have to arrange locally for the union dues to be collected individually.

6 The UDM balloted its 10,000 members on strike action for the first time in its nine-year history. It is almost certain to get a positive result and **(f)** is asking businesses in Nottingham to close for the day as a token of support.

7 (g) BR's chairman, Sir Bob Reid, apologised to commuters for the strike and **(h)** hoped that normal service would be resumed today. In some cases this will be impossible because trains are in the wrong position and cannot be moved in time for the first journeys on the Saturday timetable.

8 Details of **(j)** a letter from Paul Watkinson, BR's personnel director, were released yesterday, spelling out why **(k)** BR cannot give guarantees on no compulsory redundancies. He left the door open for further talks with the rail unions, but **(l)** there were hints last night that BR might adopt a tougher attitude towards staff who go on strike in future.

9 (m) The Prime Minister condemned the action as 'pointless, senseless and completely counter-productive', **(n)** sentiments echoed by John MacGregor, the Transport Secretary.

10 Ministers were delighted at what they regarded as a tactical blunder by the RMT in holding the strike on a Friday, allowing people to take a long weekend off.

11 People who came into work in London found the streets half empty, as if it were a Sunday. Elsewhere, bus and coach operators laid on extra services.

12 In the North-West, **(p)** the AA said there was no great increase in traffic. Manchester's Metrolink supertram system, which runs from Bury to Altrincham through the city centre, was continuing to operate, as was the Tyneside Metro service in the North-east, where **(q)** police reported normal traffic flows on the roads.

13 In the Midlands, **(r)** police and motoring organizations said the roads were slightly busier than normal but the M6 north of Birmingham and the M1 through Northamptonshire were heavily congested.

14 In Scotland, the strike failed to create the rush hour road chaos that had been feared.

15 There were also no traffic problems in the South and South-West.

16 In Yorkshire, an accident on the M1 blocked the northbound carriageway, causing a long tailback that hit commuters travelling into Leeds.

analysis

It may be useful to begin by listing all the speakers/writers explicitly mentioned in the text, together with the main reporting signal in each case. The letters in brackets refer to the reports.

union leaders – threatened (b)
Jimmy Knapp – said (c)
Arthur Scargill – told (d)
Kevan Hunt – described (e)
It (the UDM) – is asking (f)
Sir Bob Reid – apologised (g)
Sir Bob Reid – hoped (h)
a letter from Paul Watkinson – spelling out (j)
BR – give guarantees (k)
The Prime Minister – condemned (m)

John MacGregor – echoed (n)
the AA – said (p)
police – reported (q)
police and motoring organizations – said (r)

There are also two unattributed reports, where there is a reporting signal but no speaker is mentioned.

threatened (a)
hints (l)

Perhaps the first thing to mention is that all the speakers/writers are 'important' people – compare this with the second newspaper story on the strike, below. In fact, on the same page as this news story was another article about the strike, in which a different journalist described her own journey to work and reported what 'ordinary' people had said to her. This newspaper has therefore deliberately divided its description of the strike into the official account above and a private, personal account.

The speakers/writers fall into three groups: the trade unions, representing one side of the dispute (b,c,d,f); the employers and the government, representing the other side of the dispute (e,g,h,m,n); and the police and motoring organizations, who give neutral information about the effects of the strike (p,q,r). A roughly equal amount of space is allotted to each of these three groups. This suggests that the journalist is trying to present his account of the strike as reasonably balanced.

The journalist uses a fairly wide range of reporting structures, although it is perhaps surprising in this kind of news story that there is very little direct quoting.

a partial quote (m)
reported 'that'-clauses (c,d,h,p,r)
a reported 'to'-infinitive clause (f)
a reporting noun followed by a reported 'that'-clause (l)
reporting verbs with a summary of the message in
prepositional phrases (e,g,m) and noun groups (b,n,q)
a reporting verb followed by a summary of the message in a 'wh'-clause (j)

One way in which reporters may reveal their own attitudes is by using full quotes or reported clauses for the people whose opinions they value and only summaries (prepositional phrases and noun groups) for the people whose opinions they do not value. This can suggest that only the opinions of the first group are worth hearing in full. However, in this text, there is again little evidence that the journalist is biased towards one side or the other. There is no clear pattern in the way the different types of structure are used to report what each side said.

In addition to the clear reports listed above, there are also a number of cases where there may be indirect reports without a reporting signal. In paragraph 2, the report of what Jimmy Knapp said seems to end with the word *tactics* – note the change of tense in the second part of the sentence.

Jimmy Knapp, leader of the Rail, Maritime and Transport Union, said his executive would be meeting on Monday to discuss tactics, <u>although another stoppage is unlikely next week.</u>

However, what follows in the rest of the paragraph might also be a report of information provided by Jimmy Knapp.

In paragraph 10, there is an example of the ambiguity of reporting other people's feelings.

Ministers were delighted at what they regarded as a tactical blunder.

It is not clear whether the account of the ministers' 'delight' is based on a report of what the ministers said or an interpretation by the journalist of how they behaved. The second possibility is the more likely. No doubt the ministers were in fact delighted, but it would be foolish of them to say publicly 'We are delighted that the union has made a mistake'.

In paragraph 12, the first sentence is clearly an indirect report, but the status of most of the second sentence is less clear.

In the North-west, the AA said there was no great increase in traffic. Manchester's Metrolink supertram system...was continuing to run.

The choice of the continuous verb form (*was continuing*) rather than the simple form ('continued') suggests that it is also an indirect report.

If all these cases are accepted as indirect reports, then over half the text is made up of reports of one kind or another. This is not surprising, since the first ten paragraphs deal mostly with language events: reactions to the strike rather than the events of the strike itself. Even in the last six paragraphs, which describe the effects of the strike, the journalist explicitly mentions the sources of his information. The journalist clearly wants to present himself as a neutral passer-on of information.

There is one point in the text where there may be a subtle indication of the journalist's own views. This is in paragraph 9, where the journalist chooses a partial quote to give the Prime Minister's opinion on the strike. In order to see the effect of choosing a partial quote in this way, you can imagine other ways in which the same message might have been expressed. Making only minimal changes, you might expect one of the following:

The Prime Minister condemned the action.

The Prime Minister condemned the action as pointless, senseless and completely counter-productive.

The Prime Minister said: 'This action is pointless, senseless and completely counter-productive.'

The first version above gives no information about the words that the Prime Minister used, and would perhaps suggest that his opinion was not worth reporting in detail (anyone could predict that he would condemn this kind of action).

In the second version, on the other hand, the report does not explicitly show whether the Prime Minister actually used the words *pointless, senseless and completely counter-productive* or whether these words are the journalist's interpretation of what he said. This might suggest that the journalist agreed with the Prime Minister's view, or would at least leave open the possibility that he did.

The third version is in some sense the opposite of the first: by using a full quote, it suggests that the Prime Minister's opinion is worth hearing in full in its original form.

The final version, the one which appears in the text, strikes a balance between the first and third versions in the importance it gives to the Prime Minister's views. In addition, by using quote marks it explicitly signals that these are the words that the Prime Minister used, and that the journalist is therefore not to be held responsible for them.

The differences between these possible choices are, of course, fairly small, and it could be argued that the writer did not think of them in making his choice. In paragraph 4, for example, there is a very similar structure expressing a very similar opinion, *Kevan Hunt...described the strike as futile*, but there are no inverted commas around the word *futile*. However, the differences are there and can be exploited by writers if they wish. This text is careful to report both sides of the argument, and the journalist does not openly use the manipulative possibilities of reporting. As you will see, the following text is more openly manipulative, and the kinds of differences outlined here are deliberately exploited.

Another form of reporting which can be exploited to convey a biased view is unattributed reports. There will be examples of this in the following text; but in this text the two unattributed reports seem fairly innocent. The word *threatened* in the title has no speaker.

More action threatened...

But the first sentence of the text repeats the word and makes it clear who the speaker is. The title probably omits the speaker mainly in order to save space.

The second unattributed report, in paragraph 8, is a little more mysterious.

...but there were hints last night that BR might adopt a tougher attitude...

Who precisely gave these *hints*? Was it one person giving several hints, or several people giving a hint each? Also, since these were *hints* rather than 'threats', how much is the journalist interpreting what was said? Would the original speaker(s) agree with this interpretation?

It is clear that the hints must have come from the management of BR. One factor which may have influenced the journalist's choice of expression here is that the *hints* may have been given by someone who did not want to be named, in order to avoid trouble with the unions. There is a convention in journalism that 'important' people can give their comments 'off the record'. This means that the journalist can report the comments but is not supposed to reveal who made them. Impersonal structures like *there were hints* are useful for doing precisely that.

The overall impression that the journalist aims at is therefore of careful, impartial reporting, and he mostly makes his sources of information clear. The most obvious evaluations of the event (e,m,n) are those of other people, not of the journalist himself. Interestingly, these evaluations come from people opposed to the strikes, and are strongly negative; and yet the general attitude of the journalist does not appear to be anti-union. This is probably due to the fact that the reporting is balanced as a whole. (Of course, some readers might accuse the journalist of bias because, for example, he does not report the opinions of the strikers.)

Not all journalism tries to appear as impartial as this, as the following text will illustrate.

This text deals with the same rail strike, but is from a different newspaper with a rather different view of the event.

STAYAWAY DAY AS RAIL STRIKE HITS THE BUFFERS

(a) By PAUL HARRIS

1   If you had to drive to work yesterday, there was a serious danger of finding a parking space.

2   (b) Chaos had been predicted as the rail unions staged their one-day strike, but some of the roads were as deserted as the Marie Celeste.

3   In the great British tradition, those who had to get to work usually found a way. Others simply worked from home. Or took the day off.

4   All across the country, people spent the rush hour in bed. Some took their wives out to lunch for the first time for years; and for many, those little jobs that needed doing around the house were finally completed.

5   (c) Pick up the kids from school? (d) Certainly.

6   To cap it all, the sun was shining.

7   The stoppage was designed to bring the country to its knees, the first real flexing of a union muscle which withered and nearly died during the Thatcher years.

8   Suddenly (e) all those clichéd strike phrases returned again – there on our TV screens again was rail union leader Jimmy Knapp, (f) speaking of mandates to strike, of members' aspirations, getting round the negotiating table and of 'rock solid support'.

9   But it wasn't the kind of action likely to bring down a Government.

Commuters

10   On one railway line into London – the driver-only Chiltern Turbo, which continued to operate from Marylebone to Aylesbury in Buckinghamshire and to Banbury in Oxfordshire – it didn't even bring down the signals.

11   Elsewhere, main line stations were deserted, but (g) the threatened chaos never materialised. At Birmingham New Street, 600 trains a day normally ferry 70,000 passengers in and out of the city. Yesterday, there was not a commuter in sight.

Use

12 In Scotland, **(h)** a railway spokesman said people had taken the stoppage in their stride. **(j)** 'People have been taking alternative transport and getting to where they have to. We haven't had any **(k)** complaints from the general public.'

13 Indeed, **(l)** the biggest question the strike action posed was this: where do hundreds of thousands of commuters go when they don't go to work?

14 **(m)** The answer was found in pubs, shopping centres and golf courses around the country. With many schools breaking up for a two-week Easter holiday, starting it a day early was an opportunity too good to miss.

15 **(n)** The stayaway day was urged by Ministers seeking to minimise the impact of the union action and by employers' groups anxious to limit disruption to business and industry.

16 **(p)** The Institute of Management advised firms to give staff the day off or let them work from home, and many appeared to have got **(q)** the message.

17 **(r)** The Association of London Authorities said that up to 400,000 people **(s)** were thought to have stayed away from the capital. But **(t)** its estimate that the strike would cost £70 million in lost trade **(u)** was challenged by business organizations which believed that many would be keeping their companies ticking over by working from home.

18 This was made possible largely because of technological advances achieved since the strikes which halted Britain in the late Seventies – the fax machine, the mobile phone and the computer.

19 **(v)** 'Teleworking' – likely to be a feature of the next century – came a few years early as the office workers logged on at home or sat down with files and contact books brought out the night before.

20 **(w)** Paul Moorcroft, a 39-year-old assistant finance director for an export firm in London, set up a makeshift office in his child's playroom at home in Crawley, West Sussex, and worked from there. Yesterday **(x)** he said: 'I've got a laptop computer. If the boss sends me all my **(y)** rollickings by fax, I need never go to work again.'

21 Like many commuters, Mr Moorcroft decided to stay at home because although his train service is usually reliable, driving can be a nightmare. Not yesterday.

22 **(z)** The AA said most roads were no busier than normal and **(aa)** on many it was 'like a Sunday'.

23 In South Wales, coach companies reaped a bonanza by putting on extra services for their London motorway route.

24 Further north, they were more adventurous.

25 Businessman Simon Timperley travelled to his office in Ashton-under-Lyne, Greater Manchester, on a pair of motorised roller skates. On a higher plane, salesman Mark Law flew a microlight over the Pennines from Heywood, near Rochdale, to land in a field next to his office in Halifax.

26 For others, the day was more leisurely.

27 **(bb)** Sales officer Michelle Bate's boss told her to have a long weekend instead of battling to work. So Michelle, 23, from Haslemere, Surrey, spent the morning on her local golf course.

28 **(cc)** She said: 'It was OK for me because my boss is generous, but I feel sorry for people who had to lose a day's holiday or miss out on their wages through no fault of their own.'

29 Others felt the urge to spend. **(dd)** Big out-of-town shopping centres reported 'excellent business' and **(ee)** some garden centres said trade was 'more like a weekend'.

30 **(ff)** Railmen's leaders will meet on Monday to decide the next step in their campaign, writes DAVID NORRIS.

158

31 (gg) The executive of the Rail, Maritime and Transport Union could order further one-day strikes – but that now seems unlikely. The main victims of yesterday's action can only be the railmen themselves. It cost in-the-red BR £10 million in lost revenue and could drive even more lucrative freight traffic away from trains and on to the roads.

32 Yesterday's self-inflicted-wound strike was over **(hh)** BR's refusal to **(jj)** guarantee that there will be no compulsory redundancies. **(kk)** BR says **(ll)** such an assurance cannot be given.

33 The action coincided with a similar own-goal strike by Arthur Scargill's NUM, over pit closures. It stopped coal production at all but 13 of Britain's 50 collieries. The working ones were mainly in the rival UDM areas.

34 (mm) British Coal said it could only damage the industry.

analysis

The speakers/writers who are explicitly named in the text can be listed under the headings below. The main reporting signal in each case is also given. The letters in brackets refer to the reports.

● **'important' people**

Jimmy Knapp – speaking (f)
a railway spokesman – said (h)
Ministers and employers' groups – urged (n)
the Institute of Management – advised (p)
the Association of London Authorities – said (r)
the Association of London Authorities – estimate (t)
business organizations – challenged (u)
the AA – said (z)
shopping centres – reported (dd)
garden centres – said (ee)
the executive of the Rail, Maritime and Transport Union – order (gg)
BR – refusal (hh)
BR – guarantee (jj)
BR – says (kk)
BR – an assurance given (ll)
British Coal – said (mm)

● **'ordinary' people**

general public – complaints (k)
Paul Moorcroft – said (x)
the boss – rollickings (y)
Michelle Bate's boss – told (bb)
Michelle Bate – said (cc)

It is also made clear that the text was written by two different journalists.

● **journalists**

Paul Harris – By (a)
David Norris – writes (ff)

In addition, there are the following signals of reports where no speaker/writer is mentioned.

● unattributed

predicted (b)
phrases (e)
threatened (g)
question (l)
answer (m)
thought (s)
'teleworking' (v)

The question and answer in paragraph 5 can also be included as an unattributed report (they are discussed below).

The writer of the main part of the text, Paul Harris, is introduced in a conventional way (technically called a 'by-line') which is not directly connected with reporting structures. However, the writer of the final section is introduced in a different way (ff), in a clear reporting structure. This raises the question of who the reporter is here – that is, who has written the reporting signal *writes David Norris*. Presumably, it is one of the copy-editors of the newspaper, although this is not made clear.

In this text, there is a much wider range of different report structures than in the first text.

direct quotes (j, x, cc)
partial quotes (f, aa, dd, ee)
an indirect quote (c, d)
reported 'that'-clauses (h, r, z, ee, kk, mm)
reported 'to'-infinitive clauses (p, bb)
a reported main clause with the reporting clause following (ff)
reporting verbs with the message carried by prepositional phrases or noun groups (b, f, n, u, dd, gg)
reporting nouns followed by a reported 'that'-clause (t) and a 'to'-infinitive clause (hh)
reporting nouns with no information about the message (e, k, q, y, ll)
a reporting adjective (g)
reporting signals as subjects (l, m)

The most complex reporting occurs in paragraphs 17 and 32, where there are 'embedded' reports – that is, reports of people talking about what someone else has said.

> *But its <u>estimate</u> that the strike would cost £70 million in lost trade was <u>challenged</u> by business organizations.*
> *BR <u>says</u> such an <u>assurance</u> cannot be given.*

In 17, for example, the *business organizations* are reported as saying that they disagree with what the Association of London Authorities has said about the probable cost of the strike. This kind of embedding is relatively frequent in newspaper reporting, since a lot of news deals with people's comments on what other people have said.

It is also worth mentioning the inverted commas around *'teleworking'* (v). This particular use of inverted commas with unattributed quotes means one of two things. Firstly, a writer can use the inverted commas to signal 'This is the word that other people might use, but I don't agree with this use, I am only using it ironically'. This is the way that inverted commas are being used in this chapter around the words 'important' and 'ordinary' (people). In these cases, the inverted commas are sometimes called 'scare quotes'. Secondly, the inverted commas can be used to signal 'This is the word that experts use, but I think that it may be an unfamiliar word for you, the reader'. This is the way in which the quote marks are used in 'teleworking'.

The way in which reporting is used in the text appears at first sight to present a fairly straightforward account of the strike, with reports of the reactions of the organizations involved (the unions, employers, government, traffic organizations) and of some 'ordinary' people affected by the strike. If we examine the text more closely, however, we can see that the reporter has made very interesting choices about the people he reports and the ways in which the reports are given. These choices give the reader a particular view of the strike.

The basic message of the text as a whole, already signalled in the title, is that the strike was a failure because its aim was to cause chaos and it failed to do this.

The two references to the *chaos* (b, g) both have reporting signals with no speaker. The reader can guess that it was the unions who *threatened* chaos (g), though it is more difficult to decide who exactly *predicted* it (b). (In fact, in the days preceding the strike the newspapers themselves played a large role in making people expect that the strike would cause chaos.) One reason for not giving a full report including the speakers in these cases is probably because the journalist takes it for granted that his readers already know about the predictions/threats. These are simply part of the background to the story, which focuses on the fact that the predictions were not fulfilled. This is also suggested by the way that in (b) the prediction is mentioned in a full clause, although without a speaker, whereas in (g) the report of the threat is only an adjective *threatened* in a noun group – the idea that chaos had been predicted has already been mentioned and it is now treated as an established fact.

The different ways in which the 'important' people are reported show a great deal about the journalist's political sympathies. This journalist reports much more of the opinions of one side in the dispute – the employers and government – than those of the trade unions. In several places where the trade unions' views might have been reported – especially in paragraphs 30 to 34 – the journalist chooses not to do so. The only clear reporting structure used in the last section (*could order further one-day strikes*) is a report of the journalist's own guess at what might happen rather than a report of an actual language event.

The journalist's attitude is especially clear in the way that the trade union views are reported when he does report them. As an example, look at how Jimmy Knapp is reported in paragraph 8.

> *Suddenly all those clichéd strike phrases returned again – there on our TV screens again was rail union leader Jimmy Knapp, speaking of mandates to strike, of members' aspirations, getting round the negotiating table and of 'rock solid support'.*

The paragraph begins with an unattributed signal of a report: *all those clichéd strike phrases*. In this case, not only is the speaker missing, but there is no information about the message (what exactly are the words in these *phrases*?). As you read on, you see that the speaker (Jimmy Knapp) and the message (*mandates to strike*, and so on) are in fact given. The effect of using this kind of reporting structure is to label in advance whatever Jimmy Knapp (or any other trade union leader) says as merely *clichéd phrases* – bits of language with no real meaning. It is also noticeable that the *phrases* are not presented as spoken but as acting by themselves – they *returned*. This almost suggests that the phrases have a life of their own, appearing by themselves without the speaker having to think of them. Again, the implication is that speakers who use them are not really saying anything meaningful.

Even when the journalist tells you about Jimmy Knapp's message, he chooses to do so in a prepositional phrase (*of mandates to strike...*) rather than in a reported clause or direct quote. The reader does not need to know exactly what Jimmy Knapp said (since it is only *clichéd phrases*); it is enough to be given a summary of the kinds of things he (always) talks about. This structure also allows the writer, amongst other things, to make *mandates* plural. It is certain that, if Jimmy Knapp in fact talked about this subject at all, he did not say 'mandates' but 'a mandate'; and if the journalist had chosen to use a reported clause or quote, this would have been clear. By making the noun plural, the writer can reinforce the suggestion that this is the kind of thing that Jimmy Knapp always talks about and that it is not really worth listening to him.

The paragraph ends with a partial quote, *'rock solid support'*. It was mentioned above that a partial quote may be used to imply that the reporter wants to distance himself from the opinion expressed. This may not always be the case. In paragraph 29, for example, the partial quotes seem neutral, simply what the shopping centres and garden centres said. But in paragraph 8, the partial quote is less innocent.

It has probably been chosen instead of a full quote because a full quote would be a separate sentence, and would imply that the message was worth hearing. The partial quote, on the other hand, is grammatically part of the prepositional phrase, and the journalist therefore implies that it is as unimportant as the rest of the phrase. By putting quote marks around it, the writer signals something like 'These are the words Jimmy Knapp used (the sort of words he always uses), but they are not the words that I would use' (this is therefore similar to the way 'scare quotes' are used). In other words, the writer suggests that Jimmy Knapp may be mistaken or even lying about the support that he has from the members of his trade union.

If this analysis seems to you to find too much deliberate distortion in the writer's choices in paragraph 8, you might find it interesting to try to rewrite the paragraph as a direct quote, recreating as far as possible what Jimmy Knapp might have said, beginning: *Interviewed on television last night, Jimmy Knapp, leader of the rail union, said: 'Our members have given us a mandate to strike...'.* The effect, as you will see, is very different.

Another feature which contributes to the overall effect of the text is the way in which the journalist uses reporting to show that he has sympathy with the 'ordinary' people. Firstly, he has decided to include reports of what a number of 'ordinary' people said: Paul Moorcroft in paragraph 20, and Michelle Bate (and her boss) in paragraphs 27 and 28. Even some of the organizations which he quotes are connected with 'ordinary' people rather than the strike itself: shopping centres and garden centres (29).

But he also uses less direct ways of showing his attitude. For example, look at the indirect quote in paragraph 5.

Pick up the kids from school? Certainly.

This can be identified as an indirect quote because the first sentence is a question which is clearly not being asked directly by the journalist. From the context, it can be assumed that the speaker is one of the *people* mentioned in paragraph 4 who is offering to do something that he does not usually have time to do. (Interestingly, the writer believes that the only *people* in Britain who work have wives – that is, they are all men.) Paragraph 5 is therefore an indirect quote of a husband echoing his wife's request to pick up the kids and agreeing to do so. However, because it is an indirect quote, the writer does not directly signal that these are not his own words. This gives the effect of the writer speaking on behalf of 'ordinary' people, as if he were one of them. It is probably not an accident that this attempt by the journalist to identify himself with the reader – and therefore to encourage the reader to identify with him and his opinions – comes just before the most explicit indication in the text of his own views, in paragraphs 7 to 9.

In paragraphs 13 and 14, the writer again uses reporting structures to give his point of view and to suggest that it is also the reader's point of view.

Indeed, the biggest question the strike action posed was this: where do hundreds of thousands of commuters go when they don't go to work? The answer was found in pubs, shopping centres and golf courses around the country.

In these paragraphs we have two reporting signals as subjects (underlined above). These are unusual structures in this kind of text, because the person asking the question must be the journalist himself and, as noted earlier, journalists do not often report their own words. The fact that the sentences are unusual gives them an added force. They suggest that what people do instead of going to work is the main newsworthy issue raised by the strike. This is clearly an unimportant question compared with the possible issues, such as the effect of the strike on labour relations or the economy. The writer thus implies that the strike itself was unimportant.

The person asking the question is the journalist, but at the same time it is the journalist who knows the answer. Therefore, the journalist must be asking the question on behalf of someone else – the reader. The underlying message here is 'I know that you, the reader, must be wondering by now what people do when they don't go to work. I can tell you the answer.' Again, the journalist is identifying himself with the reader: he is close enough to the reader to know the questions that the reader will ask. The question assumes that the strike is trivial; so the reader is being encouraged to accept this assumption.

The analysis as a whole suggests a rather less straightforward picture than the first outline given above. The journalist shows a strong anti-trade-union bias and presents the strike as trivial, unsuccessful, and led by people who say nothing worth listening to. He also encourages the reader to identify with him as just another typical 'ordinary' person, and therefore to identify with his views.

Not all reporting is as manipulative as this, of course; but this example has been chosen in order to give some idea of the ways in which reporting can be used, in certain contexts, to try to impose a particular view of events on the hearer or reader.

Conversation

context

It is more difficult to outline the context of reporting in conversation than in journalism, novels, or academic articles, because there are fewer obvious 'rules' concerning what can be talked about or the ways in which you can talk. However, even in conversation the speaker and listener do share certain expectations about the kinds of reporting that will occur.

Of course, the term 'conversation' is a very vague one which covers many kinds of language events. The expectations of the speaker and listener depend to a large extent upon the sort of conversation that is going on. A parent chatting to a young child will talk in a different way, and use reporting in a different way, from a business manager discussing her timetable with her secretary. Here, for example, is a parent using a direct quote to tell the child what their pet cat is saying.

Look, he's hungry. He's saying, 'I want some of those prawns.'

This dramatic use of reporting is obviously less likely to occur in the business context. For various reasons, the speaker here is in fact more likely to use indirect reports, as in the following example.

Oh, I've had a note back from Keith saying that the company will put six hundred quid towards my Malaysia trip.

The kind of conversation that has been chosen for analysis here is narrative. This has been chosen because people quite often tell stories in ordinary conversation (often very short ones) and because they tend to use a lot of reporting when they tell a story.

Stories in conversation frequently deal with events in which the narrators themselves have taken part. (If they have not taken part in the events, then the whole story is typically a report of what they have been told by someone else.) The narrators report what they themselves said and thought. Even if the story mainly concerns someone else, the narrators are likely to evaluate the events and to comment on the point of the story.

Narrators also report what the other people involved said and, to a lesser extent, what they thought. Although narrators cannot in fact go inside other people's heads as a novelist can, they often interpret what another person is thinking or feeling. In this case, the narrators can signal that this is their interpretation by using expressions such as 'obviously' or 'it seemed as though'.

It is noticeable that when people tell stories they quite often use direct quotes. Unlike a journalist, who usually tries to note down or record exactly what people say, ordinary story-tellers clearly cannot be sure that they are quoting accurately, even if it is their own words. In this case, you might expect them to use indirect reports, giving the meaning of what was said without trying to give the exact wording; but direct quotes are often used instead.

The listeners do not in fact expect direct quotes to be accurate. Narrators sometimes give a direct quote of the same speech more than once, using different words each time. In most cases, the listeners are unlikely to stop the narrator and demand to know which of the versions is the accurate one.

The main purpose of using direct quotes is to make the story more lively and dramatic. In this way, part of the narrative is acted out in front of the listeners so that they can get more of the flavour of the events as they happened.

In general, the kinds of reporting that people expect to find in stories in conversation are to some extent similar to those in novels. There is likely to be quite a lot of reporting which will help the action move forwards and tell the listener something about the personality of the reported speakers. Story-tellers will also use reporting to comment on and evaluate the events, particularly by reporting what they themselves said and thought at the time of the events. Neither narrator nor listener expects direct quotes to be entirely accurate in wording: they recognize that their main purpose is dramatic.

background to the text

The text that is analysed below is taken from a conversation between Violet (V), Charles (C), her husband, and Richard (R), her son-in-law. Violet is fairly deaf, especially in one ear.

In this extract from the conversation, Violet is talking about what her friend Mary did when she and her husband Harold moved to a new town, Chester (*she* in the first sentence is Mary). She compares Mary's behaviour with her own. (The Townswomen's Guild and the Young Wives are organizations run by and for women.)

You will see that Violet uses certain dialect forms (she comes from the north of England). For example, she says *she were* where a speaker of Standard English would say 'she was'; and she says *owt*, which is a Northern English dialect word for 'anything'.

The text of the conversation has been tidied up, to make it easier to read. Brief signals from the listeners that they are listening (e.g. 'Yeah', 'Mmm') have been left out, and so have hesitations, repetitions, and false starts. Occasionally two people spoke at the same time, but this is not shown here. Punctuation, including paragraph breaks, has been added to make the conversation easier to follow.

1 V: The first thing she did when she got there, she moved one Monday, the following Monday she were in the Townswomen's Guild. Because she'd always been in it at Durham.

2 Now I've never bothered with owt like that. When I was young I used to be in the Young Wives – well, I'm an old wife now, aren't I? But it used to be a nightmare, because **(a)** I couldn't hear half of what went on, and you were fed up of **(b)** going 'Hee! hee!' You know what I mean? **(c)** The chaplain from Walton were talking. I didn't know **(d)** what the hell he were talking about. And to me it were more bother than it were worth.

3 But **(e)** she said, didn't she, that she didn't want to walk in Chester and not be able **(f)** to speak to anybody. Well, I can walk down Old Lane every day and **(g)** nobody speaks to me, except them next door – do they, Charles?

4 C: And **(h)** even if they did you wouldn't hear them –

5 V: No. And so what I'm saying is...

6 C: Violet goes through the middle of Sheffield, and **(j)** everybody there: 'Hallo, Mrs Wilson!'

7 R: **(k)** 'Hallo, Violet!'

8 C: **(l)** 'Hallo, Violet!'

9 R: **(m)** 'How are you, Violet?'

10 C: And she walks straight through, taking no notice at all.

11 R: And when they get away from her, **(n)** they say, 'Stuck-up woman!'
12 V: When I go on the bus there's always **(p)** someone manages to speak to me.
13 R: Into your deaf ear.
14 V: But **(q)** what I'm saying is, **(r)** she said, 'I'm not going to walk through Chester and not know anybody.'

analysis

The reporting in this conversation falls into three main types. First, there are the reports with little or no information about what was said:

> *...I couldn't hear half of what went on* (a)
> *The chaplain from Walton were talking* (c)
> *...what the hell he were talking about* (d)
> *...not be able to speak to anybody* (f)
> *...nobody speaks to me* (g)
> *And even if they did you wouldn't hear them* (h)
> *...someone manages to speak to me* (p)

These are all referring to situations where what is said is not important for the conversation: the topic is whether or not people talk to each other, irrespective of what they say. In addition, the fact that Violet is hard of hearing means that in any case she usually does not hear what people say to her. She could nevertheless report the kinds of things that are or were said, since, as noted above, quotes in conversation do not have to be accurate (see the discussion of the reports (j) to (n) below). However, her description of her difficulties would clearly be less effective if she quoted the words spoken, when the point of her story about herself is that she could not hear them.

The second kind of reporting in the conversation is indirect report structures. There are only two examples in the story:

> *But she said...that she didn't want to walk in Chester and not be able to speak to anybody.* (e)
> *But what I'm saying is, she said, 'I'm not going to walk through Chester and not know anybody.'* (q)

The first can be compared with the direct quote version of the same utterance (r), which is embedded in (q). They are very close in meaning and even in wording. The probable reason why Violet included both versions is discussed below. The second has a report signal as subject (compare 'I am saying (that) she said...'). It is a self-report which refers to the time of telling the story rather than the time of the events. The function of this in context is also discussed below.

The third kind of reporting is direct quotes.

> *... you were fed up of going 'Hee! hee!'* (b)
> *... everybody there: 'Hallo, Mrs Wilson!'* (j)
> *'Hallo, Violet!'* (k)
> *'Hallo, Violet!'* (l)
> *'How are you, Violet?'* (m)

... they say, 'Stuck-up woman!' (n)

... she said, 'I'm not going to walk through Chester and not know anybody.' (r)

The first of these (b) is Violet's description of her own reaction to not being able to hear properly. Whereas she does not try to report what was said to her, she uses a direct quote for her own utterance – even though these are not actually words. *Hee! hee!* is Violet reporting herself giggling in a silly way every time she was spoken to, in order to hide the fact that she could not hear what was said.

The direct quotes (j) to (n) are a joke told collaboratively by Richard and Charles. There is only an incomplete reporting signal for the first of the quotes; and the next three have no explicit reporting signals. In all cases, the speakers signal the quotes by using quoting intonation (see 1.15) and by speaking more loudly.

The point of the joke is again that Violet does not hear what the people say to her; but this time it is being told from outside, not by Violet herself. The words quoted are, of course, no more accurate than any which Violet might have quoted: the speakers are not claiming that they have actually heard people saying 'Hallo, Violet!'. But the story is being told from the other side, from the side of the people trying to speak to Violet. Therefore the speakers quote the words that they imagine being spoken, to contrast them with Violet's imagined silence. This is, of course, exactly the opposite of the way Violet presents her own situation in the conversation.

The final direct quote, (r), is the conclusion of Violet's story about Mary. In telling this story, Violet keeps switching to the contrast with her own attitude. She begins the story about Mary in paragraph 1, and brings it to a first conclusion in paragraph 3 with the indirect report of Mary's words. However, without allowing time for this 'punchline' to have its effect, she immediately goes back to the contrast with herself, still in paragraph 3. This prompts Richard and Charles to interrupt with their joke about her. Finally, Violet returns to her original story in paragraph 14.

She obviously feels that her first version of the story did not end dramatically enough. She therefore uses an emphatic structure with the reporting signal as subject:

> *But what I'm saying is, she said, 'I'm not going to walk through Chester and not know anybody.'*

Note that she chooses to emphasize her own words (*what I'm saying is*). She could emphasize Mary's words instead: 'What she said was "I'm not going to walk through Chester and not know anybody."' But the emphasis on her own words signals 'This is the main point of the story I am telling you'.

Violet also uses a direct quote instead of an indirect report. The effect of this is to make the conclusion more dramatic and therefore more effective. Violet and her listeners were clearly happy with this second attempt at a 'punchline': the conversation at once turned to a different topic.

Novels

context

One of the main features of novels is that they are, normally, concerned with imaginary events. As far as reporting is concerned, this means that there is usually no previous language event to report. The writer does, of course, write as if the events had taken place and as if he or she were reporting actual conversations and thoughts. But, unlike in journalism and academic writing, for example, it makes no sense to ask questions such as how accurately the report conveys the words or meaning of the original language event or the intentions of the original speaker or writer.

The functions of reporting in novels are therefore rather different, though equally important. You usually expect novels to contain a great deal of reported language, much of it in direct quotes. Indeed, some novels consist almost entirely of dialogue between characters in the story; others are made up of letters written by the characters to each other, or of narratives told by the characters. However, the majority of novels contain a fairly balanced mixture of direct quotes, indirect reporting, and narration of events.

The reader expects speech that is quoted or reported in the novel to have two main functions: to contribute to the development of the plot and to reveal something about the nature of the person speaking. The novel writer may give extra information about what is said: he or she may, for example, tell the reader that the speaker was lying or not saying everything openly. On the other hand, the writer may simply report the words spoken and allow the reader to interpret their significance.

Novels also typically contain a great deal of reporting of thoughts, feelings, and opinions. The writer can enter the minds of the characters in a way that is not possible in real life, and can even quote the words passing through a character's mind. In many novels, the writer actually reports the thoughts of only one of the characters. In this case, the events of the novel will probably be seen through the eyes of that character, and the reader's knowledge of the events will be restricted to what that character knows. Thus the writer can use reporting, amongst other things, to give or to keep back information. One reason for keeping back information is to puzzle and interest readers so that they continue reading to find out the rest of the information. When a detective in a novel interviews someone suspected of murder, for example, the novelist may report the detective's thoughts, but you rarely find out what the suspect is thinking.

A further function of reporting in novels is to add complexity and interest. Rather than just one point of view – that of the writer – the reader is presented with a variety of points of view. The characters in the novel can express ideas and opinions that the writer does not in fact agree with. Part of the enjoyment of the novel comes from the reader's attempts to decide what point of view they themselves should accept.

If the writer chooses to report the thoughts of one or more of the characters, those characters obviously have a more important influence on the reader's interpretation of events in the novel. Sometimes, the characters' thoughts guide the reader to the interpretation that the writer wishes to convey. In more sophisticated writing, on the other hand, the writer may imply, without explicitly stating it, that the reported viewpoint of the main characters is not necessarily the correct one. The reader in this case gets pleasure from the writer's skill in telling the story from one point of view while suggesting a different point of view.

Another way in which reporting can add interest to the novel is by allowing a variety of voices and therefore styles. This can be done simply by making the characters speak in distinctive ways – Dickens, for example, delights in using different styles in direct quotes for many of his characters. Alternatively, it can be done by mixing the voices of the characters with that of the writer. This is done especially through the use of indirect quotes, of speech and thoughts. It may sometimes be very difficult, if not impossible, to decide exactly who is speaking or thinking in a particular part of the text: the writer or one of the characters.

Thus the kinds of reporting that the reader expects to find in a novel are very varied. At the most general level, though, the reader expects that there will be a lot of reporting of speech (and, to a lesser extent, writing) and thoughts, and that any reported speech or thought will have at least two layers of possible interpretation: what it means for the characters in the novel at that point, and what it means for the reader in terms of the development and significance of the novel as a whole.

background to the text

The following extract is taken from *The Good Terrorist* by Doris Lessing. The novel deals with a group of people living in a 'squat' – that is, an unused building where they have no legal right to stay. The main members of the group are left-wing political activists, some of whom are prepared to use violence for political ends. The main character is Alice, who has rebelled against her middle-class upbringing. Her closest relationship is with Jasper, who is younger and more idealistic (perhaps fanatical), and who frequently quarrels with her because she still behaves in some ways like a member of the middle class. In the scene below, Alice hears about a political demonstration at which Jasper has been arrested.

1 It was getting dark when Alice woke. She heard Bert's laugh, a deep ho, ho, ho, from the kitchen. **(a)** That's not his own laugh, Alice thought. I wonder what that would be like? Tee hee hee more likely. No, he made that laugh up for himself. Reliable and comfortable. Manly. Voices and laughs, we make them up ... Roberta's made-up voice, comfortable. And that was Pat's quick voice and her laugh. Her own laugh? Perhaps. So they were both back and that meant that Jasper was too. Alice was out of her sleeping bag, and tugging on a sweater, a smile on her face that went with her feelings for Jasper: admiration and wistful love.

2 But Jasper was not in the kitchen with the other two, who were glowing, happy, fulfilled, and eating fish and chips.

3 (b) 'It's all right, Alice,' said Pat, pulling out a chair for her. 'They arrested him, but it's not serious. He'll be in court tomorrow morning at Enfield. Back here by lunchtime.'

4 (c) 'Unless he's bound over?' asked Bert.

5 (d) 'He was bound over for two years in Leeds, but that ended last month.'

6 (e) 'Last month?' said Pat. Her eyes met Bert's, found no reflection there of what she was thinking – probably against her will, Alice believed; and, so as not to meet Alice's, lowered themselves to the business of eating one golden crisp fatty chip after another. This was not the first time Alice had caught **(f)** suggestions that Jasper liked being bound over – needed the edge it put on life. **(g)** She said apologetically, 'Well, he has had to be careful so long, watching every tiny little thing he does, I suppose...' She was examining Bert **(h)** who, she knew, could tell her what she needed to know about the arrest. Jasper was arrested, but Bert not; that in itself...

7 Pat pushed over some chips, and Alice primly ate one or two, thinking about cholesterol.

8 (j) 'How many did they arrest?'

9 (k) 'Seven. Three we didn't know. But the others were John, Clarissa and Charlie. And Jasper.'

10 (l) 'None of the trade union comrades?'

11 (m) 'No.'

12 A silence.

13 Then **(n)** Bert, 'They have been fining people twenty-five pounds.'

14 (p) Alice said automatically, 'Then probably Jasper will get fifty pounds.'

15 (q) 'He thought twenty-five. I gave him twenty so he'd have enough.'

16 Alice, who had been about to get up, ready to leave, **(r)** said quickly, 'He doesn't want me down there? Why not? What did he say?'

17 (s) Pat said, carefully, ' **(t)** He asked me to tell you not to come down.'

18 (u) 'But I've always been there when he's been arrested. Always. I've been in court every time.'

19 (v) 'That's what he said,' said Bert. ' **(w)** Tell Alice not to bother.'

20 Alice sat thinking so intently that the kitchen, Bert and Pat, even the house around her vanished. She was down at the scene of the picket. The van loaded with newspapers appeared in the gates, its sinister gleaming look telling everyone to hate it; the pickets surged forward, shouting; and there was Jasper, as she had seen him so often, his pale face distorted with a look of abstracted and dedicated hate, his reddish crop of gleaming hair. **(x)** He was always the first to be arrested, she thought proudly, he was so dedicated, so obviously – even to the police – self-sacrificing. Pure.

21   But there was something that didn't fit.
22 (y) She said, 'Did you decide not to get arrested for any reason, Bert?'
23   Because, if that had been so, one could have expected Jasper too to have returned home.
24 (z) Bert said, 'Jasper found someone down there, someone who might be very useful to us.'
25   At once the scene fell into shape in Alice's mind. **(aa)** 'Was he one of the three you didn't know?'
26 (bb) 'That's it,' said Bert. 'That's it exactly.' He yawned. **(cc)** He said, 'I hate to have to ask, but could you let me have the twenty pounds? **(dd)** Jasper said I should ask you.'
27   Alice counted out the money. She did not let her gaze rise from this task.
28 (ee) Pat said nicely, 'That little bundle won't last long at this rate.'
29 (ff) 'No.'
30 (gg) Alice was praying: Let Bert go. Let him go upstairs. I want to talk to Pat. She was thinking this so hard that she was not surprised when he stood up
and **(hh)** said, 'I'm going to drop around to Felicity's and get myself a real bath.'
31 (jj) 'I'll come in a minute,' said Pat.
32   Bert went, and the two women sat on.

analysis

The scene mainly consists of the conversation between Alice and Bert and Pat, in which Alice finds out what has happened to Jasper. The reporting of the conversation is interrupted at certain points by narrative sections, mostly describing Alice's thoughts and reactions.

Much of the conversation itself is given in direct quotes, with minimal reporting signals. Nine of the quotes (d, j, k, l, m, q, u, aa, and ff) appear with no reporting clause; one (n) has a speaker but no reporting verb; nine (b, e, v, y, z, bb, cc, hh, jj) have simply 'X said' or 'said X' and one (c) simply 'asked X'. The focus is on what was said, with, where necessary, a simple identification of the speaker. In (k) and (m), the identity of the speaker could be ambiguous (Pat or Bert); but in the context it seems clear that it is Pat who is being friendly and informative at this point rather than Bert. The question of who says what is important for the interaction, but Lessing, having by this stage of the novel established the different characters and the kinds of events that are significant, is content to leave the reader to imagine and interpret much of the scene with little interruption.

Lessing does give some guidance as to how speeches are to be interpreted through the use of adverbs: *apologetically* (g), *automatically* (p), *quickly* (r), *carefully* (s), *nicely* (ee). Although these refer mainly to the speakers' manner of speaking, the fact that their manner is mentioned encourages the reader to think about why they have said these words in this way. Lessing does not give definite answers to the question why, and in some cases the answers would be fairly complicated.

For example, in (ee), the adverb *nicely* has several possible interpretations.

Pat said nicely, 'That little bundle won't last long at this rate.'

This might mean that Pat wants to be kind and friendly because Alice is obviously running out of money. It might mean that she merely wants to sound kind and friendly (perhaps with an implied criticism of Alice and/or Jasper for spending so much). Or it might mean that she speaks in a middle-class way (and therefore perhaps that she must be speaking in an insincere way). A further possible interpretation is discussed below.

The important point with the quotes that have been mentioned so far is that Lessing often offers just the external evidence (what was said and, sometimes, the way in which it was said) and leaves the readers to interpret it. The readers are ready to do this because they expect that what characters in a novel say and how they say it is particularly important in revealing their personality and reactions.

In this novel, Lessing does not generally aim for very different styles of speech for each character to indicate their personality. Some of the characters use more political terms than the others, but mostly the characters speak more or less in the same way (although Alice's language is, in fact, an important exception – see below). It is the content of what they say which shows what the speakers are like. In this scene, Pat is more sympathetic towards Alice – as she is throughout the novel – whereas Bert is more businesslike and less sensitive. In (b), for example, Pat is clearly trying to reassure Alice.

'It's all right, Alice...They arrested him, but it's not serious...Back here by lunchtime.'

Bert, on the other hand, (c) mentions things which might make the situation worse.

'Unless he's bound over?'

(Sometimes people are 'bound over' by a court when they have committed an offence; if they commit another offence within a certain time, they are then punished more severely.)

Before moving on to look at the reporting of thoughts, it is worth mentioning three other kinds of reporting of speech in the scene. It is noticeable that the conversation is reported entirely in direct quotes; but indirect reporting clauses are used at two points. The first is in (f), following the reporting noun *suggestions*.

This was not the first time that Alice had caught <u>suggestions that Jasper liked being bound over</u> – needed the edge it put on life.

The reported clause here does not report something said in the conversation; it sums up the kinds of things that Alice has heard or understood about Jasper over a long period of time. Therefore a direct quote would not be possible, since it is not a single speech event which is being reported.

The other point where indirect reported speech is used is when Pat and Bert are telling Alice what Jasper said. In (t), Pat uses an embedded report to make it clear that this is Jasper's instruction to Alice, not her own.

Pat said, carefully, 'He asked me to tell you not to come down.'

She may be embarrassed at having to tell this to Alice, because she softens it a little by using *asked* (compare 'He told me to tell you...' or 'He told you not to...'). However, when Alice seems to be ready not to obey, Bert changes to a direct quote of Jasper's words to reinforce the order.

'That's what he said,' said Bert. 'Tell Alice not to bother.'

The difference in the way they report Jasper's words also reinforces the impression that the reader has of the difference in the way Pat and Bert treat Alice, and therefore of their different personalities.

In (dd), Bert uses an indirect reporting structure, *Jasper said I should ask you*, again perhaps to cover embarrassment, because he is asking Alice for money: Bert makes it clear that the idea is Jasper's rather than his own.

A different kind of reporting of speech occurs in (h), within an indirect report of Alice's thoughts:

Bert...could tell her what she needed to know about the arrest.

Here, the reporting verb is followed by a 'wh'-clause giving a summary (see 3.53) of a message. The function is to signal to the reader what Alice hopes to learn from the conversation that will follow. Clearly Lessing could not use an indirect reported clause here, because as yet Alice herself does not know what Bert will say. But, from the reader's point of view, the summary serves to arouse interest by making it clear that Alice has a particular purpose in the rest of the conversation. The reader can therefore understand better why Alice asks certain questions, and is waiting – like Alice – to find out the important facts about Jasper's arrest.

Although the story is not told in the first person, it is immediately obvious that it is told from Alice's point of view. She is the only character whose thoughts are reported. It is possible to identify some clear reports of Alice's thoughts: there are direct quotes of her thoughts in (a) and (gg).

That's not his own laugh, Alice thought. I wonder what that would be like?
Alice was praying: Let Bert go.

And an indirect report in (x).

He was always the first to be arrested, she thought proudly, he was so dedicated, so obviously – even to the police – self-sacrificing.

However, a close examination reveals that a great deal of the text – perhaps most or even all of it – is to be interpreted as a report of Alice's thoughts.

The first clear signal of Alice's thoughts is in (a): *That's not his own laugh, Alice thought.* The present tense ('s) shows that this is a direct quote, although without quote marks. The following sentence is also a direct quote of her thoughts (shown by the pronoun *we*, the present tense and the interrogative form).

> *Voices and laughs, we make them up...Roberta's made-up voice, comfortable. And that was Pat's quick voice and her laugh. Her own laugh? Perhaps. So they were both back and that meant that Jasper was too. Alice was out of her sleeping bag, and tugging on a sweater, a smile on her face that went with her feelings for Jasper: admiration and wistful love.*

By the end of the paragraph the narration has moved outside Alice's head and the reader is given an external picture of Alice's actions and the expression on her face; but it is not completely clear where the change has occurred. The change of tense in the sentence *And that was Pat's quick laugh* indicates that the direct quoting has finished. This sentence may be an indirect quote (implying that Alice thought 'And that is Pat's quick laugh'), or a report of Alice's perceptions (what she heard rather than the words that she thought). The interrogative form of the next sentence and the following answer to the question *Perhaps* suggest that these are indirect quotes, or even direct quotes. The next sentence begins with the conjunction *So*, which suggests that it is also an indirect quote (see 1.64). The last sentence of the paragraph then appears to be the writer describing Alice, with no reporting.

In paragraph 6, there is a similar difficulty in deciding exactly whose point of view is being reported.

> *Her eyes met Bert's, found no reflection there of what she was thinking – probably against her will, Alice believed; and, so as not to meet Alice's, lowered themselves to the business of eating one golden crisp fatty chip after another.*

Lessing appears to move inside Pat's head by reporting her perceptions (*found no reflection there of what she was thinking*) and intentions (*so as not to meet Alice's*). However, there is also a report of Alice's opinion (*probably against her will, Alice believed*) commenting on Pat. The effect is to imply that the reader is still being given Alice's view of the scene. The fact that Alice can interpret Pat's thoughts, perceptions, and intentions therefore indicates to the reader that Alice feels close to Pat. It is noticeable that there is no similar point where Alice interprets Bert's thoughts.

There is a slightly different use of indirect quoting of thoughts in paragraphs 21 and 23.

> *But there was something that didn't fit.*
> *Because, if that had been so, one could have expected Jasper too to have returned home.*

The tense in both sentences shows that they are not direct thoughts, but the fact that they both begin with conjunctions suggests that they are indirect quotes (see 1.64). They present the parts of Alice's train of thought which are not expressed in her speech.

Paragraphs 22 and 23 are interesting in another way as well. They effectively integrate direct quote and non-reported comment into a single unit.

She said, 'Did you decide not to get arrested for any reason, Bert?' Because, if that had been so, one could have expected Jasper too to have returned home.

Lessing's aim is to give the impression of a continuing train of thought, but one which is partly expressed in spoken and partly in unspoken words. The quote and the comment are given in separate sentences – separate paragraphs, in fact – but the effect is of one grammatical structure, since the 'because'-clause clearly depends on the quote as its main clause. The written text is in fact imitating Alice's thoughts by imitating spoken language.

The frequent use of direct and, in particular, indirect quotes of Alice's thoughts means that the reader is never completely sure how much of the text is directly told by the writer and how much is actually Alice's view of events. This affects the way in which the reader interprets the text.

For example, in the analysis of paragraph 1 above, it was mentioned that the reader can take the last sentence as a description of Alice by the writer.

Alice was out of her sleeping bag, and tugging on a sweater, a smile on her face that went with her feelings for Jasper: admiration and wistful love.

This implies that the sentence gives a 'true' description of her. However, since most of this paragraph is a report of Alice's thoughts, it is also possible that this is a disguised report of Alice's own view of her actions and appearance. In other words, Alice believes that she is smiling in a way that expresses 'admiration and wistful love'. Whether she really is or not is a question for the reader, which Lessing deliberately leaves unanswered. Perhaps Alice has an unrealistically romantic view of herself.

Similarly, in paragraph 28 it is not clear whether the description of Pat's manner of talking (*nicely*) is Lessing's choice of word or Alice's. If the reader interprets it as Alice's choice, the choice can be looked at from two different angles. On the one hand, 'nicely' shows Alice's view of Pat as being friendly and sympathetic. On the other hand, the fact that Alice uses this particular word tells the reader something about Alice. 'Nice' is a word which is strongly 'middle-class', and which would almost certainly not be used by the more political characters in the novel.

There are other subtle but important signs in the language of Alice's thoughts that she has a middle-class style: for example, the pronoun *one* in paragraph 23.

...*one could have expected Jasper too to have returned home.*

This aspect of the language used to report Alice's thoughts is deliberate, and in fact guides the reader towards understanding what the novel is about.

One of the main themes of the novel is the tension between Alice's conventional middle-class upbringing and her present violently anti-middle-class opinions. Although she has consciously rejected her upbringing, she cannot get rid of the influence it still has on her behaviour and opinions. She has successfully removed most traces of the upbringing from her speech, but they still occur in her thoughts, which are less under her conscious control. Therefore Alice represents at the same time two apparently contradictory sets of beliefs and values: the bourgeois and the revolutionary. This contradiction allows Lessing to explore the nature of the two sets of beliefs more deeply.

This theme is sometimes explicitly indicated by the characters, who criticize Alice for her bourgeois behaviour. However, it is mainly conveyed through the language which Lessing chooses in reporting Alice's thoughts, reactions, and opinions. Lessing does not simply describe Alice's personality, just as she does not simply describe the personalities of the other characters in the novel. As was mentioned above, the characters are brought to life mainly by what they say and how they say it. In the same way, Alice is brought to life by the way in which her thoughts and reactions are reported. By reporting Alice's thoughts as well as her spoken words, Lessing can implicitly show the difference between her public and her private personality. The difference is not in *what* she thinks and says, but more importantly in *how* she thinks and says it.

In a sense, therefore, the whole novel is a report; and much of the meaning of the novel for the reader comes from that fact. By conveying so much through the way the reporting is done rather than by explicit explanation to the reader, Lessing leaves the task of interpretation to the reader. This increases the reader's pleasure through the sense of discovery. The indirect way in which the meaning of the novel is conveyed also adds to the complexity of the novel, because it suggests many possible interpretations without imposing any single one as 'correct'. This kind of indirection is highly prized in present-day Western literature.

The way in which reporting is used in *The Good Terrorist* is extremely subtle, but typical of its genre – or at least of sophisticated examples of the genre.

Academic writing

context

Reports of other books and articles play a very important role in academic writing. The readers of an academic text expect the author to refer to the work of many other people who have written on the same topic. The author may also refer to his or her own previous work.

Note that this is not necessarily true of textbooks. A textbook is written by experts for people who are not (yet) experts. A textbook which is intended for near-beginners in the field (e.g. school children) will probably contain very few reports of other writers. The author of the textbook will certainly use information which is based on what other people have written, but she is not expected to point this out each time. In a textbook for a more advanced audience, you are more likely to find a larger number of reports: a textbook for university students will often contain nearly as many references to other writers as an academic book.

Academic books or articles are intended for other experts in the subject, and the reporting in them has three main functions.

The first function is to show how the information in the text fits in with what experts already know about the subject. This has two aspects.

First, the author is expected to repeat the facts that people already know and the main ideas that people agree on. One important way of doing this is to report other work which has already discussed and established those facts and ideas.

Secondly, the author has to show what people do not yet know or do not agree on. This indicates why her present work is necessary and useful: the author can present the work as helping to fill the gap in knowledge or to settle the disagreement. Again, reporting the work of other people is an important way of doing this. The author can point out questions that the other people have not yet investigated, or can criticize other people's ideas as wrong or unsatisfactory and therefore needing to be improved.

Together, these provide the foundation on which the author's work is built up: what people know, which leads to what people do not know, which leads to what the author has discovered. The introduction section of an academic text often has these three steps, and therefore you often find many reports in this section.

The second main function of reporting in academic texts is to help the author's line of argument. If the author wants to strengthen a point she is making, she can often report other writers who have expressed the same idea. If the author wants to show that the results of her study are probably correct, she can report other people's results which more or less agree with hers, or report other people's theories which predict that her results should happen. Of course, the ideas and theories of the other writers are not necessarily correct; but at least the author can feel less alone and less open to criticism.

Alternatively, the author may report other writers in order to contradict their ideas, using this as a starting point to develop a new argument.

The third main function is to show that the author is an expert in the subject and that her text is therefore worth reading. The author does this by showing that she has read as many as possible of the books and articles that have already been written about the subject. If the author is a recognized expert, she may not need to do this: it is noticeable that some authors who are particularly famous in their subject often use fewer reports of other people's work than less well-known authors.

It is clear from this outline that the authors and readers of academic texts generally place a high value on the shared nature of knowledge. This sharing is signalled especially through referring to what other people have already written about the subject. In a 'good' academic text, readers normally expect to find a balance of interesting new ideas and reported 'old' ideas. They expect the reported ideas to be fitted neatly into the author's argument, preparing for the argument and helping it develop.

This means that they also expect the author to show whether she agrees or disagrees with the reported ideas. In telling a story in conversation, you might just report what someone else said without commenting on whether that person was right or wrong. In academic writing, on the other hand, you are normally expected to show your attitude in some way to anything that you report.

background to the text

The article from which the extract below is taken deals with a fairly controversial subject, since it involves questions of race. The subject is children 'in care': that is, children who have been taken away from their family and are looked after by professional workers in special homes, or by approved foster parents. The author is particularly interested in black children in care. In her article, she wants to show that previous studies have tended to ignore the question of whether or not the children in care are black. In order to fill this gap, she wants to present detailed information which she has gathered on this question through her own research. She then wants to use this information to support her argument that the people who decide whether black children should be taken into care are often influenced by racism.

The extract is a slightly shortened version of the introductory section of the article.

Black children in local authority care: admission patterns

Ravinder Barn

1   Child care is an area of much interest and concern in the personal social services. **(a)** Policy, practice and provision is essentially said to be directed to meet the interests of the child. In the last few decades **(b)** much has been written on the subject of children in care but it would appear that scant attention has been given to the situation of black children.

2   In 1985, **(c)** an HMSO report summarised the findings of nine DHSS funded studies in **(d)** a report entitled 'Social Work Decisions in Child Care'. **(e)** These studies explored the various aspects of the care career process (Packman et al 1986; Milham et al 1986; Vernon and Fruin 1985; Fisher et al 1986; Rowe et al 1984; Sinclair 1984; Hilgendorf 1981; Adcock et al 1983; Stevenson and Smith 1982). It is pertinent to **(f)** point out that **(g)** not one of these nine studies focussed on the 'race' dimension. This is perhaps also a reflection of the 'colour blind' approach which continues to exist in the personal social services.

3   **(h)** There have been a few research studies which have focussed on the issue of black children's admission into the care system. **(j)** These have principally shown that black children are much more likely to come into care than white children.

4   **(k)** A group of studies which indicate the greater likelihood of admission for black children were carried out by researchers at the University of Bradford who observed the admission patterns of children into Bradford Social Services Department. **(l)** The first study conducted in the late 1960s found that children of 'mixed-origin' were eight and a half times more likely to come into care than 'white indigenous' and 'Afro-Caribbean and Asian' children (Foren and Batta 1970). **(m)** A subsequent study conducted in 1975 obtained similar findings (Batta, McCulloch and Smith 1975). **(n)** Both studies revealed that children of 'mixed-origin' came into care at an earlier age and tended to stay in care for longer periods. **(p)** A third study of Bradford's child care population conducted in 1978 confirmed the findings of the earlier research with regard to children of 'mixed-origin' (Batta and Mawby 1981).

5   Although **(q)** research studies have asserted the high presence of black children in the care system, it is not clear whether black children are in fact disproportionately represented. Furthermore, little is known of the initial referral stage to the social services and the actual factors which precipitate black children's admission into care. It appears that **(r)** black families are much more likely to be referred by agencies such as the police, health and education (Boss and Homeshaw 1974; McCulloch, Batta and Smith 1979). However, the actual reasons for black children's admission into care are less well known. **(s)** A report by the Commission for Racial Equality (1977) suggested demographic and geographical factors as well as the lower socio-economic position of black families. **(t)** Boss and Homeshaw found: '...disturbing indications of a heavy-handed approach by both the police and the courts towards coloured children, particularly West Indians' (1975: 355). Moreover, **(u)** they also found that: '...proportionally more care orders and supervision orders were made on this particular group than was consistent with their overall numbers of court appearances' (1975: 355).

6   Despite the above findings, **(v)** the researchers feel that since black families are predominantly young, demographic reasons alone could account for the high proportions of black children in care. **(w)** Other studies have also offered explanations which are primarily related to the nature and type of families (McCulloch, Batta and Smith 1979; Fitzherbert 1967). The picture is one therefore where **(x)** the structures and lifestyles of black families are viewed in negative terms and **(y)** are perceived to be the major contributory factors which result in black children's admission into care. It appears that **(z)** the socio-economic conditions factor mentioned in the 1977 CRE report is one felt most by the black families themselves. **(aa)** It has been found that while **(bb)** social workers are more likely to explain the admission of black children into care in terms of individual or family pathology, **(cc)** parents themselves de-emphasise such factors and **(dd)** highlight their poor socio-economic situation (Pinder and Shaw 1974; Adams 1981).

7 In recent years, **(ee)** social work practitioners have begun to acknowledge the importance of cultural factors in social work decision-making. In an atmosphere of 'family pathology', **(ff)** it is increasingly being said that the strengths of black families (**(gg)** which, it is argued, survived the onslaught of slavery, colonialism and imperialism) need serious recognition (Small 1984; Liverpool 1986). **(hh)** It is also felt that social workers lack an understanding of black families and their cultural patterns (Ahmed 1981; Arnold 1982). **(jj)** Thus it is argued that black children can sometimes be unnecessarily taken into care. **(kk)** Arnold states:

> **(ll)** The West Indian parent who threatens to beat the living daylights out of a disobedient child, or who **(mm)** asks him to leave 'if he thinks himself a man' seldom means to be taken literally. These are his or her attempts at imposing a discipline in the hope that threats will serve as a deterrent for the delinquent behaviour. (1982: 109)

analysis

Perhaps the most noticeable difference between reports in academic texts and those in other kinds of texts is the set of special conventions for signalling reports. There are several different sets that are used: the one used in the extract is called the 'author/date' method.

The basic convention when you want to refer to another text in this method is that you give the name of the writer and the year when the text was published. In the vast majority of cases, you give only the writer's surname, not the first name or initials. Normally, you do not mention the title of the book or article – you will notice that in the extract there are 27 references to specific works, but only one title is mentioned, in paragraph 2.

'Social Work Decisions in Child Care'

If the text was written by three or more writers, you usually give the name of the first writer followed by *et al* (this is an abbreviation of Latin words meaning 'and others'). For example, the reference in paragraph 2:

Packman et al 1986

was actually written by J. Packman, J. Randall, and N. Jaques.

There are two main patterns for mentioning the writer's name and the date of publication. You can include the writer's name as grammatically part of the sentence, with the date of publication in brackets immediately after the name. The author does not choose this option in the extract, but here is an example from another part of her text. As often happens in this pattern, the reported writer is the subject of the sentence and the main verb is a reporting verb.

Rowe and Lambert (1973) found that 552 children in their sample group were black.

The other main pattern is the one that the author uses very frequently in the extract. After you have reported or summarized what another writer said, you give the name and date in brackets at the end of the sentence. In this case, there is often no clear reporting verb in the sentence.

It appears that black families are much more likely to be referred by agencies such as the police, health and education (Boss and Homeshaw 1974; McCulloch, Batta and Smith 1979).

As this example shows, you can refer to more than one work in this way. Here the report clearly gives a summary of conclusions drawn from both the texts mentioned in brackets. There is an even more striking example in paragraph 2, where nine works are summarized in a single sentence.

If you give a direct quote from the other writer you often use the writer as subject, but put the date in brackets at the end of the quote. You also give the page number in the book or journal where the quote is taken from.

Boss and Homeshaw found: '...disturbing indications of a heavy-handed approach by both the police and the courts towards coloured children, particularly West Indians' (1975: 355).

When the quote is fairly long (usually longer than two lines), you use a special layout:

Arnold states:

> *The West Indian parent who threatens to beat the living day-lights out of a disobedient child, or who asks him to leave 'if he thinks himself a man' seldom means to be taken literally. These are his or her attempts at imposing a discipline in the hope that threats will serve as a deterrent for the delinquent behaviour. (1982: 109)*

Note that the quote is indented from both sides and that there are no inverted commas around the quote. The lines are also usually closer together.

It has been mentioned above that you normally give only the writer's name and the date of publication in the text. You give full information about the writer's book or article at the end of your text, in the 'References' or 'Bibliography'. This is a list of all the other works that you have referred to in your text. The list is arranged in alphabetical order according to writers' surnames.

In one of the examples discussed above, there was a reference to two other works:

It appears that black families are much more likely to be referred by agencies such as the police, health and education (Boss and Homeshaw 1974; McCulloch, Batta and Smith 1979).

Here is how the first of those works is listed in the References at the end of the article.

Boss, P. and Homeshaw, J. (1974) Coloured Families and Social Services Departments, Research Report School of Social Work, University of Leicester

Note that the writers' initials are given, following the surname. The title of the work is also given. Since it is a book rather than an article, the title is in italics (or underlined). The publisher and place of publication is given at the end.

Here is how the second work is listed.

McCulloch, J., Batta, I. and Smith, N. (1979) 'Colour as a Variable in the Children's Section of a Local Authority Social Services Department', New Community 7(2): 78–84

This reference is to an article; the title of the article is given in inverted commas, followed by the title of the journal in which it appeared (*New Community*) in italics or underlined. The numbers at the end (*7(2): 78–84*) tell you exactly where the article appeared: on pages 78 to 84 in the 2nd issue of the 7th volume of the journal (each volume is made up of all the issues which appear in one year).

This is a very brief outline of one common method of giving references in academic texts. As mentioned above, there are other methods; and some writers, journals, and books use slightly different conventions even in this method. However, all the methods are designed to tell the readers of the text exactly where they can find the other works referred to if they want to read them.

Having set out the special conventions used in academic texts in general, it is time to look back at the particular text given above and see how these conventions are used to convey the author's meaning.

Here is a list of all the reports in the extract where the source of the information is explicitly mentioned. Where there is another reporting signal (e.g. a reporting verb), this is also given in the list.

an HMSO report – summarised (c)
a report – entitled (d)
These studies: (Packman *et al*...) – explored (e)
not one of these nine studies – focussed on (g)
a few research studies – have focussed on (h)
These – have shown (j)
A group of studies which – indicate (k)
The first study: (Foren and Batta 1970) – found (l)
A subsequent study: (Batta, McCulloch and Smith 1975) (m)
Both studies – revealed (n)
A third study: (Batta and Mawby 1981) – confirmed (p)
research studies – have asserted (q)
(Boss and Homeshaw 1974; McCulloch, Batta and Smith 1979) (r)
A report by the Commission for Racial Equality (1977) – suggested (s)
Boss and Homeshaw: (1975: 355) – found (t)
they: (1975: 355) – found (u)
the researchers – feel (v)

Other studies: (McCulloch, Batta and Smith 1979; Fitzherbert 1967) – have offered explanations (w)
in the 1977 CRE report – mentioned (z)
(Pinder and Shaw 1974; Adams 1981) – It has been found (aa)
social work practitioners – have begun to acknowledge (ee)
(Small 1984; Liverpool 1986) – it is being said (ff)
(Small 1984; Liverpool 1986) – which it is argued (gg)
(Ahmed 1981; Arnold 1982) – It is felt (hh)
Arnold: (1982: 109) – states (kk)

There are also a number of unattributed reports.

is essentially said (a)
has been written (b)
point out (f)
are viewed (x)
are perceived (y)
Thus it is argued (jj)

Finally, there are reports of what 'ordinary' people say. These are all included within reports of other works; and although they are interesting in themselves, they will not be referred to in the analysis following.

social workers – explain (bb)
parents themselves – de-emphasise (cc)
parents themselves – highlight (dd)
The West Indian parent who – threatens (ll)
The West Indian parent who – asks (mm)

The lists above show that over 80% of the extract is signalled as being a report of what other people have said.

This remarkably high proportion is not unusual for introduction sections. As mentioned earlier, the author is expected to begin by reviewing what other experts have written and by showing how her work adds to theirs.

There is therefore very little comment directly from the author (only four of the thirty-two sentences in the text seem to have no explicit reporting in them). Nevertheless, the author is constantly showing her attitude towards the reported information and opinion, and thus preparing the ground for her own study.

The first two reports in the text, in paragraph 1, are unattributed reports.

Policy, practice and provision is essentially said to be directed to meet the interests of the child. (a)
In the last few decades much has been written on the subject of children in care. (b)

These summarize very briefly the current position. Note that the way in which the first report is expressed – *is said to be* – implies that this claim may not be true; and the second report is immediately followed by *but* to introduce the gap in knowledge that the author wants to fill:

...but it would appear that scant attention has been given to the situation of black children.

The reports in paragraph 1 are unattributed in order to show that this is what people in general have said or written about. The author is outlining the situation in a way which signals that she is probably going to disagree with the general view.

In paragraph 2, the reporting verbs in the first two sentences are carefully neutral: the studies mentioned *summarised* (c) and *explored* (d) the situation. The contents of the studies are summarized extremely briefly, since they are not directly relevant to the author's work. The author mentions these ten studies partly, no doubt, to show that she has done all the expected reading, but also in order to stress that the studies have all ignored an important question (the question that she is going to explore, of course).

In the third sentence, there is a reporting verb which shows a positive attitude (see 2.40).

> *It is pertinent to point out that not one of these nine studies focussed on the 'race' dimension.* (f)

Although the verb does not have an explicit subject, it is clear that it is the author herself who is 'pointing out' this gap. She is using a **performative verb** (see 4.72) to emphasize her own purpose. The use of a positive verb is reinforced by the fact that so far the author has used reporting verbs which are neutral or possibly negative (*is said to be*).

In paragraphs 3 and 4, the author reports several studies in a way which shows that she accepts what they say as true.

> *These (studies) have principally shown...* (j)
> *A group of studies which indicate...* (k)
> *The first study conducted in the late 1960s found...* (l)
> *A subsequent study conducted in 1975 obtained similar findings...* (m)
> *Both studies revealed...* (n)
> *A third study of Bradford's child care population conducted in 1978 confirmed...* (p)

The reporting verbs which are used all show a positive attitude (*indicate* is perhaps a little more neutral than the others, but the general impression is that the author accepts all these findings). The author is reporting the factual results of earlier studies, which are reasonably certain.

In paragraphs 5 and 6, on the other hand, the author begins to report the conclusions of earlier studies – the other writer's interpretations of their results. Basically, she does not agree with their conclusions, and she begins using a different kind of reporting verb. The reporting verbs are now mostly neutral.

> *...research studies have asserted...* (q)
> *A report by the Commission for Racial Equality (1977) suggested...* (s)
> *Despite the above findings, the researchers feel...* (v)
> *Other studies have also offered explanations...* (w)

185

...the structures and life styles of black families are viewed in negative terms and are perceived to be... (y)

The fact that the author does not signal that she accepts these conclusions leaves her free to disagree with them. Although she does not yet explicitly say that she disagrees, the change from positive to neutral reports suggests that disagreement is coming soon.

This attitude of accepting the findings but not the conclusions is in fact signalled fairly clearly at the end of paragraph 5 and the beginning of paragraph 6. The author reports some findings using the positive verb *found*.

Boss and Homeshaw found... (t)
Moreover, they also found... (u)

She then explicitly tells her readers that she thinks that Boss and Homeshaw came to the wrong conclusions on the basis of the findings.

Despite the above findings, the researchers feel... (v)

Note that she switches to a neutral reporting verb *feel*. If she accepted the conclusions, she would probably use another positive verb here, such as 'point out'.

At the end of paragraph 6, there is another positive report:

It has been found... (aa)

This report of findings which the author again accepts as true prepares for paragraph 7. The whole of this paragraph consists of reports of conclusions which are more or less based on these findings and which she does in fact agree with. Interestingly, there is only one positive reporting verb.

In recent years, social work practitioners have begun to acknowledge... (ee)

The other reporting verbs are all neutral. It is also very striking that, except for the last one, they all have **introductory 'it'** as subject.

...it is increasingly being said... (ff)
...which it is argued... (gg)
It is also felt... (hh)
Thus it is argued... (jj)
Arnold states... (kk)

At this point, the author is doing two things. She is outlining a general view which is different from the general view that she outlined at the beginning of the article; and at the same time she is leaving herself space to show that even this second view still needs improving (this is what her article will do).

The author is setting up a contrast between two different sets of opinions about black children in care. She has described one set and suggested that the people who hold those opinions have collected accurate information but have interpreted it wrongly. Here she is describing another set of opinions. She uses introductory 'it' to show that this second set is not simply the opinions of a small and therefore unimportant group of people. The four writers that she mentions (Small, Liverpool, Ahmed, and Arnold) are presented as representatives of a larger group. For example:

It is also felt that social workers lack an understanding of black families and their cultural patterns (Ahmed 1981; Arnold 1982). (hh)

If she changed this to make the writers subjects of the reporting verbs, the implication that this is the opinion of many people would disappear: compare 'Ahmed (1981) and Arnold (1982) feel that social workers lack an understanding of black families and their cultural patterns'.

In the next part of the text, the author in fact makes it clear that she agrees with this second view in general. However, she does not want to show that she agrees completely with their conclusions, because that would take away the usefulness of her own study. Therefore she uses neutral reporting verbs, which leave her free to agree or disagree with the opinions reported.

What the author has done, therefore, in this introduction, is to establish a new consensus of opinion. Her message could be summarized as: 'Many experts in our field have ignored the position of black children in their studies. Now, however, there are many experts who understand that this is wrong. I am one of these experts (and I am going to show that I am right in this article).'

If you look back at the extract, you can see how much more subtly (and politely!) the author conveys this message. She does this very largely through an extremely skilful use of reporting. Like the novelist, the academic writer has to develop the skill of using reporting to convey her own meanings. It is one of the most important 'tricks of the trade' that academic writers have to master.

Exercises

Exercise 1 (Section 1.8)

The following direct quote structures have reporting clauses before or after the quote. Decide on at least one place where you could put the reporting clause in the middle of the quote.
Mark the position with an asterisk (*). The first one has been done for you.

1) Peter Beardsley admitted: 'We didn't play well * and we are all disappointed.'

2) 'But I can assure you that you couldn't do better than him,' he added.

3) 'Sara, what is it?' he asked quietly.

4) The manager said: 'With the growing financial problems there is a need to save as much money as possible.'

5) 'Go away, I can't cope with this now,' I shouted.

6) 'The thing is I don't remember anything about the journey,' he told Jane.

7) 'The Japanese attitude to the Emperor is similar to the way Britons view the Queen,' said Professor Sato.

8) Tim pointed out: 'The main question is whether we'll get there in time.'

9) 'What do you think I ought to do?' I asked.

10) 'But in my opinion it's worth the trouble,' she said.

Exercise 2 (Section 1.20 – 1.21, 1.24)

Punctuate the following direct quotes. In the last three sentences, the underlined words are quotes within quotes (Section 1.24). The first one has been done for you.

1) It looks like it's worth a fortune Cecil said
   'It looks like it's worth a fortune,' Cecil said.

2) Where have you been asked the manager

3) Watch out he said

   ....

4) Well he admitted there are still some things I haven't told you

   ....

5) My name's Bill he said finally what's yours

   ....

6) The man turned to me and whispered do you think this is going to go
   on for a long time

   ....

7) Mr Clark said last night we will do everything in our power to prevent
   this happening again

   ....

8) He admitted people often look at me and say <u>you look terrible</u>

   ....

9) He said she just kept asking me <u>where's the way out</u>

   ....

10) If people ask you <u>why do you do it</u> she said just say <u>because I want to</u>

   ....

Exercise 3 (Section 1.61)

Here are some indirect quotes. Report what was said using a 'normal'
indirect report structure (there may be several possible versions). The
first one has been done for you.

1) What, he asked, should he do when he'd made the beds?
   He asked what he should do when he'd made the beds.

2) Had she finished? the manager wanted to know. Well, it wasn't as easy
   as it seemed, she said.

   ....

3) The weather, he said suddenly, was just like in Sicily, wasn't it? Oh yes,
   they agreed, just like in Sicily.

   ....

4) He thought for a moment before replying. Why had he given up?
   Because he'd been sick and tired of the whole thing – that was why.

   ....

5) How stupid of him, he said to himself, not to realize what she was trying
   to do. What a fool he'd been!

   ....

Exercise 4 (Sections 1.67 – 1.74)

Change the reports below so that you use reporting adjuncts instead
of reporting clauses. The kind of reporting adjunct you should use
is given in brackets. The first one has been done for you.

1) Frank said that the shops close at 6. (According to)
   According to Frank, the shops close at 6.
   ....

2) People have told me that she's had at least two face-lifts. (Apparently)

   ....

3) Carter (1988) points out that low-cost housing is not always the best
   answer to the problem. (As)

   ....

4) The nineteenth-century philosopher von Humboldt said: 'Language
   cannot really be taught'. (To quote)

   ....

5) The dogs were well-trained and safe, their owner assured us.
   (According to)

   ....

6) 'The opera isn't over till the fat lady sings,' an old saying tells us.
   (In the words of)

   ....

7) The scientist von Frisch noted that 'The bees have no word for "up" in
   their language'. (As)

   ....

8) She hated her husband, people claimed, and wished she could get away. (Allegedly)

....

9) One commentator said that our football is 'as bad as our economy'. (As ... put it)

....

10) It is said that many teenage girls are obsessed by the idea that they are overweight. (Apparently)

....

Exercise 5 (Section 1.100)

Pick out the reporting signal and the message in each of the reports below, and identify what kind they are. The first one has been done for you.

1) However, doctors say the adverts should carry a health warning.
   reporting signal: *doctors say (reporting clause)*
   message: *the adverts should carry a health warning (reported 'that'-clause)*

2) 'Well, in that case,' says the lady, 'do be careful'.
   reporting signal: ....
   message: ....

3) The writer's aim, Simenon said, was a search for himself through his characters.
   reporting signal: ....
   message: ....

4) The judges have threatened to go on strike.
   reporting signal: ....
   message: ....

5) He was asked whether he would get back his record for scoring most
   goals.
   reporting signal: ....
   message: ....

6) On the way back to the hotel, I asked Jeremy what they'd been
   talking about.
   reporting signal: ....
   message: ....

7) In fact, as one TV critic puts it, the programmes are 'one long TV
   commercial'.
   reporting signal: ....
   message: ....

8) The man denied being involved in any violence.
   reporting signal: ....
   message: ....

9) She was complaining about the high cost of electricity.
   reporting signal: ....
   message: ....

10) Despite his insistence that the deal is on schedule, it looks
    certain that it will not go ahead.
    reporting signal: ....
    message: ....

11) He started his campaign with a promise to create more jobs.
    reporting signal: ....
    message: ....

12) The town is in an area which geologists say is likely to be hit
    by earthquakes in the near future.
    reporting signal: ....
    message: ....

Exercise 6 (Section 2.10)

Match each quote with the most suitable reporting verb from the list according to the speaker's purpose. The first one has been done for you.

1) 'Yes, I stole the money,'   a) she insisted

2) 'I'll hit you if you don't shut up,'   b) she announced

3) 'I said he was wrong and I still think   c) she admitted
   he's wrong,'

4) 'I'll bring your book back tomorrow,'   d) she suggested

5) 'There will be an economic recession   e) she warned him
   next year,'

6) 'Don't worry, everything will be OK,'   f) she complained

7) 'This food is horrible – I can't eat it!'   g) she promised

8) 'What about a nice cup of tea?'   h) she pleaded

9) 'Please, please help me,'   i) she predicted

10) 'The train has now arrived,'   j) she reassured him

1) _C_ ....   6) ....

2) ....   7) ....

3) ....   8) ....

4) ....   9) ....

5) ....   10) ....

Exercise 7 (Sections 2.28 – 2.32)

Complete the sentences below, using the most suitable reporting verb from the list. The first one has been done for you.

praise	tell off	nag	apologize	accuse
compliment	congratulate	blame	dismiss	quarrel

1) She _accused_ .... him of stealing her handbag.

2) Bill .... to Kate for forgetting her birthday.

3) I .... with Sue about doing the washing up.

4) He .... her for the accident.

5) They .... me on the way I looked.

6) I .... him on passing his exams.

7) Politicians .... the announcement as meaningless.

8) The parents .... her for her bravery.

9) She .... her husband about mending the lamp.

10) The teacher ....her .... for biting Joe.

Exercise 8 (Sections 2.75 – 2.80)

Report the following without mentioning the speaker. First use the passive structure with 'it' as subject; then use the passive structure where the reporting verb appears inside the reported message. Use the reporting verb given in brackets. The first one has been done for you.

1) 'He is extremely lazy.' (say)

   a) *It is said that he is extremely lazy.*

   b) *He is said to be extremely lazy.*

2) 'She is in New York now.' (report)

   a) ....

   b) ....

3) 'He got married for the third time yesterday.' (rumour)

   a) ....

   b) ....

4) 'They attempted to bribe their prison guards.' (allege)

   a) ....

   b) ....

5) 'These drugs are not dangerous.' (claim)

   a) ....

   b) ....

6) 'There are only two of these vases in the world.' (say)

   a) ....

   b) ....

Exercise 9 (Section 2.98 – 2.100)

Change the following quotes into reporting nouns followed by a reported clause, and use them to complete the sentences below. The first one has been done for you.

1) 'The fire was probably caused by an electrical fault,' he argued.

I wasn't convinced by *his argument that the fire was probably caused by an electrical fault.*

2) 'The talks will resume tomorrow,' the Prime Minister announced.

The main news tonight is ....

....

3) 'Oh, Nick, you're really very stupid,' she remarked.

Nick was upset by ....

....

4) 'Why don't we take both cars?' she suggested.

I agreed with ....

....

5) 'Take me to your leader,' he demanded.

They ignored ....

....

6) 'We have the sunniest beaches in Britain,' the town claims.

It's hard to check ....

....

7) 'You ought to take out life insurance,' he advised her.

She decided to follow ....

....

8) 'OK, I'll send the contract by fax,' he promised.

The new contract didn't arrive, despite ....

....

9) 'Don't forget that you've got to see Mike at 4 o'clock,' Maureen reminded him.

He was grateful for ....

....

10) 'I can come and babysit for you,' she offered.

They accepted ....

....

Exercise 10 (Sections 3.14 – 3.40)

Use an appropriate indirect report structure to report these quotes. The beginning of the report is given in brackets. The first one is done for you.

1) 'I'm afraid I've spilt some wine on the carpet.' (He confessed)
   He confessed that he'd spilt some wine on the carpet.

2) 'This is the only possible solution.' (He insisted)

   ....

3) 'I saw him throw stones at the dog.' (She claimed)

   ....

4) 'We found the car hidden near the park.' (The police reported)

   ....

5) 'Have they finished yet or not?' (She asked the foreman)

   ....

6) 'Aren't these shoes too big for your son?' (I asked her)

   ....

7) 'Do you think I should sell my car?' (I asked him)

   ....

8) 'It was really hot in the cinema.' (She said)

   ....

9) 'Make sure these letters are sent off immediately.' (She told him)

   ....

10) 'I'll never touch another drop of alcohol.' (He swore)

   ....

Exercise 11 (3.77 – 3.107)

In the following reported clauses, identify the reference features (including tense) which are probably not the same as in the original language event. Underline these features. (You may not need to underline anything in some of the reports.) The first one has been done for you.

1) He promised that <u>he would</u> telephone <u>her the next day.</u>

2) Angela then shouted that she never wanted to see them again.

3) Sources close to the Secretary of State warned that it is too early to speculate about whether the company can be saved or not.

4) A parliamentary research assistant claimed that she had had a relationship with him two years ago.

5) I asked the Vice Chancellor why they were still there.

6) I asked her what method of assessment she proposed to use in teaching. She answered that hers is not the kind of subject that you can easily assess.

7) The Liberal Democrat MP said that questions must be asked about the operation of all submarines in waters around the British Isles.

8) Ferguson said I could ask for a transfer if I still don't like it after six months.

9) Noel told the children that they should welcome this opportunity to try out their French.

10) Welch muttered that he had to collect his bag from his room that afternoon but would be back by 4 o'clock.

Exercise 12   (Sections 4.13, 4.34 – 4.35)

Where possible, express the following reports of opinions in three different ways:
a) using a 'to'-infinitive clause;
b) using the passive structure with 'it' as the subject;
c) using the passive structure where the reporting verb appears inside the reported idea.
In some cases, it may not be possible to use all three structures.
The first one has been done for you.

1) People think he is completely mad.

   a) *People think him to be completely mad.*

   b) *It is thought that he is completely mad.*

   c) *He is thought to be completely mad.*

2) Everyone considers that she is the best candidate for the job.

a) ....

b) ....

c) ....

3) People assumed that the government's policies were good for the economy.

a) ....

b) ....

c) ....

4) They took it for granted that he was going to win the championship.

a) ....

b) ....

c) ....

5) We all seriously doubted that they would arrive in time.

a) ....

b) ....

c) ....

Exercise 13 (Section 4.60 – 4.61)

Ask your listener's opinion about the following questions. The first one has been done for you.

1) Where is he? (think)
   Where do you think he is?

2) How long should we stay here? (think)

   ....

3) What has happened to the kids? (think)

   ....

4) What time are they arriving? (reckon)

   ....

5) Which kind of soap powder does she want us to buy? (suppose)

   ....

6) How many people are likely to attend the concert? (believe)

....

7) What possible reason could she have for saying that? (think)

....

8) What on earth are you playing at? (think)

....

Exercise 14 (Sections 4.69 – 4.71)

Use 'wonder' or 'suppose' to ask questions or make suggestions in a polite or tentative way. The first one has been done for you.

1) You want your friend to lend you her car. You think she might refuse.

   I wonder if you could lend me your car?

   I don't suppose you could lend me your car?

2) You want to ask someone a question.

   ....

   ....

3) You want to suggest to your family that you have the kitchen redecorated, but you think they might disagree.

   ....

   ....

4) You want to ask your teacher if you can hand in your essay next week instead of today. You think the teacher might not be happy with this.

   ....

   ....

5) A window in your home has been broken. You want to suggest that it was broken by the children next door, but you are not sure.

   ....

   ....

6) You want someone you do not know very well to have dinner with you tomorrow.

....

....

Exercise 15 (Chapter 5)

Below are two texts for you to analyze. The suggested steps in each analysis are:

1. Identify and underline any report structures

2. Decide on the type of report structure

3. Try to decide why the speaker or writer used that kind of report

structure at that point in the text

Text A

This is part of the same conversation as in Chapter Five. Violet is talking about two telephone calls to Mary ('she' in the text). The main purpose is to arrange a visit to Mary and Harold's house. Harold ('he' in most of the text, although 'he' sometimes refers to Charles) has been ill.

1 And when they'd finished I asked Charles, 'Have you asked about him being in hospital?', because in the letter she'd said he'd been in hospital for ten days in February with unstable angina.

2 And, erm, I said to Charles, 'Did you ask about him being in hospital?' He said, 'No' – typical man. I thought, 'Ooh my God,' you know, 'she won't be a bit pleased', because I wouldn't have been either, you know.

3 Anyway, later we rang them back, didn't we? And we said, 'Is it all right if we come?' And she said, 'Well, you can come during the week if you want.' But we like to go back home, you see – we don't want to stay there overnight.

4 And Charles said, 'No, it's horrendous during the week.' You know, like when we came on Friday, it was busy and we wouldn't have wanted to go back the same day. I think it's too much when you're getting old, you know. I mean, there were lorries to the right of us and lorries to the left of us, and all sorts, on Friday, but at least we only had one journey, you know. So he said, 'No, I don't want that.'

5 Anyway, I said to her, I said, 'What's all this about him being in hospital?' And then she started – it seemed as though I'd asked the right question, you see.

Text B

This is a slightly shortened version of a newspaper article about a speech given by Queen Elizabeth II, after a year in which the newspapers had criticized her and members of her family. The notes below the text show what she in fact said, so that you can compare this with the report in the newspaper. For the analysis of this text, you will need to add a fourth step to the three listed above: deciding what the report structures tell you about the journalist's attitude towards the Queen and her speech.

The Queen opens her heart as never before

PLEASE BE KIND TO US

By DAVID WILLIAMS and GORDON CRAIG

1 THE Queen opened her heart as never before yesterday to ask for a change in the way Britain treats the Royal Family.

2 In a remarkable personal plea after months of turmoil in her family, she used literary Latin to dismiss 1992 as an 'annus horribilis' – a horrible year.

3 She appealed for more understanding and, though the language was coded, appeared to hint that changes might be on the way.

4 The Queen chose a Guildhall lunch intended as a glittering celebration of the 40th anniversary of her accession to reach out to her subjects.

5 Without referring specifically to the controversies that have rocked the monarchy, she admitted for the first time that her family is not above criticism. And she appeared to acknowledge public anxieties by adding that it was such 'questioning' which triggered change.

6 Whitehall suggested last night that the Queen was opening up a new dialogue with her people to signal that she was prepared for reform.

7 There was no reference, however, to the issues which have been dominating public debate: whether she will contribute to the estimated £60million cost of restoring Windsor Castle after last week's fire and whether she should pay income tax.

8 Speaking in a barely audible croak because of a heavy cold and remaining expressionless throughout, she told the Corporation of London lunch: 'There can be no doubt, of course, that criticism is good for people and institutions that are part of public life.

9 'No institution – City, monarchy, whatever – should expect to be free from the scrutiny of those who give it their loyalty and support, not to mention those who don't.

10 'But we are all part of the same fabric of our national society and [that] scrutiny, by one part or another, can be just as effective if it is made with a touch of gentleness, good humour and understanding.'

11 Pondering on how 1992 would be looked back on*, she said: 'I dare say that history will take a rather more moderate view than that of the contemporary commentators. Distance is well-known to lend enchantment even to the less attractive views. After all, it has the [inestimable] benefit of hindsight.

12 'But it can also lend an extra dimension to judgment, giving it a leavening of moderation and compassion – even wisdom – that is sometimes lacking in the reaction of those who[se] task it [is] in life to offer instant opinions on all things great and small.'

13 Many had expected her to use the Guildhall platform to attack the Press, but it was seen as significant that she made no overt criticism.

14 What she did say was: 'No section of the community has all the virtues, neither does any have all the vices. I am quite sure that most people try to do their jobs as best they can, even if the result is not entirely successful.

15 'He who has never failed to reach perfection has a right to be the harshest critic.' The Queen, who received a standing ovation, ended by thanking everyone whose prayers had sustained her through the years.**

* 'I sometimes wonder how future generations will judge the events of this tumultuous year.'
** 'It [the hospitality] is an outward symbol of one other unchanging factor which I value above all - the loyalty given to me and my family by so many people in this country, and the Commonwealth, throughout my reign.'

Answer Key

Exercise 1

Possible but less likely positions are marked with #.

1) Peter Beardsley admitted: 'We didn't play well * and we are all disappointed.'
2) 'But # I can assure you * that you couldn't do better than him,' he told Jane.
3) 'Sara, * what is it? he asked quietly.
4) The manager said: 'With the growing financial problems * there is a need to save as much money as possible.'
5) 'Go away, * I can't cope with this now,' I shouted.
6) 'The thing is * I don't remember anything about the journey,' he added.
7) 'The Japanese attitude to the Emperor * is similar to the way Britons view the Queen,' said Professor Sato.
8) Tim pointed out: 'The main question *is # whether we'll get there in time.'
9) 'What * do you think I ought to do?' I asked.
10) 'But # in my opinion * it's worth the trouble,' she said.

Exercise 2

In the sentences where the reporting clause comes first, you can use a comma or a colon after the reporting clause.

1) 'It looks like it's worth a fortune,' Cecil said.
2) 'Where have you been?' asked the manager.
3) 'Watch out!' he said.
4) 'Well,' he admitted, 'there are still some things I haven't told you.'
5) 'My name's Bill,' he said finally. 'What's yours?'
6) The man turned to me and whispered, 'Do you think this is going to go on for a long time?'
7) Mr Clark said last night: 'We will do everything in our power to prevent this happening again.'
8) He admitted: 'People often look at me and say, "You look terrible." '
9) He said, 'She just kept asking me, "Where's the way out?" '
10) 'If people ask you, "Why do you do it?" ' she said, 'just say, "Because I want to." '

Exercise 3

The indirect report versions below are only suggestions: other versions are possible.

1) He asked what he should do when he'd made the beds.
2) The manager wanted to know if/whether she had finished.
   She said/replied that it wasn't as easy as it seemed.
3) He said suddenly that the weather was just like in Sicily. They agreed that it was (just like in Sicily).
4) He replied that he had given up because he'd been sick and tired of the whole thing.
5) He said to himself that he had been very stupid not to realize what she was trying to do.

Exercise 4

The reporting adjuncts (especially one-word adjuncts such as 'apparently') can also appear in different positions from those shown below.

1) According to Frank, the shops close at 6.
2) Apparently she's had at least two face-lifts.
3) As Carter (1988) points out, low-cost housing is not always the best answer to the problem.
4) To quote the nineteenth-century philosopher von Humboldt: 'Language cannot really be taught'.
5) According to their owner, the dogs were well-trained and safe.
6) In the words of the old saying, 'The opera isn't over till the fat lady sings'.
7) As the scientist von Frisch noted, 'The bees have no word for "up" in their language'.
8) Allegedly, she hated her husband and wished she could get away.
9) As one commentator put it, our football is 'as bad as our economy'.
10) Apparently many teenage girls are obsessed by the idea that they are overweight.

Exercise 5

1) reporting signal: doctors say (reporting clause)
   message: the adverts should carry a health warning (reported 'that'-clause)
2) reporting signal: says the lady (reporting clause)
   message: 'Well, in that case,' 'do be careful' (quote)
3) reporting signal: Simenon said (reporting clause)
   message: The writer's aim was a search for himself through his characters (reported main clause)
4) reporting signal: The judges have threatened (reporting clause)
   message: to go on strike (reported 'to'-infinitive clause)
5) reporting signal: He was asked (reporting clause)
   message: whether he would get back his record for scoring most goals (reported 'wh'-clause)

6) reporting signal: I asked Jeremy (reporting clause)
message: what they'd been talking about (reported 'wh'-clause)

7) reporting signal: as one TV critic puts it (reporting adjunct)
message: the programmes are 'one long TV commercial' (main clause, with partial quote)

8) reporting signal: The man denied (reporting clause)
message: being involved in any violence (reported '-ing' clause)

9) reporting signal: was complaining (reporting verb)
message: about the high cost of electricity (prepositional phrase)

10) reporting signal: his insistence (reporting noun)
message: that the deal is on schedule (reported 'that'-clause)

11) reporting signal: a promise (reporting noun)
message: to create more jobs (reported 'to'-infinitive clause)

12) reporting signal: geologists say (reporting clause)
message: (an area) which is likely to be hit by earthquakes in the near future (relative clause functioning as reported clause)

Exercise 6

1) c
2) e
3) a
4) g
5) i
6) j
7) f
8) d
9) h
10) b

Exercise 7

1) accused
2) apologized
3) quarrelled
4) blamed
5) complimented
6) congratulated
7) dismissed
8) praised
9) nagged
10) told off

Exercise 8

1) a) It is said that he is extremely lazy.
   b) He is said to be extremely lazy.
2) a) It is reported that she is in New York now.
   b) She is reported to be in New York now.
3) a) It is rumoured that he got married for the third time yesterday.
   b) He is rumoured to have got married for the third time yesterday.
4) a) It is alleged that they attempted to bribe their prison guards.
   b) They are alleged to have attempted to bribe their prison guards.
5) a) It is claimed that these drugs are not dangerous.
   b) These drugs are claimed not to be dangerous.
6) a) It is said that there are only two of these vases in the world.
   b) There are said to be only two of these vases in the world.

Exercise 9

1) I wasn't convinced by his argument that the fire was probably caused by an electrical fault.
2) The main news tonight is the Prime Minister's announcement that the talks will resume tomorrow.
3) Nick was upset by her remark that he was really very stupid.
4) I agreed with her suggestion that we (should) take both cars.
5) They ignored his demand that they (should) take him to their leader/his demand to be taken to their leader.
6) It's hard to check the town's claim that they have the sunniest beaches in Britain/the town's claim to have the sunniest beaches in Britain.
7) She decided to follow his advice to take out life insurance.
8) The new contract didn't arrive, despite his promise to send it by fax.
9) He was grateful for Maureen's reminder to see Mike at 4 o'clock/ Maureen's reminder that he had to see Mike at 4 o'clock.
10) They accepted her offer to come and babysit for them.

Exercise 10

1) He confessed that he'd spilt some wine on the carpet.
2) He insisted that this was the only possible solution.
3) She claimed that she saw/ had seen him throw stones at the dog or She claimed to have seen him throw stones at the dog.
4) The police reported that they had found the car hidden near the park or The police reported finding the car hidden near the park.
5) She asked the foreman whether or not they had finished yet or She asked the foreman whether they had finished yet or not.
6) I asked her whether those shoes weren't too big for her son.
7) I asked him if/whether he thought I should sell my car or I asked him whether to sell my car.
8) She said how hot it was in the cinema or She said that it was really hot in the cinema.
9) She told him to make sure those letters were sent off immediately.
10) He swore never to touch another drop of alcohol or He swore that he would never touch another drop of alcohol.

Exercise 11

In some cases, it is not possible to be sure whether the reference feature has been changed. A question mark in brackets (?) shows these features.

1) He promised that he would telephone her the next day.
2) Angela then shouted that she never wanted to see them(?) again.
3) Sources close to the Secretary of State warned that it is too early to speculate about whether the company can be saved or not.
4) A parliamentary research assistant claimed that she had had a relationship with him two years ago.
5) I asked the Vice Chancellor why they were still there(?).
6) I asked her what method of assessment she proposed to use in teaching. She answered that hers is not the kind of subject that you can easily assess.
7) The Liberal Democrat MP said that questions must be asked about the operation of all submarines in waters around the British Isles.
8) Ferguson said I could(?) ask for a transfer if I still don't like it after six months.
9) Noel told the children that they should welcome this opportunity to try out their French.
10) Welch muttered that he had to collect his bag from his room that afternoon but would be back by 4 o'clock.

Exercise 12

1) a) People think him to be completely mad.
   b) It is thought that he is completely mad.
   c) He is thought to be completely mad.
2) a) Everyone considers her to be the best candidate for the job.
   b) It is considered that she is the best candidate for the job.
   c) She is considered to be the best candidate for the job.
3) a) People assumed the government's policies to be good for the country.
   b) It was assumed that the government's policies were good for the country.
   c) The government's policies were assumed to be good for the country.
4) a) not possible
   b) It was taken for granted that he was going to win the championship.
   c) not possible
5) a) not possible
   b) It was seriously doubted that they would arrive in time.
   c) not possible

Exercise 13

1) Where do you think he is?
2) How long do you think we should stay here?
3) What do you think has happened to the kids?
4) What time do you reckon they're arriving?
5) Which kind of soap powder do you suppose she wants us to buy?
6) How many people do you believe are likely to attend the concert?
7) What reason do you think she could have for saying that?
8) What on earth do you think you're playing at?

Exercise 14

Here are some possible ways of making the requests or suggestions.

1) I wonder if you could lend me your car?
   I don't suppose you could lend me your car?
2) I wonder if I could ask you a question?
3) I don't suppose we could have the kitchen redecorated?
   I suppose we couldn't have the kitchen redecorated?
4) I wondered if I could hand in my essay next week.
   I suppose I couldn't/I don't suppose I could hand in my essay next week, could I?
5) You don't suppose it was the children next door who broke it, do you?
6) I was wondering if you'd like to have dinner with me tomorrow.

Exercise 15

It is difficult to give an answer to these activities without writing a complete analysis. Overleaf are versions of the two texts with the report structures underlined. Check that in your answer you have identified all these structures.

Answer Key

Text A

1 And when they'd finished I asked Charles, 'Have you asked about him being in hospital?', because in the letter she'd said he'd been in hospital for ten days in February with unstable angina.

2 And, erm, I said to Charles, 'Did you ask about him being in hospital?' He said, 'No' – typical man. I thought, 'Ooh my God,' you know, she won't be a bit pleased', because I wouldn't have been either, you know.

3 Anyway, later we rang them back, didn't we? And we said, 'Is it all right if we come?' And she said, 'Well, you can come during the week if you want.' But we like to go back home, you see – we don't want to stay there overnight.

4 And Charles said, 'No, it's horrendous during the week.' You know, like when we came on Friday, it was busy and we wouldn't have wanted to go back the same day. I think it's too much when you're getting old, you know. I mean, there were lorries to the right of us and lorries to the left of us, and all sorts, on Friday, but at least we only had one journey, you know. So he said, 'No, I don't want that.'

5 Anyway, I said to her, I said, 'What's all this about him being in hospital?' And then she started – it seemed as though I'd asked the right question, you see.

Text B

The Queen opens her heart as never before

PLEASE BE KIND TO US

By DAVID WILLIAMS and GORDON CRAIG

1 THE Queen opened her heart as never before yesterday to ask for a change in the way Britain treats the Royal Family.

2 In a remarkable personal plea after months of turmoil in her family, she used literary Latin to dismiss 1992 as an 'annus horribilis' – a horrible year.

3 She appealed for more understanding and, though the language was coded, appeared to hint that changes might be on the way.

4 The Queen chose a Guildhall lunch intended as a glittering celebration of the 40th anniversary of her accession to reach out to her subjects.

5 Without referring specifically to the controversies that have rocked the monarchy, she admitted for the first time that her family is not above criticism. And she appeared to acknowledge public anxieties by adding that it was such 'questioning' which triggered change.

6 Whitehall suggested last night that the Queen was opening up a new dialogue with her people to signal that she was prepared for reform.

7 There was no reference, however, to the issues which have been dominating public debate: whether she will contribute to the estimated £60million cost of restoring Windsor Castle after last week's fire and whether she should pay income tax.

8 Speaking in a barely audible croak because of a heavy cold and remaining expressionless throughout, she told the Corporation of London lunch: 'There can be no doubt, of course, that criticism is good for people and institutions that are part of public life.

9 'No institution – City, monarchy, whatever – should expect to be free from the scrutiny of those who give it their loyalty and support, not to mention those who don't.

10 'But we are all part of the same fabric of our national society and [that] scrutiny, by one part or another, can be just as effective if it is made with a touch of gentleness, good humour and understanding.'

11 Pondering on how 1992 would be looked back on, she said: 'I dare say that history will take a rather more moderate view than that of the contemporary commentators. Distance is well-known to lend enchantment to even the less attractive views. After all, it has the [inestimable] benefit of hindsight.

12 'But it can also lend an extra dimension to judgment, giving it a leavening of moderation and compassion – even wisdom – that is sometimes lacking in the reaction of those who[se] task it [is] in life to offer instant opinions on all things great and small.'

13 Many had expected her to use the Guildhall platform to attack the Press, but it was seen as significant that she made no overt criticism.

14 What she did say was: 'No section of the community has all the virtues, neither does any have all the vices. I am quite sure that most people try to do their jobs as best they can, even if the result is not entirely successful.

15 'He who has never failed to reach perfection has a right to be the harshest critic.' The Queen, who received a standing ovation, ended by thanking everyone whose prayers had sustained her through the years.

Index

Items in **bold** are technical terms. Items in roman are categories of words that are discussed in the text. Items in *italic* are lexical words that are discussed in the text. Numbers refer to the chapter and section, except where it is stated otherwise.